ESSAYS ON BIBLICAL METHOD AND TRANSLATION

ESSAYS ON BIBLICAL METHOD AND TRANSLATION

by
Edward L. Greenstein

Scholars Press
Atlanta, Georgia

ESSAYS ON BIBLICAL
METHOD AND TRANSLATION

Library of Congress Cataloging-in-Publication Data

Greenstein, Edward L.
      Essays on biblical method and translation.
      (Brown Judaic studies ; no. 92)
      1. Bible. O.T.—Hermeneutics. 2. Bible. O.T. —
      Translating. I. Title. II. Series.
      BS476.G73   1989   221'.07   87-6018
      ISBN 1-55540-122-8 (alk. paper)

Paperback edition published 2006 by Brown Judaic Studies
ISBN 1-930675-35-6 (paperback : alk. paper)

Printed in the United States of America
on acid-free paper

To my parents, Samuel and Goldie Greenstein, with love

Contents

Preface

With respect to topic, the present volume comprises two short books. One, a critical reflection on Biblical studies in its various disciplines, deals with the impact of synchronic paradigms on a field that traditionally has been oriented historically. The second, a critical analysis of different modern approaches to Bible translation, treats the problem of translation within the larger questions of language and literature. With respect to theme, I suggest that we have here one book: an examination of the relations between theory and practice in Biblical criticism in general and in Bible translation in particular. In the nineteenth century critics argued for the unity of form and content in art. The way that the Romantics saw the work of art as a fusion of substance and style, contemporary critics see the act of making sense as an interplay of theory and method. As there is no form without content and no content without form, there is no theory without application and no application uninformed by an array of philosophical positions and presuppositions. It is my object in this book to unpack some of the underlying principles of Biblical criticism and Bible translation; to explain how attention to theory can affect practice in both areas; and to contribute toward a more pluralistic vision of the field. Before one can claim really to know something, one must be able to explain how one knows what one knows. That is a primary function of criticism, and one I wish to treat.

Knowledge increases through discovery. In popular thinking, discovery follows from new finds. Though this is sometimes the case, it is not usually so. Discovery comes more often with new finding – new perspectives, seeing in a different way. Early in the summer of 1987 a fragment of the famed Colossus of Rhodes was discovered in the Aegean Sea.[1] In short time the Colossus was unfound. The same piece of rock was first a part of the legendary statue, later insignificant. What changed was not the material evidence but the way the evidence was interpreted. The process of this reevaluation can serve as a model of hypothesis construction and deconstruction. Divers observed markings on the rock. They had been led to the site of the find by a clairvoyant, so they were expecting to discover remnants of the Colossus. The grooves on the rock they initially interpreted as knuckles from a finger of the giant statue. The evidence

---

[1] "Rhodes Find Not Part of Colossus but Work of Mechanical Digger" (Reuters), *Jerusalem Post*, July 8, 1987, p. 3.

suited the hypothesis. Under further scrutiny, observers identified the rock type as sandstone – the wrong material – and attributed the grooves to a machine digging in the harbor. Raising different questions, looking from a different perspective, transforms the nature of the evidence. The divers who first made the discovery of the rock, found the Colossus. That is what, for all intents and purposes, they saw. When the divers were trained to interpret the markings differently, they began to see something else. How we think about what we study affects the results of our study no less than how much material we (re)cover.

One of my teachers once chastened me for spending so much time reading works of general theory and criticism. I would do better, he benevolently suggested, to invest more time in studying primary sources. My response was, and is, that our work as scholars, as in virtually any trade, is shaped by our manner of thinking, organizing, and analyzing material no less than by the amount of material we study and the depth in which we study it. If I am classifying trees, and my criteria are flawed, it does not help to have greater discipline in collecting specimens and more trees at my disposal. In saying this I do not mean to underestimate the critical importance of gathering data and scrutinizing it intensively. I only wish to stress that thinking about how we think about what we think about is another essential means of self-criticism, of checking our work.

My reflections on how I have worked may not have dramatically affected my writing. Yet, there is a noticeable difference between my earlier and later work. After I submitted my essay, "Theory and Argument in Biblical Criticism," for anonymous review in a journal, one of the referees figured out, on the basis of earlier publications, that I must be the author. The reviewer objected that in this essay I took one particular critical stance different from what I had written previously elsewhere. I saw, and see, no problem in this. To the contrary: as one grows and changes in the information that one knows, one may also develop in one's philosophy and outlook. Indeed, the careful reader of this book may detect certain differences in perspective between the essays I wrote earlier in the '80s and those I completed later – even after making revisions. One might characterize this change as one from a greater positivism to postpositivism, or from a focus on the object – what's out there – to the thinking of the subject – what's in here. I have learned that the objects of my attention do not signify anything to me by themselves; I am responsible for what I make of them.

In order to ascribe greater authority – objectivity – to what we think or feel, we locate the sources of our perceptions, or conceptions, in the world out there. In the interpretation of texts, for example, we endow our object with the ability to communicate. Personifying "the text," we say that it speaks. We defend our readings by appeal to what "the text says."[2] My students in recent years are by

---

[2] See further Chapter Three.

now used to my demonstration that such rhetoric is only metaphorical, a figure of speech with the purpose of objectifying our interpretations. I open my Hebrew Bible, place it on the table, and bid my class listen to what the text says. It soon becomes clear amid the silence that whatever meaning we make of the text follows from our reading of it. And, since none of us is born reading, what we read follows from how we have been taught to read. We are educated to make sense in certain ways. Training in reading, not only in the deciphering of script but in the complex of hermeneutical strategies by which we "comprehend" what we read, becomes so traditional, in whatever culture(s) to which we belong, that it may seem like the only correct way to do it. But what is "correct" depends upon conventions that are somewhat arbitrarily set and must be learned.

I noticed in a certain museum exhibit that a cuneiform tablet was displayed upside-down. Whoever placed it in the case had not been trained in the conventions of cuneiform studies. There is nothing "objective" even about how to position a text, let alone how to read it. Yemenite Jews, I am told, learned to read the Hebrew Bible from different angles because they would gather in groups around a single book. Whichever side one was on, one would read from that perspective. Beginning with the simplest strategies and proceeding to ever more sophisticated ones, we build up our power of reading, our power to make sense. Let us return for the moment to our upside-down cuneiform tablet. I indicated to the curator of the exhibit that the tablet was inverted. Recognizing me as an expert on such things, the curator repositioned the tablet. Why? Since no other visitors had seemed to mind the way the tablet looked, why should the curator straighten it out? Even if we acknowledge that how we read is the product of convention, that is no criticism. It could not be otherwise. Everything we do depends on accepted conventions; we respect conventions. So long as there is a standard convention of how to position cuneiform for reading, people will defer to those who are conversant with it.

In Biblical studies, whatever consensus on how to read (or work) may have once existed has broken. New approaches, often adapted from other disciplines, have opened up new possibilities for making meaning. Unsatisfied with earlier methods or results, scholars explore alternate paradigms for constructing our knowledge. The older conventions can no longer be taken for granted. In most areas of contemporary Bible studies there is no single authority or school to which to defer. Some fear that this opens the door to anarchy and a lack of standards. Acceptance of a variety of research models appears to be unrestrainedly relativistic. Anything, so it would seem, goes.

In fact, serious philosophers of science like Paul Feyerabend argue that science has always advanced through undisciplined discovery.[3] He advocates anarchy as the only hope for future progress. Without committing myself to such an extreme position, it is in order to indicate that relativism need not be

---

[3]See Paul Feyerabend, *Against Method* (London: Verso, 1978).

free and unlimited.[4] Relativism may deny that any truth can correspond directly to an objective world, that statements can be inherently valid by appealing to an absolute Truth. Many proponents of relativism, however, view all truth-claims within a given framework of principles and values. Standards for assessing an argument are developed within a system of conventions. To be true is to conform to the accepted rules. To be a relativist is to recognize the claims to legitimacy of different frameworks and different sets of rules.[5]

Within Biblical studies there are already a number of competing analytical paradigms. The two most general categories, the diachronic (historical) and the synchronic, have been the most pronounced, and the ones most often contrasted in this book. In Part I, I shall be describing the background and effects of these two general methodologies. I shall contend that the two research paradigms operate on different presuppositions; if so, one cannot criticize the one according to the standards of the other. The differences are not so much in how the two approaches work as in where they are coming from (and what they are intended to do). Indeed, as I have said above, theory and method interpenetrate and feed each other as they draw on each other. They are inseparable. One might even propose abandoning the distinction were it not, like "form" and "content," a heuristically useful opposition. In Part II, I shall examine the philosophical and literary underpinnings of the contrasting approaches to Bible translation, primarily the "literal" and the "idiomatic." While defending the honor of the former, which has been frequently defamed of late, I shall try to explain the functions of and the need for both. As I did in Part I, I shall maintain that because each mode of translation works according to its own assumptions and goals, it cannot be fairly evaluated except on its own terms. Throughout the book, I hope to show that scholars, like other people, act on beliefs of various sorts. As specialists, scholars, like musicians, learn skills and practice technique. But one's initial assumptions and predispositions, are, like a musician's feel for the music, personal and unsusceptible to "objective" challenge. By coming to recognize the assumptions underlying one's own work and that of others, and by delineating one's premises and principles as clearly as one's arguments, discussion can take place over fundamental issues and conflicting positions can be better understood, if not reconciled.

Six of the essays gathered here have been or will be published in an earlier form. Chapter One, "The State of Biblical Studies, or Biblical Studies in a State," will appear in *The State of Jewish Studies*, to be published by Wayne

---

[4]For a presentation of varieties of relativism and their critiques, cf. Michael Krausz and Jack W. Meiland, eds., *Relativism: Cognitive and Moral* (Notre Dame: University of Notre Dame Press, 1982).

[5]For a much deeper exploration of these and related issues, see Michael Polanyi, *Personal Knowledge: Towards a Post-Critical Philosophy* (New York: Harper & Row, 1964).

State University Press; Chapter Two, "The Torah as She Is Read," appeared in *Response* 47 (Winter 1985), pp. 17-40; Chapter Three, "Theory and Argument in Biblical Criticism," in *Hebrew Annual Review* 10 (1987), pp. 77-93; Chapter Four, Part One, a review of *Poetics and Interpretation of Biblical Narrative,* will appear in the *AJS Review*; Chapter Four, Part Two, a review of *Biblical Semantic Logic,* appeared in the *Journal of the American Oriental Society* 105 (1985), pp. 735-36; Chapter Four, Part Three, a review of *Hapax Legomena in Biblical Hebrew,* in the *Journal of the American Oriental Society* 107 (1987), pp. 538-39; Chapter Four, Part Four, a review of *The Torah: A New Commentary,* in the *Journal of Reform Judaism* 29 (Summer 1982), pp. 80-86; Chapter Five, "Theories of Modern Bible Translation," in *Prooftexts* 3 (1983), pp. 9-39; Chapter Six, "The Job of Translating Job," in the *AJS Newsletter* no. 30 (October 1981), pp. 6-7. I am grateful to the editors of *Response,* the *AJS Review,* and the *Journal of Reform Judaism*; to the American Oriental Society; to the Jewish Theological Seminary of America and Wayne State University Press; and to the Johns Hopkins University Press for permission to reprint versions of these publications here. Versions of Chapter Seven have been presented at the annual meeting of the American Academy of Religion in 1986 and at the sesquicentennial jubilee conference held at Union Theological Seminary in 1987.

I am grateful, too, to the Jewish Theological Seminary of America and its Abbell Research Fund for stipends supporting some of the work included here; and to the Max Richter Foundation for a grant assisting me in the preparation of the manuscript for the press. Mr. Lorne Hanick has provided helpful research assistance.

I am particularly indebted to Professor Jacob Neusner for having encouraged me to assemble a book of essays and for welcoming the finished product into the Brown Judaica Series. Thanks, too, to Professor Neusner and his associate editor, Professor Ernest Frerichs, for their patience in awaiting my book.

Many friends and colleagues have aided me with information and references and have helped me think through some of my ideas. I hope I do not omit mention of any; if I do, I hope they will accept my apologies. For helpful criticism of an earlier draft of Chapter One, I thank Professors Shaye J. D. Cohen, Moshe Greenberg, Simon Greenberg, and Gershon Shaked. For stimulating comments on an earlier version of Chapter Three, I thank Professors Adele Berlin, Aaron Demsky, Yehoshua Gitay, Avi Hurvitz, Sara Japhet, Jacob Milgrom, Yochanan Muffs, Michael O'Connor, Uriel Simon, and Jeremiah Unterman. I am indebted to conversations with Professor Stanley Fish for assistance in formulating my thoughts for the original version of that chapter. Dr. Gabriele Strauch spent many hours guiding me through the finer points of the Buber-Rosenzweig Bible translation; her assistance was invaluable for composing the first version of Chapter Five. Professor Theodor H. Gaster has debated with me the truth about translating over many a cup of coffee. Among the several people who provided suggestions and material concerning that essay, I especially thank Mr. Fred Bogin and Professors Baruch M. Bokser, Everett Fox, William W. Hallo, Alan Mintz, Michael P. O'Connor, Harry M. Orlinsky, Joel Rosenberg, Lou H. Silberman, and the late Gershom Scholem. My revision of Chapter Seven owes a special debt to comments and/or material from Drs. Walter Bodine, Keith R. Crim, Marcia Falk, and Harold P. Scanlin. Last, but never least, Professor David Marcus has always offered helpful criticism alongside unflagging friendship.

Abbreviations

AB   Anchor Bible (Doubleday)
ABS   American Bible Society
AJS   Association for Jewish Studies
BA   *Biblical Archaeologist*
BARev *Biblical Archaeology Review*
BiOr   *Bibliotheca Orientalis*
BR   *Bible Review*
CBQ   *Catholic Biblical Quarterly*
CCAR   Central Conference of American Rabbis
HUCA   *Hebrew Union College Annual*
IEJ   *Israel Exploration Journal*
JAAR   *Journal of the American Academy of Religion*
JANES *Journal of the Ancient Near Eastern Society*
JAOS   *Journal of the American Oriental Society*
JBL   *Journal of Biblical Literature*
JCS   *Journal of Cuneiform Studies*
JJSt   *Journal of Jewish Studies*
JNES   *Journal of Near Eastern Studies*
JQR   *Jewish Quarterly Review*
JSOT   *Journal for the Study of the Old Testament*
JSS   *Journal of Semitic Studies*
JTS   *Journal of Theological Studies*
KJV   King James (or Authorized) Version
MT   Massoretic Text
NEB   *New English Bible*
NJV   New Jewish Version (The Jewish Publication Society of America)
RB   *Revue Biblique*
SBL   Society of Biblical Literature
SBLDS   SBL Dissertation Series

SVT   *Supplements to Vetus Testamentum*
TEV   Today's English Version *(Good News Bible)*
UF   *Ugarit-Forschungen*
VT   *Vetus Testamentum*
ZAW   *Zeitschrift für alttestamentliche Wissenschaft*

Part One

THEORY AND METHOD IN BIBLICAL CRITICISM

Chapter One

The State of Biblical Studies,
or, Biblical Studies in a State

Biblical Studies has grown into a multi-disciplined field, seeming to expand in several directions at the same time. We are experiencing a somewhat dizzying development, similar to one that scholars in many other disciplines have recently undergone. Instead of building up the body of knowledge through the progressive accumulation of data and insights, practitioners have struck out centrifugally into uncharted terrain, extending the field laterally without necessarily enhancing its depth.[1] While on the one hand the exposure to new and different disciplinary approaches bespeaks a maturation of Biblical Studies as an academic field, on the other it reflects a more and more widely spreading "crisis" in our faith in the methods that have traditionally been cultivated within the confines of our own criticism.[2] In the present essay I shall examine the background and nature of the

---

[1]Cf., e.g., William E. Cain, *The Crisis in Criticism: Theory, Literature, and Reform in English Studies* (Baltimore: Johns Hopkins University Press, 1984); Donald W. Fiske and Richard A. Shweder, eds., *Metatheory in Social Science* (Chicago: University of Chicago Press, 1986).

[2]Quite presciently R. M. Polzin some time ago put his finger on the problem: "If there is a crisis in biblical scholarship today, it does not consist in the present almost healthy tension between historical and literary criticism of the Bible, but rather in the destructive self image both may have concerning their status as scholarly disciplines modeled after the natural sciences"; see Robert M. Polzin, "Literary and Historical Criticism of the Bible: A Crisis in Scholarship," in Richard A. Spencer, ed., *Orientation by Disorientation: Studies in Literary Criticism and Biblical Literary Criticism* (Pittsburgh: Pickwick Press, 1980), pp. 99-114; here, p. 100. I must register here my dissent from Polzin's assumption that synchronic (or any other) analysis can operate without any preconceived theories; see further Chapter Three.

In the end Polzin attributes the "true crisis" to the fact that through historical criticism "so many...believe that they are actually understanding the Bible's claims on its own terms, when in fact they are not" (p. 108). While I agree with this assessment, it must be acknowledged that synchronic or ahistorical critics are no more free of presupposition than the historians; see further below and cf. Alan Cooper, "On Reading the Bible Critically and Otherwise," in Richard E. Friedman and H. G. M. Williamson, eds., *The Future of Biblical Studies: The Hebrew Scriptures* (Atlanta: Scholars Press, 1987), pp. 61-79.

"crisis" state in the Biblical field and explore the foundations underlying the sorts of historical and ahistorical approaches that various scholars take. Rather than bemoan an apparent lack of direction, I shall in the end celebrate the rich, new possibilities that have opened up to us for the construction of meaning.

In 1964 the Anchor Bible published the first volume in its popular series, E. A. Speiser's *Genesis*. In one of his most original suggestions in that commentary, Speiser contended that the story in Genesis 14 of the battle between the four kings from the North and East and the five kings from the Dead Sea region represents a Hebrew transformation of an authentic non-Israelite chronicle, probably composed in Akkadian, from a time close to the events themselves, the eighteenth century B.C.E.[3] "The narrative," Speiser concluded, "...has all the ingredients of historicity."[4] Among the foundations on which Speiser based his argument were certain linguistic features that struck him as Akkadian and the resemblance between the names of some of the protagonists in Genesis 14 and the names discovered on three cuneiform tablets, the so-called Spartoli texts, known by Bible scholars as the Chedorlaomer Texts since the early twentieth century. What was at stake for Speiser in presenting this hypothesis he himself made clear: "If Abraham was cited in a historical or quasi-historical narrative that was written not by Israelites but by outsiders, it necessarily follows that Abraham was not a nebulous literary figure but a real person who was attested in contemporary sources."[5]

At about the same time M. Astour published a lengthy and highly detailed study of Genesis 14 in which he concluded that the Biblical narrative is a piece of late Deuteronomistic historiography.[6] He reached this finding through two general lines of investigation. On the one hand, he compared the narrative style of Genesis 14 with specimens of Deuteronomistic writing in 2 Kings. On the other, he examined the onomastics and typologies in Genesis 14 and found them to reflect a genre of late date in Mesopotamia. The Spartoli tablets, which Astour like Speiser connects with the Biblical text, come from the second century B.C.E. and represent originals that cannot be dated earlier than the seventh century. Genesis 14, in this view, is not a genuine historical document from 1700 B.C.E. but a symbolic fiction of no earlier than 700 B.C.E.[7]

Anyone acquainted with Biblical scholarship knows well that the antithesis between early and late dating of the patriarchal narratives is altogether typical of

---

[3]E. A. Speiser, *Genesis*, AB 1 (Garden City, NY: Doubleday, 1964), pp. 105-9.
[4]Ibid., p. 109.
[5]Ibid., p. 108.
[6]Michael C. Astour, "Political and Cosmic Symbolism in Genesis 14 and in Its Babylonian Sources," in Alexander Altmann, ed., *Biblical Motifs* (Cambridge, MA: Harvard University Press, 1966), pp. 65-112.
[7]On Genesis 14, see further J. A. Emerton, "The Riddle of Genesis XIV," *VT* 21 (1971), pp. 403-39, with bibliography; John Van Seters, *Abraham in History and Tradition* (New Haven: Yale University Press, 1975), pp. 296ff.

the state of the field. Some seek to establish the authenticity of the patriarchal period and accordingly look for parallels to the accounts in Genesis in ancient Near Eastern documents of the second millennium. Others, like Van Seters, seek to establish the lateness of Genesis' composition and accordingly look for parallels to the accounts of Genesis and its literary style in the mid-first millennium.[8] Such a situation does not inspire confidence in the student who would like to know the history of Israel in the early Biblical period. Skepticism has earned a respectable place in the field.[9]

This skepticism is hardly new. Contemporary Biblical Studies still hold largely to the assumptions of Wellhausen and other scholars of a century ago.[10] Virtually axiomatic in Wellhausen's approach was that narratives reflect events, or reflect events accurately, only when they are composed near the time in which the events are supposed to have transpired. Facts are recorded in writing. What is not recorded in writing is suspect and unreliable for historical reconstruction. As M. Noth put it in the middle of this century, "History can only be described on the basis of literary traditions, which record events and specify persons and places."[11] More recently, Van Seters, who conceives of history somewhat differently from Noth, cannot conceive of it apart from the medium of writing.[12] The patriarchal stories bear no presumption of reliability because, among other things, no one believes they were written down in the period they are said to represent.

Now one might think that the influence of Gunkel in the early part of this century had weakened scholars' attachment to Wellhausen's axiom. Gunkel argued eloquently for the existence of prior stages of oral transmission of traditions preceding the writing down of Biblical texts.[13] Gunkel has made a lasting impact on the way some historians of ancient Israel do their work. W. F. Albright and his students J. Bright, F. M. Cross, and others, have attempted to

---

[8]Cf. Van Seters, *Abraham*; see also T. L. Thompson, *The Historicity of the Patriarchal Narratives* (Berlin: W. de Gruyter, 1974).

[9]Consider, e.g., both the contents and tone of the following remarks by a historian of the Biblical period: "It is time we stopped kidding ourselves; the patriarchal and conquest narratives represent at best the traditions of the end of the Late Bronze and the beginning of the Iron Age with thorough reworking in the late monarchy and beyond"; Anson F. Rainey, Review of *The Tribes of Yahweh* by N. K. Gottwald, *JAOS* 107 (1987), pp. 541-43; here, p. 542b.

[10]See esp. Julius Wellhausen, *Prolegomena to the History of Ancient Israel* (Cleveland: Meridian Books, 1957; first published 1878).

[11]Martin Noth, *The History of Israel*, rev. ed. (New York: Harper & Row, 1960), p. 42.

[12]Van Seters, *Abraham*; idem, *In Search of History: Historiography in the Ancient World and the Origins of Biblical History* (New Haven: Yale University Press, 1983).

[13]Esp. Hermann Gunkel, *Genesis* (Göttingen: Vandenhoeck & Ruprecht, 1966; first published 1901); idem, *The Legends of Genesis* (New York: Schocken Books, 1966; first English ed., 1901).

posit years and sometimes centuries of oral transmission, more specifically epic narration, prior to the composition of Biblical prose narratives.[14] Like the Israeli scholar Cassuto,[15] many scholars of the so-called Albright school interpret units of parallelistic verse in the Torah and the Deuteronomistic History as evidence of an earlier Israelite historical epic. They will look to ancient Near Eastern models and typologies for explaining the historical and literary contexts of Biblical materials, arguing for their antiquity on the grounds of these parallels. Yet, in working this way even the Albright school displays the pervasive effects of Wellhausen's methodology.

Let us turn briefly to a recent historiographic effort by a former student of Cross. In *The Emergence of Israel in Canaan* B. Halpern tries to reconstruct what he can of the "premonarchic" history of Israel.[16] He readily avers that the narratives of the Books of Joshua and Judges betray tendentious stories that read later monarchic institutions and ideology back into the earlier periods. "It is impossible to determine," he writes, "whether a character named Joshua ben-Nun led more than a few souls...into the Aijalon Pass."[17] Distrusting whatever orally transmitted traditions might lie behind that story (and I do not mean to imply that I put any stock in them either), Halpern establishes his conclusions on what he can glean from written documents. In this case they are the El Amarna letters from the fourteenth century, the Song of Deborah and the Song at the Sea – which, following Albright, Halpern dates to the so-called Period of the Judges – and large parts of the Deuteronomistic History that he ascribes to the early sources of that later historiographic composition. Tellingly, Halpern writes that the Song of Deborah "marks the beginning of the period for the recovery of which Israelite sources are of significant value (and basically historical character)."[18]

For similar reasons G. W. Ahlström locates the beginning of the national entity named Israel in the period of Saul, the first who attempted to unify the

[14]E.g., William F. Albright, *From the Stone Age to Christianity*, 2nd ed. (Garden City, NY: Anchor Books, 1957); idem, *Archaeology and the Religion of Israel*, 5th ed. (Garden City, NY: Anchor Books, 1969); John Bright, *A History of Israel*, 3rd rev. ed. (Philadelphia: Westminster Press, 1981); Frank M. Cross, *Canaanite Myth and Hebrew Epic* (Cambridge, MA: Harvard University Press, 1973). For Gunkel's influence on Albright, see the latter's introduction to the 1966 edition of the former's *Legends*.

[15]See esp. Umberto Cassuto, "The Israelite Epic," *Biblical and Oriental Studies*, trans. I. Abrahams (Jerusalem: Magnes Press, 1975), vol. 2, pp. 69-109. Note the criticism of Van Seters, *In Search of History*, pp. 226-27; but see, too, Chapter Three.

[16]Baruch Halpern, *The Emergence of Israel in Canaan* (Chico, CA: Scholars Press, 1983).

[17]Ibid., p. 8.

[18]Ibid., p. 32; cf. p. 8.

people that took upon itself the name Israel.[19] It is hardly a coincidence that Ahlström regards the Biblical traditions about Saul to be the earliest that are historically reliable.

Virtually all modern Biblicists accept the overall historicity of the narratives from the monarchy on. In large measure this is because so many believe that the story of David and the succession to his throne was composed close to the time of David, perhaps during the "golden" era of Solomon.[20] The David story has been understood by many as an eyewitness version that served as a primary source for the Deuteronomist.[21] Its reliability is directly bound up with the theory that Israelite history writing began formally in the era of David and Solomon. Gottwald, who radically diverges from the Bible's account of the conquest and settlement of Canaan,[22] treats the Bible's account of the early monarchy with a high degree of credibility. Gottwald does recognize the genre of the David story as a novella of sorts[23]; yet, in his synthesis of Israelite history, he accepts the particulars of the Biblical sources. Unsurprisingly, Gottwald attributes the first great Israelite history writing to the period of David and Solomon.

> A connected story of Israel's beginning from the creation of the world to at least the verge of Israel's entrance into Canaan was composed ca. 960-930 B.C.E., during the reign of Solomon, in the view of many scholars, although others date it later by as much as a century or more....We do not know the name of the writer. Apparently it was someone in governmental favor – if not actual government service – who provided a kind of "national epic" for the young kingdom of David and Solomon.[24]

Gottwald, in line with conventional scholarship, is referring, of course, to J.[25]

---

[19]Gösta W. Ahlström, *Who Were the Israelites?* (Winona Lake, IN: Eisenbrauns, 1986).

[20]Cf., e.g, Gerhard von Rad, "The Beginnings of Historical Writing in Ancient Israel," *The Problem of the Hexateuch and Other Essays*, trans. E. W. Trueman Dicken (Edinburgh: Oliver & Boyd, 1966), pp. 166-204, esp. p. 195.

[21]For a literary critique of this position, see Yair Zakovitch, "Story Versus History," *Proceedings of the Eighth World Congress of Jewish Studies*, Panel Sessions, Bible Studies and Hebrew Language (Jerusalem: World Union of Jewish Studies, 1983), pp. 47-60.

[22]Norman K. Gottwald, *The Tribes of Yahweh: A Sociology of the Religion of Liberated Israel, 1250-1050 B.C.E.* (Maryknoll, NY: Orbis Books, 1979). See also his more synoptic presentation in "The Israelite Settlement as a Social Revolutionary Movement," in Janet Amitai, ed., *Biblical Archaeology Today: Proceedings of the International Congress on Biblical Archaeology, Jerusalem, April 1984* (Jerusalem: Israel Exploration Society, 1985), pp. 34-46.

[23]Norman K. Gottwald, *The Hebrew Bible: A Socio-Literary Introduction* (Philadelphia: Fortress Press, 1985), pp. 317-18.

[24]Gottwald, *The Hebrew Bible*, p. 137.

[25]Cf. this recent summary of contemporary thinking: "There seems to be plenty of reason to argue that J was created for and reflects the enthusiastic achievement of

A leading scholar who more than most exhibits the strong influence of Gunkel is R. Rendtorff. In his recent *The Old Testament: An Introduction*, Rendtorff's historical synthesis hews closely to the Bible's own historiography.[26] He endeavors to combine traditional source criticism with a history of traditions.[27] Following Noth and von Rad, Rendtorff identifies the earliest sources in the tradition as the earliest written embodiments of particular traditions. He posits the preliterary, oral transmission of traditions as "fact."[28] He does not account to the preliterary "sagas," however, the historical value that he ascribes to the narratives that might have originated in writing – the history from David onward. He believes the sagas' reports that Israel's ancestors led a "nomadic life-style,[29] but the "various and sometimes independent traditions from the nomadic sphere" possess an inchoate form until they are "introduced into the later cult of all Israel."[30] This seems just another way of saying that whatever authentic traditions may be preserved in Biblical narrative, they have been made over in the period after Israel had become a nation state, after the monarchy was established.

Rendtorff's historical reconstruction is founded almost entirely on the Biblical text: "the OT largely remains our only source for the history of Israel."[31] What the texts do not relate, we do not know: "the texts themselves do not make reference to the matter, so that in my view a tolerable historical reconstruction is impossible."[32] How do we know when the text is giving an authentic account of a tradition? Here Rendtorff trusts in the god of consistency. If two passages report the same thing, the truth of the thing is established. For this purpose extra-Biblical documents may also be adduced.[33] When Rendtorff asserts that "the periods into which [the Bible] divides [its] history have been confirmed in all essential points,"[34] what he is saying is that powerful traditions

---

Davidic-Solomonic nationalism. To date it anytime during the period of the Divided Kingdom, and even after refugees from the North have been assimilated into the Hezekian community, seems less than satisfactory"; Simon J. De Vries, "A Review of Recent Research in the Tradition History of the Pentateuch," in Kent H. Richards, ed., *Society of Biblical Literature 1987 Seminar Papers* (Atlanta: Scholars Press, 1987), pp. 459-502 at 500.

[26]Rolf Rendtorff, *The Old Testament: An Introduction*, trans. John Bowden (Philadelphia: Fortress Press, 1986).

[27]For a comprehensive survey of tradition historical work, see now De Vries, "A Review of Recent Research" (see n. 25 above). De Vries is far more conventional than Rendtorff, however, and remains mystified at the latter's departures from normative source theory.

[28]Rendtorff, *The Old Testament*, p. 79.

[29]Ibid., p. 86.

[30]Ibid., p. 20.

[31]Ibid., p. 5.

[32]Ibid., p. 70.

[33]Ibid., pp. 11, 19, and passim.

[34]Ibid., p. 5.

are historically valid. This is effectively no different from affirming one's credence in the historicity of Biblical traditions.[35]

For many Biblicists the early nineteenth century "Quest for the Historical Jesus" has turned into the Quest for the Historical Abraham, or, that having mainly failed, the Quest for the Historical David. It must be remembered that a historian who trusts all traditions that one cannot disprove is no more or less predisposed than a historian who distrusts all traditions that one cannot corroborate or deduce with conviction. In scholarship, cynicism is no worse than credulity. A scion of the Albright school, and a believer in the Bible's historical reliability, P. K. McCarter, Jr., begins from a position of trust. He writes, for example:

> The stories of David's rise to power and the rebellion of Absalom *seem easiest to understand* [my emphasis] in the context of David's own lifetime. They were composed as attempts to sway public opinion in his favor and, more specifically, to defend him against charges or suspicions of wrongdoing – thus, to legitimate and solidify his claim to the throne.[36]

Note in McCarter's statement that he merges his view of the story's essential historicity with his estimation of its dating to the period of David. One wonders whether McCarter and others would accept the historicity of the David narratives were they convinced that those narratives were set in writing at a much later date.

In characteristically maverick fashion, Van Seters has argued that the source-critical analysis of the Book of Samuel that segregates an early, Davidic or Solomonic stratum in the David story, is wrong.[37] Van Seters endeavors to demonstrate that the very passages that earlier scholars had assumed to be ancient show signs of having been produced *de novo* by the Deuteronomist historian. More precisely, Van Seters finds the story of David's early career to be of a piece with Deuteronomistic historiography. The so-called Court History of David is, in Van Seters' judgment, "a bitter attack upon the whole royal ideology of a 'sure house' for David."[38] Since the Deuteronomist is pro-Davidic, the Court History must have been added to the David narrative in the post-exilic period. It should go without saying that Van Seters puts little store in the reliability of the Davidic "history." Written late, it is not based on historical sources; it is contrived.

---

[35]For a recent positivistic assertion that the Bible's historical reliability should be presumed, see now Tomoo Ishida, "Adonijah the Son of Hagith and His Supporters: An Inquiry into Problems about History and Historiography," in Friedman and Williamson, eds., *The Future of Biblical Studies*, pp. 165-87.

[36]P. Kyle McCarter, Jr., "The Historical David," *Interpretation* 40 (1986), pp. 117-29; here, p. 118.

[37]Van Seters, *In Search of History*, esp. ch. 8, pp. 249-91.

[38]Ibid., p. 290.

What is curious is that critical historians of opposing positions manifest trust in Biblical traditions only when they are found in near-contemporary written documents. With all the theorizing that has gone on since Gunkel concerning the oral transmission of Biblical narratives and other traditions, even scholars like Rendtorff and McCarter will place confidence only in a written report. In this respect they are not far from Wellhausen. The believing historian, unlike the uncritical believer, does not accept the Bible as a historical witness. The believing historian by virtue of the academic discipline of history, begins from a position of distrust.[39]

Some will justify their skepticism by pointing to the literary genre of the Biblical narrative, its presumed intention. Zakovitch, for example, maintains that the extensive and multifaceted literary patterning of the Biblical "history" betrays its artificial, novelistic quality.[40] Although my own sympathies are with Zakovitch on this, the following represents a more widely shared perspective:

> Although, admittedly, the Biblical authors made use of historical facts, they did so to convince the reader of the validity of the religious, moral and social concepts being urged, and they kneaded the raw material of historical facts into the message they were trying to convey. In short, when historical facts fit into the message, the Biblical authors used them; when the historical facts did not support the message, the facts were molded by rearranging them or elaborating them until they did support the message.[41]

The author of these remarks, Y. T. Radday, goes on to delineate a large number of Biblical claims that cannot be factual, in particular matters of geography and chronology. Now if these fundamentals of historiography are unreliable, in what can the historian trust? Indeed, on what basis does Radday assert that "the Biblical authors made use of historical facts?" To what extent is what the Bible says factual, and how can one tell? We have seen above that Rendtorff applies the standard of coherence: if the same fact is reported in different texts, it may be believed.

Others adduce the confirmation of archaeological exploration. While historical geographers can often link up archaeological sites with Biblical

---

[39]For further discussion of this topic, see Ivan G. Marcus, "The Jewish Historian and the Believer," in Nina B. Cardin and David W. Silverman, eds., *The Seminary at 100: Reflections on the Jewish Theological Seminary and the Conservative Movement* (New York: The Rabbinical Assembly and the Jewish Theological Seminary of America, 1987), pp. 215-22.

[40]Zakovitch, "Story Versus History" (see n. 21 above).

[41]Yehuda T. Radday, "A Bible Scholar Looks at BAR's Coverage of the Exodus," *BARev* 8/6 (Nov./Dec. 1982), pp. 68-71; here, pp. 68-69. For the view that the Biblical history of the monarchy was less than tendentious, see now Baruch Halpern, "Biblical or Israelite History?" in Friedman and Williamson, eds., *The Future of Biblical Studies,* pp. 103-39.

toponyms,[42] the fact is that archaeology can readily be used to demonstrate the historical *un*reliability of what the Bible reports. The cases of Ha-ai and Jericho are well-known.[43] Let me illustrate with a less familiar but hardly obscure instance. Textual and artifactual evidence had convinced scholars like W. F. Albright that the camel had not been domesticated in the Levant until the twelfth century B.C.E. Accordingly, Albright viewed the references to camels in Genesis as "anachronistic."[44] Albright did not mean that the patriarchal narratives were late inventions. He thought that a later tradent replaced an earlier beast in the original narrative with a more fashionable, contemporary one. "Of course," Albright was quick to add, "such anachronisms in local color no more disprove the historicity of the underlying tradition than Tissot's painted scenes of Bible life falsify the biblical story by depicting its heroes as modern Palestinian Arabs."[45] In drawing the conclusion that the archaeological data do not indicate the time of the events being narrated in the Bible, Albright is in effect discounting the relevance of the archaeological evidence for dating or authenticating Biblical reports. Material evidence does not budge his trust in the historicity of the narratives. His initial presumption of historicity predetermined the way he handled the archaeological data.

The most recent data on the camel in the ancient land of Israel, from the excavation of numerous animal bones at Tel Jemmeh, an ancient crossroads near Gaza, indicate that camel caravans were not employed in what archaeologists call Syro-Palestine until around 600 B.C.E.[46] Thus, unless the trip of Abraham's servant in Genesis 24 and the visit of the Queen of Sheba to Solomon are but "singular events,"[47] the reference to camels in Biblical narrative are grossly anachronistic. One can argue that earlier stories were modernized by a later editor who inserted camels where there had been none in the source. But one will follow this strategy only under the presumption that the Biblical narratives are essentially historical. A historian who adds this particular anachronism to the many others that have been suggested may also also conclude that the narratives were composed at a late date, and that they are historically unreliable.

---

[42]See esp. Yohanan Aharoni, *The Land of the Bible,* rev. and enlarged by Anson F. Rainey (Philadelphia: Westminster Press, 1979).

[43]Cf., e.g., Bright, *History,* pp. 130-31. For further discussion see Roland de Vaux, *The Early History of Israel,* trans. David Smith (Philadelphia: Westminster Press, 1978), esp. pp. 475-87.

[44]William F. Albright, *The Archaeology of Palestine,* rev. ed. (London: Pelican Books, 1954), pp. 206-7.

[45]Ibid., p. 207.

[46]Paula Wapnish, "Camel Caravans and Camel Pastoralists at Tell Jemmeh," *JANES* 13 (1981), pp. 101-21.

[47]Ibid., p. 112. It should be noted that Wapnish appears rather conservative in her suggestion that the Queen of Sheba might have made an extraordinary journey to the Land of Israel in the tenth century B.C.E. by camel. Wapnish takes the narrative at its face value, in spite of its fairytale-like quality.

The archaeologist William Dever has in a number of manifestoes contended that recent studies and excavations in the near Middle East can best be explained if one does not accept the historical authenticity of the major episodes in the narrative from Genesis through Kings,[48] the so-called Primary History.[49] In his view there was no exodus of masses of Hebrews from Egypt in the thirteenth century, no sojourn in the Sinai wilderness, no military conquest of Canaan by the Israelites. Excavations by Israeli and American scholars in the Galilee and Negev in particular indicate that Israelites took up residence in places that had no preceding settlement.[50] To many, including Dever, the Israelites were Canaanites who moved to the hill country and Negev because those were sparsely populated areas that would offer them little resistance. Accordingly, Dever believes that recent archaeology conforms more closely to the settlement model proposed by Mendenhall and Gottwald[51] than the invasion model that had been favored by the Albright school, represented, for example, by Bright's *History of Israel*.[52] In the third edition of this widely used volume Bright attempts to assimilate some of the recent opposition but retains the historicity of the exodus and military conquest. He regards the events as complexes of

---

[48]For a summary and bibliography, see William G. Dever, "Syro-Palestinian and Biblical Archaeoloogy," in Douglas A. Knight and Gene M. Tucker, eds., The *Hebrew Bible and Its Modern Interpreters* (Chico, CA: Scholars Press, 1985), pp. 31-74. For a similar position, cf. now Max Miller, "Old Testament History and Archaeology," *BA* 50/1 (March 1987), pp. 55-63.

[49]For the term "Primary History," see David N. Freedman, "The Earliest Bible," in Michael P. O'Connor and D. N. Freedman, eds., *Backgrounds for the Bible* (Winona Lake, IN: Eisenbrauns, 1987), pp. 29-37.

[50]For summary discussion and bibliography, see now Moshe Kochavi, "The Israelite Settlement in Canaan in the Light of Archaeological Surveys," in Amitai, ed., *Biblical Archaeology Today*, pp. 54-60. See also, in addition to the articles by Aharoni cited there, Aharon Kempinski, "Israelite Conquest or Settlement? New Light from Tell Masos," *BARev* 2/3 (Sept. 1976), pp. 25-30. Cf. Kempinski's conclusion (p. 30b):

> The first appearance of the Israelites at Tell Masos in the northern Negev and the new cultural elements which they brought with them is in total harmony with the settlement theory of [Albrecht] Alt....Tell Masos establishes that the Israelite settlers of the second half of the 13th century B.C.E. were not simply nomads who "emerged from the desert" but were a people who already had a building tradition going back to the Bronze Age traditions of the mountainous areas.

Contrast the somewhat more traditional views of Amihai Mazar in *Biblical Archaeology Today*, pp. 61-71.

[51]George E. Mendenhall, "The Hebrew Conquest of Palestine," *BA* 25/3 (Sept. 1962), pp. 66-87, reprinted in Edward F. Campbell, Jr., and David N. Freedman, eds., *The Biblical Archaeologist Reader 3* (Garden City, NY: Anchor Books, 1970), pp. 100-20; idem, *The Tenth Generation: The Origins of the Biblical Tradition* (Baltimore: Johns Hopkins University Press, 1973); Gottwald, The *Tribes of Yahweh*.

[52]Bright, *A History of Israel*, esp. pp. 133-43.

various distinct group movements that have been telescoped, and he lowers the numbers of people involved.

The editor of *Biblical Archaeology Review*, Hershel Shanks, has correctly defined the difference between the approach of scholars like Dever and that of scholars like Bright.[53] The one begins without any commitment to the historical truth of the Biblical narrative, while the latter begins from a position of faith. Shanks maintains that "for Dever, any collision he can identify between the archaeological evidence and the Biblical evidence requires him to reject the Biblical evidence."[54] Shanks justifiably labels Dever's approach an "anti-Biblical bias."[55] If one means by that a considered distrust of the Bible's historicity concerning the early stages of Israel's history, that characterization may be valid. But Shanks also condemns Dever's approach as "a fundamental methodological error."[56] What Shanks is effectively saying is that good methodology posits the authenticity of the Biblical record, or, more generously, that good methodology must exclude bias for or against both the Biblical record and one's interpretation of archaeological data. The exclusion of bias or presupposition, however, is no more than a comforting illusion, as we have seen. One always begins from a position of greater credence or of greater skepticism. One's methodology will be fundamentally affected by that opening stance.[57]

---

[53]Hershel Shanks, "Dever's 'Sermon on the Mound'," *BARev* 13/1 (March/April 1987), pp. 54-57.

[54]Ibid., p. 57.

[55]Ibid., p. 56.

[56]Ibid., p. 57.

[57]Cf. Frederic Brandton, "The Limits of Evidence: Archaeology and Objectivity," *Maarav* 4/1 (Spring 1987), pp. 5-43, who concludes: "As it turns out, the material evidence, although exceptionally valuable, is no more intrinsically accurate or objective than any other kind of evidence" (p. 43). Concerning the non-objective use of archaeological evidence for ascertaining the historicity or date of any events reported in the Bible, one can hardly gainsay the characteristically thoughtful perspective of S. R. Driver, first published in 1904:

> The monuments, again,...though they have thrown some light on the kings' names in Gen. 14:1, and have shown that it would be no impossibility for a Babylonian or Elamite king of the 23rd century B.C. to undertake an expedition to the far West, make no mention of the *particular* expedition recorded in Gen. 14: they consequently furnish no independent corroboration of it....The case is similar in the later parts of Genesis. The argument which has been advanced, for instance, to show that the narrative of the purchase of the cave of Machpelah (ch. 23) is the work of a contemporary hand, breaks down completely: the expressions alleged in proof of the assertion are not *confined* to the age of Hammurabi; they one and all...occur, in some cases repeatedly, in the period of the kings, and even later: they consequently furnish no evidence that the narrative was written at any earlier date. There is no antecedent reason why Abraham should not have purchased a plot of ground near Hebron from the native inhabitants of the place: but to

Aware of contrary possibilities for constructing a convincing model of what early Israel looked like, Cross has candidly admitted:

> I doubt that Biblical archaeology can ever establish that the traditional events of Israel's early epic are historical, and certainly the archaeologist cannot prove these events were truly interpreted, even if established as historical.[58]

Nevertheless, while Cross acknowledges the limitations of the historical disciplines in reaching decisive conclusions, he confesses his personal outlook, what Shanks would have to call a "bias":

> Israel uniquely was plunged into history, into a perennial grappling with history as the realm of meaning, and it would not be surprising, I think, if this plunge were precipitated by Israel's own historical experience.[59]

In other words, Cross admits to his predisposition to trust the contours of the Biblical tradition. At the same time, it is evident that historians and archaeologists with different predispositions will assemble their data into different models of historical reconstruction. Data do not by themselves congeal into theories. Scholars shape the date into configurations of their own imagination.[60]

The same may be said of philological analysis. In a recent publication two Israeli scholars, Y. Klein and Y. Zakovitch, assign the Book of Ruth to two different periods, one pre-exilic and one post-exilic.[61] Zakovitch advocates the later dating on the basis of the text's affinities to post-exilic Hebrew and its putative Aramaisms; its post-classical orthography; and its morphology (e.g., no distinction between masculine and feminine in the plural possessive suffixes). Klein defends the earlier dating by pointing out that many of the text's peculiar expressions (lexical and morphological) occur in pre-exilic sources, too – and some of them only in early sources. To account for this he hypothesizes that what occurred late in written Hebrew may have developed early in spoken Hebrew.[62] The text's orthography may, in Klein's view, reflect the results of

---

suppose that this is proven, or even made probable, by archaeology, is completely to misinterpret the evidence which it furnishes"; Driver, The *Book of Genesis,* 2nd ed. (London: Methuen, 1904), pp. xlix-l.
See, too, Chapter Three.
[58]Frank M. Cross, "Biblical Archaeology Today: The Biblical Aspect," in Amitai, ed., *Biblical Archaeology Today,* pp. 9-15; here, p. 14.
[59]Loc. cit.
[60]Cf. Luis Alonso Schökel, "Of Methods and Models," *SVT* 36 (Leiden: E. J. Brill, 1985), pp. 3-13; and Chapter Three.
[61]In אנציקלופדיה עולם התנ״ך [Bible World Encyclopedia], vol. 16a, ed. Yaakov Klein (Tel Aviv: Revivim, 1987), pp. 72-73.
[62]Cf. Abba Bendavid, לשון מקרא ולשון חכמים [Biblical Hebrew and Mishnaic Hebrew] (Tel Aviv: Dvir, 1967), 2 vols.

scribal transmission, not the stage of composition. Both Zakovitch and Klein acknowledge the archaic literary style of Ruth. But for Klein it is an authentically classical style, and for Zakovitch it is deliberately archaizing. Each scholar defines and adapts the evidence according to his own point of view.[63]

Nowhere is this situation more obvious in Biblical Studies than in the state of affairs of the source critical analysis of the Bible, and of the Torah in particular.[64] Source criticism of the Torah has loomed large in modern Biblical Studies – so much so that Weinfeld has virtually equated source criticism with Biblical criticism in general in a recent encyclopedia article.[65] All questions concerning the early history of Israel and the development of Biblical religion – including the divine character of the Torah – presuppose certain conclusions about the Torah's literary origins. Both Wellhausen's and Kaufmann's almost antithetical visions of ancient Israelite religious history depend upon closely kindred theories of the Torah's literary development.[66] Both Wellhausen and Kaufmann accept the division of the Torah into four documents, J, E, D, and P – except that for Kaufmann nothing is exilic or later, and P precedes D. In assaulting Wellhausen's reconstruction of Israelite history, Kaufmann did not challenge the assumptions and methods of source critical analysis.

F. V. Winnett and his former student J. Van Seters have posed such a challenge, but only a partial one.[67] Van Seters objects not to source division but to the minute dissection of passages into small fragments; and, more significantly, he interprets the sources distinguished by documentary theorists not as parallel texts that have been redacted together but rather as literary supplements by what is often the same writer. The writer, in this view, fleshes out and revises earlier sources not by altering them but by adding to them. Alternatively, an ancient Israelite historian might compose a narrative of whole cloth, alluding to imaginary sources at times in order to give an aura of

---

[63]Were I writing on the dating of Ruth based on the linguistic evidence, rather than take one or the other side I would explain that one could for very cogent reasons formulate the evidence in either direction. We are not in a position philologically to make a call either way.

[64]Cf., e.g, John Van Seters, "Recent Studies on the Pentateuch: A Crisis in Method," *JAOS* 99 (1979), pp. 663-73; my "Sources of the Pentateuch," in Paul Achtemeier, ed., *Harper's Bible Dictionary* (San Francisco: Harper & Row, 1985), pp. 983-86; and see further Douglas A. Knight, "The Pentateuch," in Knight and Tucker, eds., *The Hebrew Bible*, pp. 263-96.

[65]Moshe Weinfeld, "Biblical Criticism," in Arthur A. Cohen and Paul Mendes-Flohr, eds., *Contemporary Jewish Religious Thought* (New York: Charles Scribner's Sons, 1987), pp. 35-40.

[66]Wellhausen, *Prolegomena* (see n. 10 above); Yehezkel Kaufmann, תולדות האמונה הישראלית [History of Israelite Religion], 8 vols. (Tel Aviv: Dvir, 1955-60); see also his גולה ונכר [Exile and Foreign Land], 2 vols. (Tel Aviv: Dvir, 1929-32), for the theoretical assumptions underlying much of his historiography.

[67]Frederick V. Winnett, "Re-examining the Foundations," *JBL* 84 (1965), pp. 1-19; Van Seters, *Abraham* and *In Search of History*.

authenticity to his work.[68] Whereas in the Torah, the former model of composition prevails, in the Deuteronomistic History one finds a mix of both types.[69] The classical Documentary Hypothesis and the Winnett-Van Seters theory apply different compositional models.[70] The Documentary theory regards the redactor of the Torah as an ancient Jewish predecessor of the author of a synoptic Gospel, redacting together two or more sources into a new version. Van Seters sees the Torah's author as a contemporary of Herodotus, composing history using similar methods. The implications of the two opposing models for the reconstruction of Israelite history are profound. Within the first model, which posits earlier sources, it is possible to assume the antiquity and historicity of various Biblical traditions. The second model obstructs any attempt to posit early historical traditions.

The theory of the Torah's composition delineated by Rendtorff is both more revolutionary and more conservative than those just discussed.[71] Instead of beginning with written sources, Rendtorff follows Gunkel, Noth, and von Rad in tracing the written materials from units of tradition. These units take literary shape independently until they are later assembled into more extensive narrative works. These are then composed into the Torah through various processes resembling at times the model of documentary redaction and at times the model of literary supplementation. It is again unsurprising that in positing ancient oral traditions behind the earliest written stages of the Torah's development Rendtorff affirms the general historicity of the Biblical traditions, as we have seen. Just as historical reconstruction depends upon a theory of literary composition, so does one's approach to literary composition reflect one's perspective on Israelite history, or the Bible's account of it.

Rendtorff considers himself to have made "a fundamental break with the traditional methods of analyzing pentateuchal texts."[72] He explains the nature of that break this way:

> Scholars usually begin their study of a pentateuchal text by dividing sources within the text....But in my opinion this is wrong because it presupposes that there must be sources running through the whole Pentateuch....According to the traditional method of literary critique it is not for the scholar to demonstrate that the respective text is not uniform and composed by different sources but it is for the text itself to prove

---

[68]Van Seters, *In Search of History*, e.g., pp. 40-49 (see the Index there for further references).

[69]Ibid., pp. 267-69.

[70]Cf. Alonso Schökel, "Of Methods and Models" (see n. 60 above), esp. pp. 5-6.

[71]Rolf Rendtorff, *Das überlieferungsgeschichte Problem des Pentateuch* (Berlin: W. de Gruyter, 1977); idem, "The Future of Pentateuchal Criticism," *Henoch* 6 (1984), pp. 1-14; cf. Erhard Blum, *Die Komposition der Vätergeschichte* (Neukirchen-Vluyn: Neukirchener, 1984). For a critique of Rendtorff's approach, see Van Seters, "Recent Studies on the Pentateuch" (see n. 64 above).

[72]Rendtorff, "The Future of Pentateuchal Criticism," p. 11.

this unity. This approach must be reversed. First of all we have to take the text as a unity and have to try and understand its structure and particular intention.[73]

Rendtorff would have us replace the dogmatism of source analysis with the dogmatism of synthesis. Viewing the text phenomenologically, from a presumption of unity, is no more or less theoretical than viewing the text as a composite. He is opposing a newer theory to the older one.[74]

Rendtorff's position is symptomatic of two important tendencies among many contemporary Biblicists. One is a disaffection from historical paradigms of Biblical study. The other, concomitant trend is attention to the text's unity, or, put differently, applying synchronic paradigms of study to the final form of the Biblical text. I shall take up these two points together because they are interdependent. The application of synchronic modes of analysis to the Bible, in step with other academic disciplines, seems often to flow from a reaction against or restlessness with the more entrenched historical methods of research.[75]

The frustration of many Biblicists with historical study is evinced in the recent introduction to the Hebrew Bible (or, in Christian terms, the "Old Testament") by Crenshaw. On account of the complicated and obscure literary development of the Biblical text, Crenshaw says:

> A purely historical analysis of the literature cannot yield satisfactory results. Efforts to specify dates for biblical books and to examine them according to their historical sequence are doomed from the start. It has become increasingly clear that no satisfactory history of the literature can be written....Thus far, no suitable criteria exist by which to separate later glosses from early writings, and every indication points to extremely active editorial work in updating ancient traditions.[76]

If we cannot with confidence distinguish historical strata in a Biblical text, we can only doubtfully engage in historical reconstruction. The Bible is, after all, our major source. We can, however, study and interpret the final form of the text, putting into practice strategies of analysis that deal with the form, style, and underlying ideas of the literature as we have it. Synchronic methods generally presuppose the integrity of the text.

The function of textual criticism has always been to restore an earlier, more original document. Versions of the Hebrew Bible, such as the Septuagint, have

---

[73]Loc. cit.; cf., e.g., Bernhard W. Anderson, "From Analysis to Synthesis: The Interpretation of Genesis 1-11," *JBL* 97 (1978), pp. 23-39; Moshe Greenberg, *Ezekiel 1-20*, AB 22 (Garden City, NY: Doubleday, 1983), pp. 18-27; idem, "What Are Valid Criteria for Determining Inauthentic Matter in Ezekiel?" in J. Lust, ed., *Ezekiel and His Book* (Leuven: Leuven University Press, 1986), pp. 123-35.
[74]See further Chapter Three.
[75]Cf. Chapter Two, with references.
[76]James L. Crenshaw, *Story and Faith: A Guide to the Old Testament* (New York: Macmillan Publishing, 1986), p. 2.

been compared in order to evaluate the Massoretic Text and correct it where necessary with readings in the versions that for various reasons seemed better to the critic. There is now, however, a newer tendency to view the versions as independent traditions. The Septuagint, too, is a textual unity.[77] Only after being studied as a total structure should a text like the Septuagint be compared with the Massoretic Text, or with a Dead Sea fragment for that matter. M. Greenberg, in an examination of the Massoretic and Greek texts of Ezekiel, regards each as an independent entity: "we have two versions, each with its own quality and its own coherence."[78] Out of respect for the integrity of the Massoretic Text, the received text is regularly compared in order to trace the literary history of the versions. Compare the following conclusion from a recent study of the Exodus scroll from Qumran Cave 4:

> [The Qumran text] represents a textual tradition that is very close to that known to us in the Massoretic text. Working from a base very much like what has come down to us as [the Massoretic text], one or several scribes expanded certain specific sections of the text, with the result that many columns of the scroll look quite similar to [the Massoretic text], while other columns – even in their present fragmentary state – have six or seven lines not found in [the Massoretic text].[79]

Implicit in these remarks are the following premises: MT is a distinct text; the Qumran scroll is a distinct text; material in the latter that is missing in the former is the result of expansion in the scroll rather than deletion in the source; and, most fundamentally, there is a historical connection between the MT and Qumran texts. We may tend to forget that the connections that we take for granted are the products of our prior hypotheses and conclusions. We do not simply see the connections; we first draw them. Our changing perspectives are not the naked fruits of new research. They are just that – "changing perspectives," a different way of looking at things.

This newer synchronic vision is most evident in our approaches to exegesis. Whatever disciplines scholars work in – whether anthropology, sociology, rhetoric, or theology – more and more analyze the Bible as a contained system of structurally related components. The models many Biblicists are increasingly adopting are structural, paradigmatic.[80] The difference in what the Bible means

---

[77]See, e.g., Emanuel Tov, "Jewish Greek Scriptures," in Robert A. Kraft and George W. E. Nickelsburg, eds., *Early Judaism and Its Modern Interpreters* (Philadelphia/Atlanta: Fortress Press/Scholars Press, 1986), pp. 223-37, esp. 229.
[78]Moshe Greenberg, "The Use of the Ancient Versions for Interpreting the Hebrew Text," *SVT* 29 (Leiden: E. J. Brill, 1978), pp. 131-48; here, p. 140.
[79]Judith E. Sanderson, *An Exodus Scroll from Qumran* (Atlanta: Scholars Press, 1986), p. 140.
[80]See, e.g., Roland Barthes et al., *Structural Analysis and Biblical Exegesis*, trans. Alfred M. Johnson, Jr. (Pittsburgh: Pickwick Press, 1974); Robert M. Polzin, *Biblical Structuralism* (Philadelphia/Missoula: Fortress Press/Scholars Press, 1977); Robert Detweiler, *Story, Sign, and Self: Phenomenology and Structuralism*

between the historical and synchronic methods of exegesis is analogous to the difference between the chronicle of a person's life and a psychoanalysis of that person.

Let me illustrate by referring to Biblical prophecy. While scholars had typically attempted to segregate what the prophet said from what later interpolators and editors had added,[81] some recent work such as the Ezekiel commentary by Greenberg and the studies of First and Second Isaiah by Gitay start with the assumption of textual order.[82] They then apply diverse literary and rhetorical strategies to account for and make good sense of the present form of the text. We then read of the "consistent trend of thought" and "distinctive style" of Ezekiel,[83] or of the "order" and "art of persuasion" of Second Isaiah.[84] Applying synchronic analysis from a sociological perspective, Robert Wilson has endeavored to examine not so much the history of prophecy in ancient Israel as the relations of Biblical prophets to their society.[85] So, too, Michael Fishbane, rather than reconstruct the development of Israelite prophecy, has summarized a phenomenology of Biblical prophecy, placing it in the context of other elements in the Bible's conceptual framework (such as covenant and

---

as Literary-Critical Methods (Philadelphia/Atlanta: Fortress Press/Scholars Press, 1978). The book *Structuralism and Biblical Hermeneutics* (Pittsburgh: Pickwick Press, 1979), ed. and trans. Alfred M. Johnson, Jr., deals directly very little with the Scriptures, and then mostly with the Christian ones. The fact, however, that the book is primarily addressed to Biblicists bespeaks the editor's presumption that structuralist methods are vital to Biblical Studies.

[81] For a recent approach to Jeremiah that attributes the book to layers of redactional work, see Robert P. Carroll, *From Chaos to Covenant: Prophecy in the Book of Jeremiah* (New York: Crossroad, 1981); *Jeremiah: A Commentary* (Philadelphia: Westminster Press, 1986). Carroll clearly distinguishes modern approaches to Jeremiah in their theoretical oppositions in his "Introduction" to *Jeremiah*, esp. pp. 38-50. For an exemplary discussion of the ways that theory and method impinge on the literary historical analysis of Jeremiah, see W. McKane, "Relations between Prose and Poetry in the Book of Jeremiah...," in Leo G. Perdue and Brian W. Kovacs, eds., *A Prophet to the Nations: Essays in Jeremiah Studies* (Winona Lake, IN: Eisenbrauns, 1984), pp. 269-84.

[82] For Greenberg, see the references in n. 73 above; Yehoshua Gitay, "Reflections on the Study of Prophetic Discourse," *VT* 33 (1983), pp. 207-21; "Isaiah and His Audience," *Prooftexts* 3 (1983), pp. 223-30; "The Effectiveness of Isaiah's Speech," *JQR* 75 (1984), pp. 162-72; *Prophecy and Persuasion: A Study of Isaiah 40-48* (Bonn: Linguistica Biblica, 1981). Although Greenberg maintains that his conclusion of the text's integrity "is no *a priori* stance" but his "critical assessment of the evidence" ("What Are Valid Criteria," p. 135), by his applying the criteria that he himself sets forth in ibid., p. 133, he could hardly have reached a different conclusion.

[83] Greenberg, *Ezekiel 1-20*, p. 26.

[84] Gitay, *Prophecy and Persuasion*, p. 232.

[85] Robert R. Wilson, *Prophecy and Society in Ancient Israel* (Philadelphia: Fortress Press, 1980); cf. idem, *Sociological Approaches to the Old Testament* (Philadelphia: Fortress Press, 1984).

worship).[86] The significance of the prophet and the meaning of his message are determined in these models by their function within a given system, be that a social or literary one.

Various forms of literary criticism largely find the meaning of Biblical texts in the linguistic configurations and or semantic and psychological deep structures that are manifest in them. Like a wave touched off by new and different disturbances in the field of literary theory, Biblical Studies has of late reacted routinely to the latest literary vibrations. We have nothing like the widespread paradigm shifts in Biblical Studies that would, in Thomas Kuhn's terminology, mark the equivalent of a "scientific revolution,"[87] but if there is any single new wave in Biblical criticism, it is the application of synchronic modes of literary interpretation. Even within historical approaches, synchronic analysis is often adduced to determine the meaning of a historical period or literary stratum, as in, for example, the studies of the Deuteronomist's work by Polzin[88] and Van Seters[89]; Harold Bloom's essays on "J," the Bible's, and perhaps the world's, most original writer[90]; and canonical criticism in general – the study of Biblical texts with regard to their position in the canon.[91]

Synchronic analysis, as the study of the text as a relatively closed system, is attractive for at least three reasons, apart from its trendiness. First, it interprets what we have – rather than a reconstructed version of it. Although interpreting what we have involves the same degree of theorizing as does interpreting what

---

[86]Michael Fishbane, "Biblical Prophecy as a Religious Phenomenon," in Arthur Green, ed., *Jewish Spirituality from the Bible through the Middle Ages* (New York: Crossroad, 1986), pp. 62-81.

[87]Thomas S. Kuhn, *The Structure of Scientific Revolutions*, 2nd ed. (Chicago: University of Chicago Press, 1970). John Dominic Crossan exaggerates in seeing a current revolution in Kuhn's sense in the Biblical field; see his "'Ruth Amid the Alien Corn': Perspectives and Methods in Contemporary Biblical Criticism," in Robert M. Polzin and Eugene Rothman, eds., *The Biblical Mosaic* (Philadelphia/Chico, CA: Fortress Press/Scholars Press, 1982), pp. 199-210.

[88]Robert Polzin, *Moses and the Deuteronomist* (New York: Seabury Press, 1980).

[89]Van Seters, *In Search of History*, pp. 249-353.

[90]E.g., Harold Bloom, "Introduction" to Martin Buber, *On the Bible*, ed. Nahum N. Glatzer (New York: Schocken Books, 1982), pp. ix-xxxii; "Criticism, Canon-Formation, and Prophecy," *Raritan* 3/3 (Winter 1984), pp. 1-20; and "Exodus: From J to K, or The Uncanniness of the Yahwist," in David Rosenberg, ed., *Congregation* (New York: Harcourt Brace Jovanovich, 1987), pp. 9-26.

[91]See esp. James A. Sanders, *Torah and Canon* (Philadelphia: Fortress Press, 1972); Brevard S. Childs, *Introduction to the Old Testament as Scripture* (Philadelphia: Fortress Press, 1979). In canonical criticism the text is read in its final form against the background of the faith community that created it. Childs' approach differs somewhat from Sanders' in that the former is more concerned with the meaning of the final form within the faith traditions that have preserved and transmitted it.

we must first reconstruct,[92] many feel more comfortable with the received text. Biblicists are only recently beginning to acknowledge the hypothetical nature of all the approaches they take. The matter has been put well by Barton:

> Biblical "methods" are *theories* rather than methods: theories which result from the formalizing of intelligent intuitions about the meaning of biblical texts. Texts are perceived as having certain sorts of meaning – or, just as interestingly, as failing to convey meaning – by reading them with certain vague expectations about genre, coherence, and consistency, which are either confirmed and clarified, or disappointed and frustrated. Then reading begins again, this time with a sharper focus; and at the end of the process there emerges a distinct impression of what the text means, together with an explanatory theory as to how it comes to mean it. But the theory – which, when codified, will become source analysis or redaction criticism or whatever – is logically subsequent to the intuition about meaning.[93]

Accordingly, preference for the received text adumbrates an epistemological position. Many trust our means of making meaning more than our means of reconstructing a text.

A second reason for the popularity of synchronic analysis is also epistemological. We find the sense of a text, or anything else, to be more significant or fuller by studying it in terms of its shape and function than by studying its historical evolution. We have touched on this matter above.

A third, rather pragmatic reason for doing synchronic analysis is that its practice requires fewer accessory disciplines than historical investigation. That is, one does not have to be as well educated in languages, scripts, archaeology, history and historiography, textual criticism, and comparative Semitic philology to analyze the Biblical text within a synchronic paradigm. The synchronic approach either depends upon the prior and fundamental work of historical scholarship, or it ignores it.[94] There is no question that synchronic methods

---

[92]It is for this reason that I would not adopt the suggestion made to me by Professor Gershon Shaked that instead of contrasting, as I do, the historical/diachronic with the phenomenological/synchronic, I should contrast the positivist with the poeticist. In my view, positivism may characterize poetic analysis as well as historical reconstruction. An example might be Meir Sternberg's magnificent *The Poetics of Biblical Narrative* (Bloomington: Indiana University Press, 1985). To positivism I would oppose a perspective more akin to relativism, pluralism, or deconstruction – terms that many will regard as apt for classifying the present essay.

[93]John Barton, *Reading the Old Testament* (Philadelphia: Westminster Press, 1984), p. 205.

[94]Neglect of historical Biblical scholarship is manifest, for example, in the work of Robert Alter, *The Art of Biblical Narrative* (New York: Basic Books, 1981) and *The Art of Biblical Poetry* (New York: Basic Books, 1985). See, e.g., the criticisms in the following reviews: Jon D. Levenson, *BA* 46/2 (Spring 1983), pp. 124-25; Baruch Schwartz, *Shnaton: An Annual for Biblical and Ancient Near*

produce rich and revealing meaning in the text, in particular with respect to the themes and typologies that have come to constitute the frameworks of the great religions that base themselves on the Hebrew Bible.[95] But in order to perform synchronic analysis on the Bible one need know only Hebrew, or even no Hebrew at all.[96]

Synchronic methods also serve us well in our teaching. We can train our students to apply literary, structural modes of analysis to the text in far less time than it would take to develop their skills in diachronic forms of analysis. Moreover, teaching historical method almost necessarily conveys a hierarchical or authoritarian view of the teacher-student relationship – that of learned master vis-á-vis ignorant disciple. Utilizing a synchronic approach, in little time the student can contribute and almost democratically participate in learning. The preference for synchronic paradigms of study by teachers and students may well reflect such an egalitarian political agenda.

If our object is to find meaning in the Bible in as many ways or on as many levels as possible, we should attempt to see the text within both historical and synchronic matrices. In his superb new introduction to the Hebrew Bible, Norman Gottwald assesses the values of the many paradigms of study – as religious testimony, historical witness, literary world, social world, to use his terms.[97] It is the merit of Gottwald's book to explain how different epistemological paradigms – what he calls "angles of vision" – yield different views of the Bible and the various parts of the world in which it was first produced. Before discussing the major Biblical themes or traditions, Gottwald does his best to place the literary sources in their historical, and if possible even their sociological, context.

That will work for Gottwald, who, as we saw above, appears relatively confident in the potential of historical reconstruction. It will not work for someone like literary critic Meir Sternberg, who would like to read the Bible against the enriching background of its historical world but does not because, as

---

Eastern Studies 5-6 (1978-79), esp. pp. 268-69 [in Hebrew]; Edward L. Greenstein, *Hebrew Studies* 27 (1986), pp. 82-91; James L. Kugel, *Journal of Religion* 67 (1987), pp. 66-79.

[95]Cf., e.g., Michael Fishbane, "The Sacred Center: The Symbolic Structure of the Bible," in M. A. Fishbane and Paul Mendes-Flohr, eds., *Texts and Responses: Studies Presented to Nahum N. Glatzer* (Leiden: E. J. Brill, 1975), pp. 6-27; Northrop Frye, *The Great Code: The Bible and Literature* (New York: Harcourt Brace Jovanovich, 1982).

[96]Distinguished examples are Roland Barthes, "The Struggle with the Angel," in Barthes et al., *Structural Analysis and Biblical Exegesis*, pp. 21-33 = Barthes, *Image/Music/Text* (New York: Hill and Wang, 1977), pp. 125-41; Mary Douglas, "The Abominations of Leviticus," *Purity and Danger* (New York: Praeger, 1966), pp. 41-58.

[97]Gottwald, *The Hebrew Bible*, esp. pp. 31-33.

he says, "when all is said and done, the independent knowledge we possess of the 'real world' behind the Bible remains absurdly meager...."[98]

Many contemporary Biblicists are experiencing a crisis in faith. I do not mean faith in the Bible's history, which, as we have seen, is hardly new; but faith in believing the results of our study. The objective truths of the past we increasingly understand as the creations of our own vision. The words of Christian Scriptures scholar John Dominic Crossan describe what we have found:

> We found not a picture but a mirror, and the dust of ages was but the images of our ancestors. In a mirror, however, we see not just ourselves but ourselves *looking*. We see our eyes before we see all else.[99]

But rather than lament our loss of absolute knowledge, Crossan relishes the new hermeneutical possibilities that we have gained by this self-awareness of our ideas and sensibilities: "the fact that the mirror is overlaid with images, with multiple interpretations, is not our failure but our success."[100]

The effect of recognizing that all scholarship relies on theories and methods that come and go, and that modern critical approaches are no more or less than our own midrash, places us, if we are informed and responsible, on the same footing as our predecessors.[101] We should do our work as well as we can, using the paradigms and tools in which we can put our trust. Those paradigms and tools will play a role that serve our objectives and concerns. Feminist critics of the Bible, for example, have learned to appreciate the value of midrashic types of hermeneutics in order to make of the Bible a text with which and by which they can live.[102] Other feminist critics, using more conventional secular approaches, may decide that within their paradigms the Bible is hopelessly androcentric and

---

[98]Sternberg, *The Poetics of Biblical Narrative* (see n. 92 above), p. 16.

[99]John Dominic Crossan, "The Hermeneutical Jesus," in O'Connor and Freedman, eds., *Backgrounds for the Bible* (see n. 49 above), pp. 15-27; here, p. 27.

[100]Loc. cit.

[101]This, for example, is the inevitable conclusion of James L. Kugel's review of the history of Biblical poetics in *The Idea of Biblical Poetry: Parallelism and Its History* (New Haven: Yale University Press, 1981). Cf., e.g., Ismar Schorsch, "Message of the Chancellor," *[Jewish Theological] Seminary Progress*, March 1987, p. 16: "Critical scholarship is the *midrash* of the modern Jew, the application of Western modes of cognition to ancient texts that resonate with sense and meaning."

[102]Cf., eg., Phyllis Bird, "Images of Women in the Old Testament," in Rosemary Radford Reuther, ed., *Religion and Sexism* (New York: Simon & Schuster, 1974), pp. 41-88; Phyllis Trible, "Feminist Hermeneutics and Biblical Studies," *The Christian Century* 3/10 (February 1982), pp. 116-18; idem, *God and the Rhetoric of Sexuality* (Philadelphia: Fortress Press, 1978); idem, *Texts of Terror: Literary-Feminist Readings of Biblical Narratives* (Philadelphia: Fortress Press, 1984).

demeaning to women.[103] Obviously, women who are committed to the centrality of the Bible will take the former approach, analogous to classical rabbinic midrash, because it will foster their personal or ideological needs. Women, or men for that matter, who lack that commitment, or who seek to dislodge the Bible from its historical position as a foundation of faith, will apply those analytical strategies that expose the Bible's anti-female bias.[104]

As a Jew, I welcome the greater freedom that issues from the crisis of faith in the older methods and conceptual constructs of Biblical Studies. For several years now, Jewish Biblicists in Israel and in the United States have pointed to the fact that so many categories in the study of Biblical literature, and its religion in particular, derive from patently Christian doctrines.[105] We are only

---

[103]Cf., e.g., Mieke Bal, *Lethal Love: Feminist Literary Readings of Biblical Love Stories* (Bloomington: Indiana University Press, 1987); J. Cheryl Exum, "'Mother in Israel': A Familiar Figure Reconsidered," in Letty M. Russell, ed., *Feminist Interpretation of the Bible* (Philadelphia: Westminster Press, 1985), pp. 73-85; Esther Fuchs, "The Literary Characterization of Mothers and Sexual Politics in the Hebrew Bible," in Adela Y. Collins, ed., *Feminist Perspectives on Biblical Scholarship* (Chico, CA: Scholars Press, 1985), pp. 117-36; idem, "Who Is Hiding the Truth? Deceptive Women and Biblical Androcentrism," in ibid., pp. 137-44; idem, "Structure and Patriarchal Functions in the Biblical Betrothal Type-Scene," *Journal of Feminist Studies in Religion* 3 (1987), pp. 7-13.

[104]Cf., e.g., Carol Meyers' review of *Feminist Interpretation of the Bible, JAAR* 54 (1986), pp. 608-9; Danna Nolan Fewell, "Feminist Reading of the Hebrew Bible: Affirmation, Resistance, and Transformation," *JSOT* 39 (Oct. 1987), pp. 77-87. Consider, for example, the contrast Fewell draws between Trible's and Fuchs' treatment of the character Ruth: "While Trible sees the character Ruth exemplifying radical commitment, Fuchs sees the character Ruth complying with patriarchal ethos..." (p. 81).

[105]See esp. Moshe Goshen-Gottstein, "Jewish Biblical Theology and the Study of Biblical Religion," *Tarbiz* 50 (1980-81), pp. 37-64 [in Hebrew]; idem, "Tanakh Theology: The Religion of the Old Testament and the Place of Jewish Biblical Theology," in Patrick D. Miller, Jr., and Paul D. Hanson, eds., *Ancient Israelite Religion: Essays in Honor of Frank Moore Cross* (Philadelphia: Fortress Press, 1987), pp. 617-44; Jon D. Levenson, "The Hebrew Bible, the Old Testament, and Historical Criticism," in Friedman and Williamson, eds., *The Future of Biblical Studies*, pp. 19-59; idem, "Why Jews Are Not Interested in Biblical Theology," in Jacob Neusner, Baruch A. Levine, and Ernest S. Frerichs, eds., *Judaic Perspectives on Ancient Israel* (Philadelphia: Fortress Press, 1987), pp. 281-307. Cf., too, Michael Fishbane, "The Role of Biblical Studies within Jewish Studies," *AJS Newsletter* 36 (Fall 1986), pp. 19-21; James L. Kugel, "Biblical Studies and Jewish Studies," in ibid., pp. 22-24.

Recently a Christian scholar, Rolf Rendtorff, has discussed the Christian orientation of "Old Testament Theology" in "Must 'Biblical Theology' Be Christian Theology?" *BR* 4/3 (June 1988), pp. 40-43. Although I appreciate Rendtorff's criticism of current "Biblical theology," I find him somewhat naive in thinking that anyone could compose a theology of the Hebrew Bible without some ideological slant. His own reading of Genesis and Exodus (p. 43), for example, omits any mention of the particularism that characterizes the covenant between YHWH and Abraham. That is – as I read it – after unsuccessful attempts to form

beginning – at least in widely circulating print – to produce a phenomenology of Biblical religion, or religions, that expresses a traditional Jewish framework.[106] It is significant, too, that Jewish scholars with historical training are attempting to reconstruct the development of classical Jewish hermeneutics from the Biblical world itself.[107] The Bible is no longer seen as a sphere apart from later Jewish tradition. For a time Jews engaging in the predominantly Christian field of Biblical Studies seemed to feel constrained from reading their own religious outlook into the earlier Scriptures. Y. Kaufmann recognized that Biblical

---

covenants with the progenitors of all humankind, YHWH initiates and cultivates a relationship with a single tribe, the Hebrews. I suspect that Rendtorff's being a Christian and my being a Jew has something to do with our difference in interpreting the trajectory of the narrative.

[106]See, more explicitly, Jon D. Levenson, *Sinai & Zion: An Entry into the Jewish Bible* (Minneapolis: Winston Press, 1985); and less explicitly, a study such as Jacob Milgrom's *Cult and Conscience: The* asham *and the Priestly Doctrine of Repentance* (Leiden: E. J. Brill, 1976). Note the assessment of the latter by Z. W. Falk in *BiOr* 39 (1982), cols. 377-79: "Thus while studying minutiae of *sancta* and ritual, the author presents us with a major insight on biblical theology. Repentance is seen as the central goal of piety and as an integral part of legal and cultic procedure....In this sense the author has discovered in the Levitical code a central idea of rabbinical law..." (col. 379).

Jewish in their orientation, too, are the articles on Biblical religion in Green, ed., *Jewish Spirituality 1* (see n. 86): David Sperling, "Israel's Religion in the Ancient Near East" (pp. 5-31); Jon D. Levenson, "The Jerusalem Temple in Devotional and Visionary Experience" (pp. 32-61); Fishbane, "Biblical Prophecy" (see n. 86 above); Joel Rosenberg, "Biblical Tradition: Literature and Spirit in Ancient Israel" (pp. 82-112); and James L. Kugel, "Topics in the History and Spirituality of the Psalms" (pp. 113-44). Cf. also many of the contributions to *Judaic Perspectives on Ancient Israel* (see n. 105 above).

I do not mean to imply that studies of Biblical religion by non-Jews are necessarily incompatible with Jewish views. I am sympathetic, to take merely one example, with aspects of John Barton, "The Old Testament," in Cheslyn Jones, Geoffrey Wainwright, and Edward Yarnold, eds., *The Study of Spirituality* (New York: Oxford University Press, 1986), pp. 47-57.

[107]Cf. Nahum M. Sarna, "Psalm 89: A Study in Inner Biblical Exegesis," in Alexander Altmann, ed., *Biblical and Other Studies* (Cambridge, MA: Harvard University Press, 1963), pp. 29-46; Michael Fishbane, *Biblical Interpretation in Ancient Israel* (Oxford: The Clarendon Press, 1985); James L. Kugel, Part One of Kugel and Rowan A. Greer, *Early Biblical Interpretation* (Philadelphia: Westminster Press, 1986); Avigdor Shinan and Yair Zakovitch, "Midrash on Scripture and Midrash within Scripture," in Sara Japhet, ed., *Studies in Bible 1986* (Jerusalem: Magnes Press, 1986), pp. 257-77; and cf. Jeffrey H. Tigay, "An Early Technique of Aggadic Exegesis," in H. Tadmor and M. Weinfeld, eds., *History, Historiography and Interpretation* (Jerusalem: Magnes Press, 1982), pp. 169-89. Pertinent, too, are the anthologies of Jewish exegesis collected by Yair Zakovitch and Avigdor Shinan: *The Story about Reuben and Bilhah* (Jerusalem: Hebrew University, 1983; in Hebrew); *And Jacob Came "Shalem"* (Jerusalem: Hebrew University, 1984; in Hebrew); *The Story of the Mandrakes* (Jerusalem: Hebrew University, 1985; in Hebrew). In each collection the editors begin with excerpts of "inner Biblical exegesis."

scholarship had in fact been presupposing certain Christian ideas, such as the priority of ethics and faith over ritual and community.[108] Kaufmann did not overly read traditional Jewish religious values into the Bible; but it is clear that his own dogmas concerning the distinctiveness of the People of Israel and their worldview went hand in glove with his strong Zionist ideology.[109]

Before concluding, it should be observed that not only Kaufmann's scholarship but historical modes of research are still prevalent in contemporary Israeli Biblical Studies.[110] While it is best to eschew the search for a single, simple explanation for this phenomenon, one should not in pondering it overlook the effect of environment, as well as ideology, on scholarship. Israelis live with the world of the Bible; its history haunts their land. The Biblical encyclopedia produced in Israel, as Simon has noted, is distinguished from scholarship elsewhere not by its disciplinary approaches but by its extraordinary attention to the archaeology and *realia* of the Land of Israel.[111] We in the diaspora find the text, the literature, closer at hand. Our milieu is the library more than the countryside.

In Umberto Eco's mystery novel, *The Name of the Rose*, the detective monk's amenuensis, Adso, asks his master, Brother William:

"Therefore you don't have a single answer to your questions?"

"Adso, if I did I would teach theology in Paris."

"In Paris do they always have the true answer?"

"Never," William said, "but they are very sure of their errors."

---

[108]See the works of Kaufmann cited in n. 66 above.

[109]Cf., e.g., Stephen A. Geller, "Wellhausen and Kaufmann," *Midstream,* December 1985, pp. 39-48, esp. 46b-47a.

[110]Cf. Uriel Simon, "לדרכה של המחלקה לתנ״ך באוניברסיטח בר-אילן" [The Approach of the Bar-Ilan University Bible Department]," *De'ot* 49 (1982), pp. 229-36, esp. 231. This observation can be confirmed by a perusal of a recently published volume representing the Hebrew University's Department of Biblical Studies – Japhet, ed., *Studies in Bible 1986* (see n. 107 above). My own conclusions concerning this volume accord with those of Ze'ev Weisman in his review in *Tarbiz* 56 (1987), pp. 291-95: "על המקרא ועל המגמתי במחקר המקראי הירושלמי." The only two common areas of interest one can discern among the seventeen contributions are Biblical law and the history and historical exegesis of the received text. Two of the essays might be typed as synchronic literary criticism. The fact that the history of ancient Israel is not directly addressed has less to do with the (non-)historical slant of the "Jerusalem School" than the relegation of "Biblical history" to departments of Jewish history, the ancient Near East, and archaeology. Japhet, in her introduction to the volume, claims that what unifies the "Jerusalem school" is its attempt to blend traditional Jewish text study with modern modes of criticism. As Weisman (p. 295) correctly observes, however, Hebrew University Bible research shares a great deal in common with scholarship elsewhere, too.

[111]Simon, loc. cit.

"And you," I said with childish impertinence, "never commit errors?"

"Often," he answered. "But instead of conceiving only one, I imagine many, so I may become the slave of none."[112]

The newer thinking in Biblical Studies is open to new disciplines and conceptual models, as well as to newly discovered tells and texts.

---

[112]Umberto Eco, *The Name of the Rose,* trans. William Weaver (New York: Warner Books, 1984), pp. 367-68.

Chapter Two

The Torah as She Is Read

It used to be taken for granted that the best way to explain the meaning of a thing would be to trace its history. To borrow an illustration, one would explain a house by recounting the stages in its planning and construction rather than by describing its architecture, the functions and interrelations of its parts, its situation in its environment, and so forth.[1] Similarly, it was assumed in such modern classics of Biblical exegesis as Speiser's *Genesis* and Sarna's *Understanding Genesis* that the best way to expound the meaning of a Biblical text, such as a story, would be to trace its history – the way that the story evolved into its present form.[2] If we could reconstruct its literary or cultural history, it was thought, we could discover its meaning or significance.

Why, for example, are there two accounts of Creation in Genesis, differing in style and substance? A historically oriented answer is: the two accounts were originally composed separately, in different contexts, from different perspectives. A redactor later juxtaposed them, leaving the original shape of each intact. Each must, therefore, be read separately. They have different and distinct meanings. What about the fact that someone has taken a great deal of trouble to incorporate both accounts, and in a certain sequence?

The problem becomes especially acute when we consider the Flood story. Here, source criticism convincingly argues, two texts have been spliced together.[3] Should each source, J and P, be read on its own – even after a redactor

---

[1]Cf. Robert M. Polzin, *Biblical Structuralism* (Philadelphia/Missoula: Fortress Press/Scholars Press, 1977), chap. 1.

[2]E. A. Speiser, *Genesis*, AB 1 (Garden City, NY: Doubleday, 1964); Nahum M. Sarna, *Understanding Genesis* (New York: Jewish Theological Seminary/McGraw-Hill, 1966).

[3]See now Richard E. Friedman, *Who Wrote the Bible?* (New York: Summit Books, 1987), esp. pp. 54-60. The literary history of this passage may, however, be more complex than the conventional source analysis allows; see, e.g., Joseph Blenkinsopp, "The Documentary Hypothesis in Trouble," *BR* 1/4 (Winter 1985), pp. 22-32, esp. 28-32. The arguments against a source analysis of the Flood story in Isaac M. Kikawada and Arthur Quinn, *Before Abraham Was* (Nashville: Abindgon Press, 1985), esp. pp. 83-106, fail for a number of reasons. To summarize, on the one hand they attack the criteria of source analysis one by one, as Umberto Cassuto had done in his *The Documentary Hypothesis*, trans. I.

has taken pains to interlace them? Yes, and no. Yes, if we are interested in the historical significance of each source.[4] No, if we want to understand the story as it has been transmitted to us in the Bible, which is, after all, the only way we know it.[5] Nobody preserved the Priestly source. The Jewish community has indeed preserved the Torah in its redacted shape. Nobody canonized JE or P or even – Josiah's Reform notwithstanding – D. If these (hypothetical) sources had been strictly canonical, they would hardly have been ravaged by the redactional process. No, it was the process of redaction that produced the sacred scripture that is the Torah.[6] If the Torah is revealed, revelation has taken place in redaction as well as in composition.

This notion is epigrammatically expressed in the formula of Martin Buber and Franz Rosenzweig: *R = Rabbenu*, "our teacher." That is to say, the redactor whom source critics designate by the siglum "R" is the one who transmitted Torah to us in its sacred, canonized form. Although R cannot be credibly identified with *Moshe Rabbenu*, "Moses, our Teacher," R is our teacher nonetheless and can be esteemed as *Rabbenu*. Our teacher was not a transcriber or author (as in novelist), but a redactor:

> It appears that a book like the Book of Genesis could not have been put together like a cheap newspaper, with the help of scissors and paste. Many expressions and turns of phrase formerly thought to be characteristic of one or another "source" increasingly reveal their meaning and their intent within a well-ordered whole. Such a rounded unity is not necessarily the finished work of a single, early author. My ear, too, distinguishes a variety of voices in the chorus. Even the most ancient memories are likely to have been preserved from a variety of motives and will accordingly have been rendered in a variety of tones....And yet this story has an amazingly homogeneous character,

---

Abrahams (Jerusalem: Magnes Press, 1961). This line of argumentation is inappropriate to documentary theory, since that theory rests on the coincidence or intersection of various criteria. It is a cumulatively constructed hypothesis and, accordingly, needs to be addressed as a whole. On the other hand, Kikawada and Quinn underestimate the several blatant contradictions in the Flood narrative, such as the discrepancy between the numbers of pure animals to be taken onto the ark and the duration of the flood. For a more extensive critical discussion of Kikawada and Quinn's book, see P. Kyle McCarter, Jr., "A New Challenge to the Documentary Hypothesis," *BR* 4/2 (April 1988), pp. 34-39.

[4]Cf., e.g., Friedman, *Who Wrote the Bible?*

[5]Cf., e.g., Bernhard W. Anderson, "From Analysis to Synthesis: The Interpretation of Genesis 1-11," *JBL* 97 (1978), pp. 23-39; Gordon T. Wenham, "The Coherence of the Flood Narrative," *VT* 28 (1978), pp. 336-48; and cf. Umberto Cassuto, *A Commentary on the Book of Genesis*, trans. I. Abrahams (Jerusalem: Magnes Press, 1961).

[6]Cf., e.g., James A. Sanders, *Torah and Canon* (Philadelphia: Fortress Press, 1972).

although the homogeniety did not exist from the beginning, but developed in time.[7]

If the Torah is so homogeneous in its story and storytelling, that does not mean that there were no sources. The Torah explicitly quotes the "Book of the Wars of YHWH" (Num. 21:14) and may attest other primary documents as well.[8] Many times the narrator acknowledges the distance in time between his material and his own situation (e.g., Gen. 2:24; 12:6; 22:14; etc.). What it does mean is that the Torah comprises a joining of material such that in the end a striking degree of literary and thematic coherence obtained. How, then, should the Torah be read to be understood? In pieces, by disintegrating its hard-won unity, or as a whole, respecting its unified form?

It is not necessarily an altogether either/or proposition. Brevard Childs, in his *Introduction to the Old Testament as Scripture*,[9] as well as in his prodigious commentary, *The Book of Exodus*,[10] first delineates the literature of the text in its historical components and then describes the redaction of that literature. He seeks to recover the ideology that underlies the form of the redaction and, further, the implications for the meaning of a text that arise from its position within the canon of a faith community. (For him, of course, that community is a Christian one.) From a literary perspective, one can assume the principle that the form of a text and its contextual placement affect its meaning. Imagine, for example, what Genesis would mean if the second Creation story preceded the first, or the way we would respond to the Golden Calf episode had it not been preceded by two injunctions against graven images (Exod. 20:3, 19). What would be the theme of the Torah had Joshua been included within it? Childs' approach is essentially historical rather than synchronic, asking most fundamentally what the text meant to the community that canonized it and transmitted it in its sacred shape.

In a similar vein, R. E. Friedman endeavors to identify the latest editorial labors in the formation of the Torah and assess their historical significance.[11] He shows how one version of the Torah reacted to earlier versions by revising and supplementing. His reconstruction and analysis operate on the assumptions and techniques of conventional source criticism. This is essential for the kind of work he is doing, but it therefore suffers from the vagaries of source-critical

---

[7]Martin Buber, *On the Bible*, ed. Nahum N. Glatzer (New York: Schocken Books, 1968; new ed.: 1982), p. 24. For the characterization of "R" as *Rabbenu*, see Franz Rosenzweig, "Die Einheit der Bibel," in M. Buber and F. Rosenzweig, *Die Schrift und ihre Verdeutschung* (Berlin: Schocken, 1936), pp. 46-54, esp. 47.

[8]See my "Sources of the Pentateuch," in Paul Achtemeier, ed., *Harper's Bible Dictionary* (San Francisco: Harper & Row, 1985), pp. 983-86.

[9]Brevard S. Childs, *Introduction to the Old Testament as Scripture* (Philadelphia: Fortress Press, 1979).

[10]Idem, *The Book of Exodus* (Philadelphia: Westminster Press, 1974).

[11]Richard Elliott Friedman, *The Exile and Biblical Narrative: The Formation of the Deuteronomistic and Priestly Works* (Chico, CA: Scholars Press, 1981); and see now his *Who Wrote the Bible?*

analysis. He must make presumptions such as the following: "surely it would would have been better to write nothing at all than to inform exiles that their channel to salvation is the building which no longer exists [that is, the Temple of Solomon]."[12] On the basis of this presumption, Friedman determines that 1 Kgs. 8:46-53 must antedate the Babylonian Exile. He may be correct in his judgment, but his reasoning is his own, unfounded in the expressed ideology of the Deuteronomistic History. Certainly the Temple was of vital importance to those exiles who felt a clear imperative to rebuild it upon their return to Jerusalem![13] Friedman similarly discriminates between a pre-Exilic edition of Deuteronomy and an Exilic revision not on the basis of language and style – which he admits are homogeneous between the two putative editions – but on the basis of his own logic. The theme of restoration after the Exile, he contends, must have emerged in the Exile and not before it. He seems not to reckon with the alternative – that it was precisely because certain pre-Exilic materials did foresee a restoration following the Exile that they served as sacred scripture for the Judeans.

Source criticism has always rested on Western presuppositions and standards about logical sequence, the unacceptability of logical contradiction, the aesthetic blemish of duplication or repetition, and the ideal of consistency. Studies of orally performed literature in preliterate societies, however, demonstrate that "repetitions, doublets, false starts, digressions, rough transitions and the like so dear to the heart of biblical critics" tend to pervade oral literature.[14] This means that the source critic's evidence of documentary difference may not represent difference at all. Without the discovery of independent documents attesting to the historical reality of sources, one simply is in no position to decide whether a discrepancy or duplication results from editorial splicing or a compositional sensibility that differs from the modern critic's.[15] The source critic must in any

---

[12]Friedman, *The Exile and Biblical Narrative*, p. 21.

[13]Cf. now Baruch A. Levine, Review of *The Israelian Heritage of Judaism*, *AJS Review* 12 (1987), pp. 143-57, esp. 156-57: "The single, legitimate temple in Jerusalem was relevant to the hope of national restoration to the Land of Israel. An exiled people whose religious fulfillment depended on access to Jerusalem would be less likely to abandon its hope of return!"

[14]Burke O. Long, "Recent Field Studies in Oral Literature and Their Bearing on OT Criticism," *VT* 26 (1976), pp. 187-98.

[15]Emanuel Tov has shown that the ancient Greek version of the story of David and Goliath in 1 Samuel 17 coincides with a source critical analysis of the text. He hypothesizes – to my mind, convincingly – that the Greek version reflects one of two primary texts that have been redacted together in the Massoretic Text; "The Composition of 1 Samuel 16-18 in the Light of the Septuagint Version," in Jeffrey H. Tigay, ed., *Empirical Models for Biblical Criticism* (Philadelphia: University of Pennsylvania Press, 1985), pp. 97-130. No matter how cogent Tov's argument, his theory remains a hypothesis; and, despite the title of the volume in which he published his study, his hypothesis is based on the theoretical coordination of discrete literary materials. It is not the sort of direct

event admit that the redactor found the end-result aesthetically acceptable. What was acceptable to an ancient redactor might also have been acceptable to an ancient author. For these and other reasons source critical conclusions must remain indecisive.[16]

Nevertheless, the presence of a number of source-critical discriminations in the same places can be adduced to suggest probable boundaries between once-discrete literary materials. The premier instance in the Torah is the Flood narrative, cited above. Attempts have been made to explain the structure of the account in Genesis 6-9 as a coherent literary unit.[17] Viewed as an outline, from what I call an aerial reading of the text,[18] the Flood story may appear smooth in its present form. But from the ground, the level at which we customarily hear or read, this narrative is jagged. We are tossed back and forth between passages by contrasts in style, jarring repetitions, and – especially – downright factual contradictions that consistently recur in the text. Here, Friedman's approach (see above) gives us some handle on the material. According to Friedman, a redactor interlaced the later P version with an earlier J story of the Flood in order to "correct" elements of the J account that were intolerable to P. For P, only a priest may make an offering to God, and then only at the ordained sanctuary and at the appointed time. In building his own altar and offering up the ritually pure animals after the Flood, Noah, from a Priestly perspective, was way out of line. So in P's version, Noah brought only two – not seven – of each of the pure animals with him onto the ark; he didn't need extras for offerings, which J's seven of each kind provided. With respect to this hypothetical literary-historical reading, where the literary form seems not artful but political – a later redactor interfering with an unacceptable version of the story – the most fruitful reading may be historical.

If P was, as would seem likely, not only the compiler of the P materials but also the redactor of the Torah – note, as a simple example, that Genesis 1 and most of Deuteronomy 34, the framework of the Torah, are P; or note that the backbone of Genesis, the ten תולדות (genealogy) passages, is P – why did P include those materials of J (and E), as well as D, alongside or intertwined with the revised P versions? It is a "mystery," Friedman confesses.[19] The answer is elusive, but one may try anyway. Friedman's own suggestion is that P incorporated other, divergent sources into the Torah because they were all traditionally ascribed to the same author, Moses. More likely, the redactor, whatever his orientation, felt compelled to include materials other than P because

---

observation of the literary process that is implied by the term "empirical"; see further, Chapter Three.

[16]See further Chapters One and Three.

[17]See the studies cited in n. 5 above.

[18]See my "Biblical Narratology," *Prooftexts* 1 (1981), p. 206.

[19]So in *The Exile and Biblical Narrative*. In his more recent *Who Wrote the Bible?*, pp. 234-45, Friedman elaborates on his earlier position.

those materials were already precious, if not sacred, to the Judean community in or after the Exile.

It is also possible to see the motivation for including divergent sources in one Torah more or less as Buber did: the art of the Torah, the structuring that created a canonized text out of hitherto profane, or unauthoritative, materials, was in redacting. Our Torah is not a painting but a collage. The final result is the art.[20] This assumes a redactor not entirely convinced of the early P ideology; but it could be accounted for by a revised Priestly orientation in the Exile.[21]

Friedman takes on a more Buberian posture when he discusses the theology that emerges from the text once it has been combined or redacted. "The juxtaposition of the JE and Priestly Creation accounts," he writes, "precipitated a narrative synthesis with exegetical possibilities which neither of the original documents possessed independently."[22] J (even JE) depicts a God intimate, personal, and doting.[23] P's God is more transcendentally perceived. He won't even use angels (thus, for example, P must tell of Jacob's renaming as Israel in Gen. 35:9-10 apart from the wrestle with God in Genesis 32). In P's Creation account in Genesis 1, a cosmic God arranges a harmonious order. JE's story of the Garden of Eden introduces a far more personal God, grappling with the conflicts of his creatures in a disorderly scene. The canonical "truth" – which comprises no less than both narratives juxtaposed – is conveyed by neither account. The ongoing tension between the ideal and the all-too-real – which comes as close as one can to the "truth" – is evinced only by pitting one story against the other.

Why couldn't the two versions be editorially combined? They would then mean something else. I would use the following analogy. Imagine a painting in which red and blue pigments were mixed and then applied to an entire canvas. Now imagine a canvas painted half red and half blue. The colors bounce off each other as though responding to and commenting upon one another. Such is the juxtaposition of the two Creation accounts.

There are, however, redacted texts in the Torah in which two (or more) sources seem to have been editorially (or compositionally) intertwined, rather than juxtaposed. How can they be read? In conventional Biblical scholarship, under the influence of source criticism, in order to read the text the putative components would first have to be isolated – thwarting, and thereby demeaning, the efforts of the redactor, *Rabbenu*. The results might be interesting if an entire

---

[20]See Joel Rosenberg, "Meanings, Morals, and Mysteries: Literary Approaches to Torah," *Response* 26 (1975), pp. 67-94.
[21]So Friedman, in *The Exile and Biblical Narrative* and *Who Wrote the Bible?*; in the latter, he revives the argument that the fifth-century Ezra was the redactor.
[22]Friedman, *The Exile and Biblical Narrative*, p. 120; cf. *Who Wrote the Bible?*, pp. 234-41.
[23]For a striking characterization of J and J's God, see the essays by Harold Bloom cited in Chapter One, n. 90.

source – all of J, for instance – could be isolated and analyzed. One could then get the sense of J. This, as mentioned above, is what Bloom has tried to do. He conceives, for example, a literary and thematic coherence to this source, which begins with YHWH shaping the first human from clods of earth and concludes with YHWH burying the greatest human, the prophet Moses, in an unmarked grave. A concentric symmetry characterizes the next circle of structure, too. In the Garden of Eden, YHWH forbade the man and woman to eat of the Tree of Knowing; before Moses' death, YHWH forbade him to cross over into the Promised Land. Not only the "uncanny" and "original" J, but even the less well-reputed P has been treated to a stylistic analysis of its narrative art.[24]

Nevertheless, the difficulties attending this method of divide and conquer are not hard to conjure up. Source criticism must first produce the text that it submits for interpretation. Much material in the Torah probably does not come down within any of the literary sources (such as J and P). The Testament of Jacob in Genesis 49 and the final songs of Moses in Deuteronomy 32-33, for example, are not attributable to a documentary source. But the most serious problem with examining the structure of any hypothetical source is that we have no idea at all about what might have been dropped out (let alone restructured) in the course of redaction. We don't know how complete are the remains of the sources in the present Torah. Crucial material might be lying on the cutting room floor. We are in a far worse position than the archaeologist. From mere fragments of a jar or a building an archaeologist can reconstruct the image of the whole of which the fragment is a part. There is a model by which to locate the piece. In the case of fragmentary literary remains, we have no way of knowing how the pieces once fit. We have no standard, no structural pattern.

From a Jewish perspective – and there is an analogous Christian one, too[25] – there is an even more serious problem. I have alluded to it above. None of the putative sources was preserved as sacred in its preredacted shape. If the Torah is sacred only in its redacted form, it is that form in which it must be read as Scripture. Isolating narrative strands will not do. What do the strands mean in their intertwined form? What is the meaning of the braid that is the text?

Approaches to the text in its unified form have found expression in the classical *midrashim*, especially in their analyses of juxtaposed passages –

---

[24]Sean E. McEvenue, *The Narrative Style of the Priestly Writer* (Rome: Pontifical Biblical Institute, 1971); cf. now David Damrosch, "Leviticus," in Robert Alter and Frank Kermode, eds., *The Literary Guide to the Bible* (Cambridge, MA: Harvard University Press, 1987), pp. 66-77.
[25]See Childs' *Introduction* (n. 9 above).

.סמיכות פרשיות[26]; in Benno Jacob's Genesis commentary[27]; in Cassuto, in Buber, and in an abundant variety of recent literary studies[28] – most popularly in Alter's *The Art of Biblical Narrative.*[29] In a chapter entitled "Composite Artistry" Alter compares the redactor's art of composition to the filmmaking technique of "montage," juxtaposing images so that we can interrelate them in our perceptions. Among the texts Alter studies are the Joseph story, Numbers 16, and the two conflicting accounts of how it was that David came to Saul's camp.

A decade before Alter's book appeared, the French critic Roland Barthes (who is egregiously omitted by Alter) endeavored to explain the meanings conveyed by the composite narrative in Gen. 32:23-33, the story of Jacob's struggle at the Jabbok.[30] Barthes described the "logic" of sequence in this composite narrative as a "metonymic montage":

> . . . the themes (Crossing, Struggle, Naming, Alimentary Rite) are *combined*, not *'developed'*....Metonymic logic is that of the unconscious. Hence it is perhaps in that direction that one would need to pursue the present study, to pursue the reading of the text – its dissemination, not its truth.[31]

The text embraces an apparent contradiction, one attributed by source criticism to different documents. According to Gen. 32:23, Jacob crossed the Jabbok; Gen. 32:24 says he crossed over his party. Did he cross, or didn't he? If he did not, the struggle connotes the triumph of a hero over the deity (demon?) who guards the

---

[26]For some comparisons of classical rabbinic exegesis and literary criticism, cf. Kalman Bland, "The Rabbinic Method and Literary Criticism," in Kenneth R. R. Gros Louis et al., eds., *Literary Interpretations of Biblical Narratives* (Nashville: Abingdon Press, 1974), pp. 16-23.

[27]Benno Jacob, *Das erste Buch der Tora: Genesis* (Berlin: Schocken, 1934). The English abridgement of this monumental work simplifies it exceedingly, leaving it thin and shallow. Jacob's Exodus commentary, more recently published by Ktav in English translation, does not compare with its predecessor.

[28]For a compendium of literary comment on the Hebrew Bible from ancient times to the present, see now Alex Preminger and Edward L. Greenstein, eds., The *Hebrew Bible in Literary Criticism* (New York: Frederick Ungar, 1986). Cf. also Alter and Kermode, eds., *The Literary Guide to the Bible.*

[29]Robert Alter, *The Art of Biblical Narrative* (New York: Basic Books, 1981). For extensive critical discussion of the book see *JSOT* 27 (1983), pp. 75-111; Alter replies on pp. 113-17.

[30]Roland Barthes, "The Struggle with the Angel," *Image/Music/Text* (New York: Hill & Wang, 1977), pp. 125-41; originally published in French in 1971, a poorer Emglish version appeared in R. Barthes et al., *Structural Analysis and Biblical Exegesis* (Pittsburgh: Pickwick Press, 1974), pp. 21-33. Cf. now, too, Stephen A. Geller, "Jacob's Struggle at the Jabbok," *JANES* 14 (1982), pp. 37-60.

[31]Barthes, *Image/Music/Text*, pp. 140-41.

river.[32] If he did cross, his struggle was a *rite de passage* – a spiritual, symbolic, psychoanalyzable wrestling, implied already in the midrash in which the combatant is שרו של עשו, "Esau's guardian angel." For Barthes, the text need not be read in an either/or fashion, by selecting one reading and benignly neglecting the other. The two readings are inextricably "tangled" together in the text. It is not for us to disentangle them but to hold them in tension. In fact, just as the text continues to refer to Jacob by both his names (Jacob: the conniver, and Israel: the one who strived with God), so the story here holds both perceptions open. If the redacted text maintains both readings, is it fitting for the audience to close one in favor of the other?

Peter Miscall asks us to leave open that which the text does not explicitly close.[33] Through a reading of several passages relating to Abraham and David, Miscall concludes that the morals of both figures are left ambiguous. We should not assume, for example, that Abraham followed the divine command to go to a new country out of any but selfish motives. After all, the text does not share his motives with us (as it does elsewhere, as recent books by Bar-Efrat and Sternberg demonstrate).[34] Miscall's arguments provide a welcome caution against overreading, assuming more than we have reason to insinuate into the text. His own readings, it must be admitted, however, are not neutral but rather super-skeptical. He distrusts the ways the Biblical narrator presents his characters to us.[35] Miscall is correct, though, in reprimanding commentators for exploiting and distorting the sense of the text in order to draw lessons from it.

Returning to the problem of reading "tangled" texts, we may ask whether we are supposed to identify or bracket different blocks of source material or different traditions within it prior to reading. Polzin, for example, has argued eloquently that the narrator of Deuteronomy both frames and comments upon the words of Moses, ultimately superseding Moses' authority in presenting God's word to the community. That way, the narrator commands the respect he needs to carry Moses' material further into the Deuteronomistic History (Joshua-Kings) and legislate for the audience living at the tail end of that history.[36] Polzin's reading, however, hinges on the audience's perception of the breaking in and dropping off of the narrator's voice, perception of which I for one am not always convinced. He sees the narrator purposely undermining the authority of Moses and the

---

[32]So Sarna, *Understanding Genesis* (see n. 2), p. 204, and many other commentators.

[33]Peter D. Miscall, *The Workings of Old Testament Narrative* (Philadelphia/Chico, CA: Fortress Press/Scholars Press, 1983).

[34]Shimeon Bar-Efrat, העיצוב האמנותי של הסיפור במקרא [The Artful Shaping of Biblical Narrative] (Tel Aviv: Sifriat Poalim, 1979), esp. pp. 48ff.; Meir Sternberg, *The Poetics of Biblical Narrative* (Bloomington: Indiana University Press, 1985).

[35]Contrast, e.g., Sternberg, *Poetics of Biblical Narrative,* who insists that the Biblical narrator is both omniscient and reliable.

[36]Robert M. Polzin, *Moses and the Deuteronomist: A Literary Study of the Deuteronomistic History* (New York: Seabury Press, 1980).

uniqueness of Israel in order to interpose his own authority and program. But whether a historical audience would have perceived this subtle argument within the rhetoric of Moses' own speeches must remain questionable.

In analyzing the Garden of Eden story, Joel Rosenberg, too, suggests that the components of the text can be identified.[37] The braid of composite Biblical narrative, to use our earlier metaphor, comprises strands of different colors. We observe their interrelation even as we retain our perceptions of the individual lineaments. Rosenberg characterizes this aspect of Biblical style as "an art of quotation," adducing various components of the Israelite traditions. The "redactional level of meaning" – the meaning one makes of the textual pieces commenting on one another – "is sometimes at odds with the story's plain or apparent meaning." He tries "to show that the logical analogies established in the story arise from relations of its traditionary units."[38] My own quarrel with such a strategy revolves around whether a reader does or should pick up textual signals that different traditions are given voice within the text.[39] When they are tightly meshed, should they be pried apart?

When I approach a "braided" text, I posit its literary unity, unless I find in it some explicit reference to its molecular structure (as in the citation of a discrete source). Without literary signals, so to speak, I would read the text straight, allow for duplication, ambiguity, and contradiction, and incorporate the effects of duplication, ambiguity, and contradiction into my interpretation. I have endeavored to exemplify this manner of reading in my analysis of the episode of Joseph's descent to Egypt.[40] There I deal in detail with Genesis 37 and subsequent passages that relate the circumstances in which Joseph went down to Egypt. The crux is familiar: did the brothers sell him to Ishmaelites, or did Midianites kidnap him from the pit? The narrative seems to intertwine two sequences of action so that it becomes impossible to tell. I approach the confusion as meaningful; I allow that the redactional process is artful.[41] Indeed, one could justify both the manner of reading and the assumption of meaningful

---

[37]Joel Rosenberg, "The Garden Story Forward and Backward," *Prooftexts* 1 (1981), pp. 1-27.

[38]Rosenberg, "The Garden Story," p. 20. It should be noted that such a reading is akin to the source-critical approach of Friedman, cited above. Friedman, however, recombines components of various passages into hypothetical sources, while Rosenberg inspects the components within a delimited passage.

[39]Cf. my "Sources of the Pentateuch" (see n. 9 above).

[40]"An Equivocal Reading of the Sale of Joseph," in Kenneth R. R. Gros Louis with James S. Ackerman, eds., *Literary Interpretations of Biblical Narratives, Volume II* (Nashville: Abingdon Press, 1982), pp. 114-25, 306-10.

[41]Cf. John A. Miles, Jr., "Radical Editing: *Redaktionsgeschichte* and the Aesthetics of Willed Confusion," in *Traditions in Transformation,* eds. Baruch Halpern and Jon D. Levenson (Winona Lake, IN: Eisenbrauns, 1981), pp. 9-31.

composition by pointing to a similar narrative structure and thematic effect in Numbers 16.[42]

We have what Barthes has called a "friction between two intelligibilities."[43] While it has been customary in Biblical criticism to settle for one "intelligibility" at the expense of the other and insist that the two narrative sequences be read distinctly – despite the efforts of the redactor to combine or harmonize them – I would deal directly and unabashedly with the integrated text.[44] I do not here repeat my interpretation of the ambiguous narrative for that is less significant than the generative principle of reading, or hearing, the text in its redacted form. If reading equivocal texts demands a poetics different from the conventions by which we read other texts, then that is one of the tasks at hand.

Most contemporary literary analysis of the Hebrew Bible seeks to find its meaning within its network of literary or stylistic features as well as its overall structure.[45] Such study takes a particular epistemological stance: the best way to know what the text means – or to make meaning of the text – is to observe its various literary patterns and devices, to see how it communicates and how it "hangs together."[46] It is held that these factors are the clearest channels for drawing out the text's significance.

This methodology challenges the comparative method, which held sway for decades. The comparative approach maintains that to know the text best I should examine it in contrast with other texts. To know Genesis 1 best, for example, I should, with Speiser, Sarna, and others (see above), study how it is distinguished from Enuma Elish or another ancient Near Eastern creation account. A literary-

---

[42]Coincidentally, Alter ("Composite Artistry," *Art of Biblical Narrative*) compares the same texts, but with a different understanding.

[43]See n. 30.

[44]In saying this I do not mean to discount the possibility of accidents in scribal transmission. I would not interpret what I consider to be an error. The act of making sense presumes an intention to mean something. To interpret scribal errors as serious, not to say sacred, text, is to interpret the typing of a chimpanzee as poetry.

[45]The amount of professional literary analysis of the Hebrew Bible has swelled to such proportions that one could hardly do justice by assembling a brief bibliography. As a sampler, in addition to the books cited elsewhere in this chapter, let me mention the following English titles: Adele Berlin, *Poetics and Interpretation of Biblical Narrative* (Sheffield: Almond Press, 1983); David J. A. Clines et al., *Art and Meaning: Rhetoric in Biblical Literature* (Sheffield: JSOT Press, 1982); Robert C. Culley, *Studies in the Structure of Hebrew Narrative* (Philadelphia/Missoula: Fortress Press/Scholars Press, 1976); Michael Fishbane, *Text and Texture* (New York: Schocken Books, 1979); J. P. Fokkelman, *Narrative Art in Genesis* (Assen: Van Gorcum, 1975); idem, *Narrative Art and Poetry in the Books of Samuel* (Assen: Van Gorcum, 1981-), 2 vols. in print, 2 projected; Jacob Licht, *Storytelling in the Bible* (Jerusalem: Magnes Press, 1978). See also periodicals such as *Prooftexts, Semeia, JSOT*, and the Indiana Studies in Biblical Literature series.

[46]Cf. Chapter One.

rhetorical method would identify the patterns and recurrent formulae in the passage, note the effects of its diction, follow its allusions (if any), and so forth. Whereas the comparative method would look for difference between Biblical and non-Biblical texts, the literary-rhetorical method looks for difference – the distinctive – within the Biblical context itself.[47] For the greatest meaning, it may be best to utilize both approaches wherever possible. But a "purely" literary method will emphasize the formal linguistic and rhetorical devices of the text. Literary analysis, then, best serves its practitioners by exposing – or hypothesizing[48] – the means by which the text communicates (from a structuralist perspective) or by which we make meaning (from a post-structuralist one).

In recent years a number of newly cultivated disciplines have been tested in Biblical exegesis. One that has proved fruitful, especially for plumbing levels of significance beneath the surface of the narrative, is structural anthropology. In order to appreciate its contribution, one must understand what anthropologists, some literary critics, and others have meant by "myth."

Literary methods tend to read the Biblical narrative not as history, but as story.[49] To the extent that the Torah's story moves in certain repeating patterns, and articulates the people Israel's perceptions of their place in the world and the meaning of their existence, as well as their concerns and anxieties, that story is "myth."[50] Myth expresses and in turn shapes the self-understanding of a group through paradigmatic stories. The rehabilitation of myth as a certain kind of narrative – and not only stories about gods – is a happy result of recent literary, anthropological, and religious studies writing.

It is obvious that the Torah does not tell everything that happened in its world, even within its own time-frame. It does not relate, for example, what Abraham did during the first 75 years of his life. Of all that Abraham did later, the Torah selects two stories in which he represents his wife as his sister. For what reason does such behavior merit a double recounting in a narrative that omits nearly all description of Abraham as father and husband? Clearly the material that was not only selected but preserved, transmitted, and variously transformed until the Torah book was produced, somehow expressed underlying ideas and concerns of the community to whom it was precious, sacred. The narratives of the Torah, and of the Former Prophets' continuation of the Torah's story, may present themselves as a form of history.[51] But they are far too

---

[47]See my "Literature, Old Testament as," in *Harper's Bible Dictionary* (n. 9).

[48]See Chapter Three.

[49]Cf. Zakovitch, "Story Versus History" (see Chapter One, n. 21).

[50]See esp. Northrop Frye, *The Great Code: The Bible and Literature* (New York: Harcourt Brace Jovanovich, 1982). For a concise discussion, see Eduardo Rauch, "Toward an Understanding of the Forgotten World of Myth – An Essay in Definition," *Melton Journal* no. 13 (Winter 1982), pp. 4, 18-19.

[51]Cf. John Van Seters, *In Search of History* (see Chapter One, n. 12).

sketchy and idiosyncratic to serve that function for an audience concerned primarily with history. The audience almost certainly responded to underlying messages and values.

To read the Torah for its deeper meaning is hardly new. Within Jewish tradition, the effort to draw out that which lies behind or concealed in the Torah is the impetus of classical midrash. Few texts make this more explicit than the thirteenth century Kabbalistic *Zohar:*

> Rabbi Simeon said: Alas for the man who regards Torah as a book of mere tales and profane matters. If this were so, we might even today write a Torah dealing in such matters and still more excellent. In regard to earthly things, the kings and princes of the world [in their chronicles?] possess more valuable materials. We could use them as a model for composing a Torah of this kind. But in reality the words of the Torah are higher words and higher mysteries....The Torah has a body, which consists of the commandments and ordinances of the Torah, which are called *gufe torah,* "bodies of the Torah." This body is cloaked in garments, which consist of worldly stories. Fools see only the garment, which is the narrative part of the Torah; they know no more and fail to see what is under the garment. Those who know more see not only the garment but also the body that is under the garment. But the truly wise...look only upon the soul, which is the true foundation of the entire Torah.[52]

How do we proceed to uncover the underlying ideas of the Torah?

First, as was said above, we read larger structures – books, blocks of books (Tetrateuch, Pentateuch, Hextateuch), series of books (Torah plus Former Prophets). Global reading affords us two advantages. Overall structure may reveal the design, the plan of the whole and its component parts. Spinoza, for example, knew that the meaning of the Torah is bound up with the fact that it forms a segment of a more or less continuous story of Israel from Creation to the Exile:

> Now, if we turn our attention to the connection and argument of all these books, we shall see easily that they were all written by a single historian, who wished to relate the antiquities of the Jews from their first beginning down to the first destruction of the city [of Jerusalem].[53]

Long before twentieth-century German Bible scholars, such as M. Noth, established the literary and ideological unity of Deuteronomy and the ensuing "Deuteronomistic History" – the latter being a narrative illustration of the program of the former – Spinoza delineated the thematic thread running through the entire history. The significance of the thread is suggested by the direction it takes and its ultimate destination, the destruction of Jerusalem in 587. The entire

---

[52]Quoted and translated in Gershom Scholem, *On the Kabbalah and Its Symbolism* (New York: Schocken Books, 1965), pp. 63-64.
[53]Benedict de Spinoza, *Theologico-Political Treatise* (New York: Dover Books, 1951), p. 126 (ch. 8).

narrative, from Genesis through Kings, explains how the Jewish nation came to suffer devastation and exile:

> . . . even as Moses had foretold. In regard to other matters, which do not serve to confirm the law, the writer either passes over them in silence, or refers the reader to other books for information. All that is set down in the books we have conduces to the sole object of setting forth the words and laws of Moses, and proving them by subsequent events.[54]

The other advantage of global reading is that only in larger structures can we determine those themes that persistently recur. If certain themes and motifs crop up time and again in diverse material, it is a token of their significance. Lévi-Strauss, for example, compares the semiotics of myth to a musical score.[55] The narrative sequence represents the horizontal unfolding of the music in time, measure after measure. What is thematically significant will repeat, directly or through transformation/variation, in the course of the music. If one were to line up all instances of particular themes or motifs in vertical columns, the bulkier columns would contain the most persistent – hence significant – ones. Therein lie at least a portion of the important ideas or concerns of the text.

The structural anthropology of Lévi-Strauss has spawned a large number of applications to the Bible.[56] Most focus on mythic patterns relating to kinship. Edmund Leach, perhaps the first to do this, finds a series of episodes in Genesis that seek to define the ideal kinship relation of a prospective wife to her husband.[57] In what seems, at least initially, a perverse claim, Leach argues that the recurrence of illicit sexual liaisons of a gross type in Genesis (Adam and his quasi-sister Eve, Cain and Abel who were apparently compelled to incest,[58] Lot and his daughters) mitigates the impropriety of Abraham's marriage to the woman he declares to be his half-sister, Sarah (Gen. 20:12). Whether or not this reading convinces, Leach valuably notes this important function of myth in mitigating conflicts between the real and the ideal, between what a society possesses and what that society professes.

Although structural anthropologists make claims about deep-seated concerns in a culture, Leach and some others lack sensitivity to the socio-historical environment in which kinship practices, rituals, and myths develop.[59] Textual analysis, in order to gain in conviction, must consider and control the pertinent

---

[54]Ibid., p. 129.
[55]Claude Lévi-Strauss, *Myth and Meaning* (New York: Schocken Books, 1979).
[56]Cf. recently, e.g., Edmund Leach and Alan D. Aycock, *Structuralist Interpretations of Biblical Myth* (Cambridge: Cambridge University Press, 1983).
[57]Edmund Leach, *Genesis as Myth and Other Essays* (London: Jonathan Cape, 1969).
[58]So in rabbinic midrash; see Louis Ginzberg, *The Legends of the Jews* (New York: Simon & Schuster, 1956), p. 56; *Bereshit Rabba* 22:7.
[59]Contrast, e.g., the approach of Norman K. Gottwald, *The Hebrew Bible: A Socio-Literary Introduction*, discussed in Chapter One.

ethnographic data. Myths' meaning can only be discerned when those myths are related to the structure of a particular society. Whereas "the interpretation of myth...is the analysis of structure, and though the rules of structuring may derive from some general properties of the human mind, the forms and contents of given structures derive from particular societies."[60] The author of that quotation, Nathaniel Wander, adopts the original program of Lévi-Strauss (who admittedly violated it himself) to perform analysis of myth within an ethnographic context. Wander then shows the rhetorical means by which the text of Genesis treats women – certain women – with the object of mitigating a practical societal tension.

But where does Wander get an ethnography of ancient Israel? Archaeology is not suited to foot so large a bill; ancient Near Eastern texts furnish only fragments and refractions of "real life." Thus, with nowhere better to turn, Wander looks to studies of modern Semitic societies, especially Middle Eastern bedouin. While some aspects of bedouin social structure have been bent by technological and geopolitical changes, kinship structures have been less susceptible to the corrosive forces of modernity. Characteristic of Semitic marriage is that the most preferred wife is one's father's brother's daughter, that is, one's first cousin on the father's side. Such a practice serves a system in which inheritance and authority in the family pass through the father's line (patrilineality). After two generations, the system gives rise to a dilemma. The father's brother's daughter turns out to be a relative through the mother's line, too. Take, for instance, Rachel/Leah, who is Jacob's cousin by his father and his mother. Women in such an ambiguous position are dangerous to the social structure because widespread misinterpretation could lead to a redefinition of the society by its members as matrilineal, or as both patri- and matrilineal.

The threat posed by such women is tamed by Israelite myths in which the text seems to go out of its way to show that what appear like father's brother's daughters are not so. Sarah's status is blurred: is she or isn't she a relative? Rebekah is a condensation of a relative and a nonrelative and gives birth to two sons, one in the lineage of Israel, one without. Leah and Rachel are a split father's brother's daughter (actually with an extra generation added, but see how the text itself skips a generation in Gen. 29:5). Jacob's marriages are described as mother's brother's daughter liaisons (Gen. 27:43-46; 28:2, 13). Esau's father's brother's daughter marriage to Basemat is disguised as a marrying out, and Lot's liaisons with his daughters abridge the generational span (FBD marriage becomes D marriage). Because Sarah, Rebekah, Leah, and Rachel are important in the lineage, they are compromised in the text – through barrenness and (except for Rebekah) substitutions by stand-in wives. Because the ideal of FBD marriage

---

[60]Nathaniel Wander, "Structure, Contradiction, and 'Resolution' in Mythology: Father's Brother's Daughter Marriage and the Treatment of Women in Genesis 11-50," *JANES* 13 (1981), pp. 75-99; here, p. 75.

suffers potential confusion and redefinition in social reality, the myths of Genesis mitigate the society's anxieties.

Wander also uncovers another tension in societies similar in structure to ancient Israel's.[61] Ideally, the oldest son receives the larger share of his father's estate. But older sons also leave home sooner. While the younger sons grow up, the father may increase his estate such that the younger sons hanging on may wind up with a share greater than that of the enterprising older son. This scenario may explain, on one level, the numerous passages in the Bible in which a younger son achieves higher station than his older brother. Such a myth in its manifold variations would function to mitigate the ideal of primogeniture and the frequent actuality of ultimogeniture.

Read this way, Genesis expresses the concerns of a largely tribal and fairly primitive culture. Was that the state of Israelite civilization at the time the Biblical narrative was formed, extending to the Babylonian Exile? No. One of the rewards of Wander's study is his argument that "myths never forget." The material in the Biblical narrative embodies mythic patterns and relations that characterized Israel's earliest stages, as well as its later stages. In the course of growth and transformation myths may take on new associations and references. But they do not lose their earlier meanings. Like rolling stones gathering moss, they acquire new layers of significance without shedding the underlayers. Thus, as we shall soon see, the theme of the younger son's domination increases in significance by extending its reference.

At its tribal stage, Israel's ethnography must be derived, if at all, by analogy to modern bedouin. As for the ethnography of Israel at the stage at which the Torah as we now have it was essentially formed, the overwhelming historical facts are the destruction of Solomon's Temple and the Exile. The latest strata of the Torah, those of P (according to a large scholarly consensus), can be dated by linguistic criteria to the sixth century B.C.E.[62] The Torah speaks to, even comforts, the exiles in many ways and on various levels. Assuming the Exile as the period in which the Torah as we know it found an audience, what does the Torah say?

---

[61]Ibid., p. 80 with n. 22, pp. 98-99 with n. 57.

[62]Robert Polzin argues for a mid-sixth-century dating; *Late Biblical Hebrew* (Missoula: Scholars Press, 1976). Gary Rendsburg's critique of Polzin in *JANES* 12 (1980), pp. 65-80, corrects a number of Polzin's arguments and claims but does not suffice to counter his overall thrust. Avi Hurvitz, in "The Evidence of Language in Dating the Priestly Code – A Linguistic Study in Technical Idioms and Terminology," *RB* 81 (1974), pp. 24-46, and *A Linguistic Study of the Relationship between the Priestly Source and the Book of Ezekiel* (Paris: Cahiers de la Revue Biblique, 1982), dates P to a period before the Exile, but not long before it. A date around 600 B.C.E. would be acceptable. See also Ziony Zevit, "Converging Lines of Evidence Bearing on the Date of P," *ZAW* 94 (1982), pp. 481-511. Zevit contends P was composed before 587, but he says we cannot tell how much earlier.

Most obviously perhaps, the Torah explains the Exile. The core of the Torah is the covenant and its regulations. The threatening curses that conclude sections of law in Leviticus and Deuteronomy promise exile for repeated infractions. In the Former Prophets, Israel is chastened with surrender to an enemy whenever it strays from the fealty God demands from his vassals. When the people repent, God delivers them. This was widespread theology in the ancient Near East. Compare, for example, this excerpt from the inscription of King Mesha of Moab:

> I, Mesha...king of Moab...made this high-place for Chemosh [the national god of Moab]...because he has saved me from all the kings and has let me see [victory] against all my enemies. Omri, king of Israel – he oppressed Moab many years, for Chemosh had been angry at his land.[63]

The destruction of the northern kingdom of Israel by Assyria in 722 presaged a similar fate for the southern kingdom of Judah. YHWH would do to his land what Chemosh had done to his, and what YHWH had done to the northern kingdom, YHWH would do to the South.

The pattern of divine command, popular disobedience, and divine punishment also shapes a large number of episodes in the Torah. I am not only thinking of the Golden Calf story and the several instances in which the people grumble and God afflicts them with fire (Num. 11:1-3) or serpents (Num. 21:4-9).[64] We may first identify the theme of threatened exile in Genesis, in the Garden of Eden. The first humans are given one prohibition by God. They blow it, and they are expelled from the Garden. The entire world is evil, they have polluted the ground.[65] In a most extreme form of expulsion, God annihilates them and the ground from beneath them by flood. God's destruction of the cities of the plain (Genesis 18-19) is a more circumscribed instance.

That this is God's way – removing people from their land for having sinned – takes on a remarkable form in Genesis 15. There God tells Abram that the latter's descendants will have to suffer a temporary exile and persecution becuase God cannot yet displace the native inhabitants of Canaan. The Canaanites have not had time to build up a sufficient record of sinfulness (see v. 16). The lesson is restated in Deut. 9:4, where Moses admonishes the Israelites:

> Do not say in your heart [i.e., think] when the Lord your God sweeps them away from before you, "By dint of my righteousness has the Lord

---

[63] For comparable Assyrian material, too, see Morton Cogan, *Imperialism and Religion: Assyria, Judah and Israel in the Eighth and Seventh Centuries B.C.E.* (Missoula: Scholars Press, 1974).

[64] See Culley, *Studies in the Structure of Hebrew Narrative* (see n. 45 above), for analysis of the "punishment stories."

[65] Tikva Frymer-Kensky, "The Atrahasis Epic and Its Significance for Our Understanding of Genesis 1-9," *BA* 40 (Dec. 1977), pp. 147-55.

brought me to possess this land," for it is by dint of the wickedness of these nations that the Lord dispossesses them before you.

Moses peppers his recounting of the Israelite history, from Deuteronomy 1 to the song in Deuteronomy 32, with reminders of Israel's apostasy and recalcitrance. When the Exile comes, Israel will know why.

It is perhaps worth mentioning in this connection that recent studies call attention to the large amount of north Israelite tradition in the Book of Deuteronomy.[66] It would then be likely that, as Ginsberg has argued, there already existed a core edition of Deuteronomy in the late-eighth century reign of Hezekiah.[67] The theology of the late-eighth century Deuteronomy would serve the function, among other things, of interpreting the destruction of Samaria to the southern kingdom. A later edition of Deuteronomy, taking into account the abominations of the seventh-century King Manasseh, would speak directly to the Judeans.

Having an explanation of the Exile would be a source of great consolation. If they knew how they got into it – by repeated violations of the covenant – they would know how to get out of it – by strict adherence to the covenant. But even so, the Judeans must have been dubious about the power of their ancestral God. The oracles of the Second Isaiah in the Babylonian Exile, mocking the pagan gods and beatifying the Lord of Israel as Creator of the world and Controller of events, are clearly addressed to such a skeptical, if not disbelieving, Judean audience. Many, if not most, Judeans must have questioned the covenantal promises, must have wondered how, if they were a special people of God – עם סגולה – they could live in such a state of humiliation and powerlessness.

In more obvious ways and less obvious ones the Torah, and many other Biblical writings, may be read as responses to those anxieties. As Clines has stressed, the Torah's narrative ends before the end.[68] Because the Torah transports the Israelites only to the threshold of the Promised Land, with the conquest by and large ahead of them, the position of the Israelites parallels that of the Judean exiles: "the promise of God stands behind them, the promised land before them."[69] The Judeans know from their Deuteronomistic History that the Israelites eventually took possession of the Land. They could hope for the same for themselves.

In a succinct but precise outline of the major themes in Genesis, Everett Fox observes that its primary concern is continuity, conveyed most concretely

---

[66]See, e.g., Alan W. Jenks, *The Elohist and North Israelite Traditions* (Missoula: Scholars Press, 1977); Friedman, *Who Wrote the Bible?*
[67]H. L. Ginsberg, *The Israelian Heritage of Judaism* (New York: Jewish Theological Seminary of America, 1982).
[68]David J. A. Clines, *The Theme of the Pentateuch* (Sheffield: JSOT Press, 1978).
[69]Ibid., p. 98.

by the חולדות lists.[70] With all its attention to continuity, however, "the undercurrent in Genesis points not to life and its continuation, but rather to its threatened extinction."[71] Genesis and the Torah as a whole (see the beginning of Exodus!) treat the threat of extinction as forever real; but they also reassure the audience that Israel's future is insured.

Like Jeremiah, the Judean exiles would want to know: "Have you rejected, rejected Judah? Are you revulsed by Zion?" (Jer. 14:19). The Lord has elevated Israel by calling them his "firstborn son" (Exod. 4:22). If Israel retains that status even in Exile, it sure doesn't look like it. Again we see a case of conflict between the ideal and the real. Israel in Exile does not resemble the firstborn but the younger, weaker, underprivileged son. In a marvelously shrewed analysis of recurrent themes in Genesis 37-Exodus 20, Alan Miller shows that the two dominant themes – twins unidentical though they be – respond precisely to this exilic anxiety.[72] Repeatedly the younger son overpowers, overshadows, or is simply more blessed than his older brother. Israel in Exile – by rights the firstborn but in reality the last in line – in the role of the younger son will eventually triumph, as did Jacob over Esau.

Nonetheless, having suffered defeat and a humbling deportation, the Judeans can hardly feel chosen. They don't look chosen. Here the second theme identified by Miller enters into play. Over and over we find in the Biblical narrative instances of deception, disguise, dissimulation. It turns up explicitly, as in the deception of Isaac by Rebekah and Jacob and the tit-for-tat deception of Jacob by Laban (and – how can she be exempted? – Leah). But we find it more subtly, too. The Lord disguised himself and surprised Moses at the burning bush. Things are not what they appear to be, the Torah reminds its audience. Israel in Exile may not look chosen, may seem fallen from divine favor. But looks are deceiving – that is a message for Israel to ponder.

A number of writers – Fox, Friedman, and Robert Cohn[73] – indicate a progression in the Biblical narrative from Genesis on in which God withdraws more and more from complete and direct control of worldly affairs and human beings must accept more and more responsibility. Using the Joseph story as an illustration, Cohn observes in addition that "directly correlated to the diminished direct divine role in events is the augmented role of human wisdom."[74] As Cohn and most of the other authors we have been discussing acknowledge, the exiles

[70]Everett Fox, *In the Beginning* (New York: Schocken Books, 1983), pp. xxxiii-xxxvii.

[71]Ibid., p. xxxiv.

[72]Alan W. Miller, "Claude Lévi-Strauss and Genesis 37-Exodus 20," in Ronald A. Brauner, ed., *Shiv'im* (Philadelphia: Reconstructionist Rabbinical College, 1977), pp. 21-52.

[73]Robert L. Cohn, "Narrative Structure and Canonical Perspective in Genesis," *JSOT* 25 (1983), pp. 3-16.

[74]Ibid., p. 13.

would hear in this message confirmation of the theology that they by rededicating themselves to the covenant can bring themselves out of it.

How? By observing Torah. It must not be neglected that the core of the Torah is not the reassuring and chastening narrative framework that runs into the Former Prophets. It is the legal code that with all its civil statutes and moral injunctions places Leviticus in the center.[75] The crisis of the Exile is that God's presence grows remote from the people. It was the divine presence in Israel's midst that defined its *raison d'être:* "in your going along with us, I and your people are distinguished from every people that is on the face of the earth" (Exod. 33:16; cf. Deut. 7:6-8; 14:2). In the Land of Israel, and in the situation the Torah imagines Israel was in in the wilderness, God's presence was housed among the people in the Dwelling, the משכן. The end of Exodus vividly describes God's taking up residence there in an environment of freshly made purity and luxury.[76] You could see God there.[77] In Exile Israel would feel the need to restore God's presence by maintaining an environment of holiness and purity. Leviticus provides the means.

Without a Temple, the cult of animal and meal offerings had to be discontinued until the Temple was rebuilt. The Temple, from the Torah's perspective, would have to be rebuilt. The many laws of purity have one preeminent purpose: to keep ritual pollution out of the sanctuary. They are virutally irrelevant without a sanctuary. The "logic" of the Torah's purity concept is this.[78] God is holy, his essence utter purity. God's purity is supersensitive to ritual pollution, so that God's immediate environment – the משכן and secondarily the camp – must be kept free of pollution. God would reject and withdraw from an accumulation of ritual pollution, as in an allergic reaction to pollen. Thus, ritual pollution, be it intentional or unintentional, has an ineluctable effect on God's presence. The priests were trained to detect pollutants in offerings and persons entering the sanctuary, and contain them. The community would be responsible for keeping the polluted out of their camp, to safeguard God's nourishing and protective presence among them. Just in case pollutants entered the holy presence of God unbeknownst to the priests, the sanctuary would be purified once a year whether it needed it or not, on יום הכפורים, "The Day of Purgation." This, as Kaufmann explained in a retort to

---

[75]I thank Susan Einbinder for reminding me of this fact. See now Damrosch, "Leviticus" (see n. 24 above).

[76]Cf. my "Biblical Law," in *Back to the Sources,* ed. Barry W. Holtz (New York: Summit Books, 1984), pp. 83-103, esp. 89.

[77]Cf. Jon D. Levenson, "The Jerusalem Temple in Devotional and Visionary Experience," in Arthur Green, ed., *Jewish Spirituality 1* (New York: Crossroad, 1986), pp. 32-61.

[78]Cf. my "Biblical Law," esp. pp. 89-95.

the Wellhausian claim that יום הכפורים was instituted in the Exile to atone for the sinfulness of the nation, was what the annual purification was about.[79]

What constitutes the holy? For the Torah the holy is that which is God's, extensions of God, things pertaining to God: God's land (his "holy territory"; Exod. 15:13), God's people (when they observe their purity), God's paraphernalia (sanctuary, ark, altar, and so forth), and – life.[80] After the Garden of Eden events, when humans acquire knowledge like that of God (Gen. 3:8), God is distinguished from mortals by the fact that he lives forever; he is, as I would say, livingness.[81] The Torah's concern for maintaining the definition of boundaries comes out most sharply in the strange, distressingly pagan, episode in Gen. 6:1-4. The God-sons have intercourse with the human daughters and produce a hybrid race of God-people. That means that there would be human beings living for a long time if not forever. God's distinctiveness would be jeopardized. God's reaction is to make his unique characteristic firmer than ever: human beings would live no more than 120 years. Read in thematic context, the episode coheres with the Torah's general concerns, despite its pagan veneer.

Because God is livingness, blood, the primary liquid of life, is God's. Humans may not take or partake of life and blood. Because blood is the quintessential material of God's, it is the one that most effectively purifies the polluted.[82] Discharges of blood or other bodily fluids pollute – when they flow from reproductive areas. While nothing pollutes more than the antithesis of livingness, death, the confusion of boundaries that ensues from leaking life from the organs of life, is a major source of pollution. Until the leaks are plugged, or the impairments repaired, life-leaks pollute.

The other quality that makes for holiness in the Torah is proximity to the state of createdness. Things can be holy when they remain close to the condition in which God made them. God demands from Israel the fresh and new; being close to their created state, they properly belong to God. God asks for the first fruits of the earth and womb (Exod. 13:1ff.; Deut. 26:5-10); an altar of unhewn stone (Exod. 20:25); a red heifer that has never borne a yoke (Deut. 21:3-4); a new cart on which to carry the ark (2 Sam. 6:3); free-flowing water for purification (Lev. 14:5, 52; 15:13).

---

[79]Yehezkel Kaufmann, *The Religion of Israel,* abridged and trans. Moshe Greenberg (Chicago: University of Chicago Press, 1960), esp. pp. 307-9.
[80]Cf. Jacob Milgrom, "The Biblical Diet Laws as an Ethical System," *Interpretation* 17 (1963), pp. 288-301. The best analysis of the Biblical mindset, though technical, is still Henry Wheeler Robinson, *Inspiration and Revelation in the Old Testament* (Oxford: Clarendon Press, 1946); cf. also Hans Walter Wolff, *Anthropology of the Old Testament* (Philadelphia: Fortress Press, 1974).
[81]Cf. my "Biblical Law," p. 91.
[82]See, e.g., Jacob Milgrom, "The Paradox of the Red Heifer," *Beth Mikra* 89-90 (1982), pp. 155-63 [in Hebrew].

God created the various species in categories, and humans must respect those categories. To violate those categories by ignoring, blurring, or mixing them would be tantamount to arrogating to oneself divine powers. To maintain the categories within their boundaries, the way God created them, is a sort of *imitatio dei*. The Torah prohibits hybrids because, in the Torah's view, they result from combining different species. This explanation of the taboo on hybrids was first articulated, so far as I know, by Rabbi Joseph Bekhor Shor, the twelfth-century French commentator.[83] The reason Israel should not mate different animal species together is that "you would have altered the act of creation...you would be making yourself like a Creator."[84] What would happen if one did create a hybrid, say a new vegetable? Deut. 22:9-11 furnishes the answer. Because a hybrid is a new creation, and creation is God's prerogative, the hybrid is automatically consecrated property (קדש), property of God. Humans may not put it to personal use.

The dietary laws concretize the principle of respecting the categories of creation.[85] In the diction of Genesis 1 one is impressed by the repetition of the verb הבדיל, "to separate." Division is the key ordering device. Israel, for its part, may eat animals that do not ingest blood (for blood belongs to God) and conform to one of three classes. The language of Leviticus 11 puts emphasis on the place in which an animal typically dwells and, in particular, the manner by which that animal moves in its domain – by walking, the appropriate locomotion for land animals; by flying, the proper method for air animals; or by flapping, the right way for water animals. The three classes, then, are: the land-grazers, the air-wingers, and the water-flappers. Animals that move about inappositely for their domain cross a boundary, so to speak, and are tainted. Fowl, which is typologically supposed to fly in the air but which walks on the ground, cannot be eaten (see Lev. 11:20). Thus, Alter, in critiquing the structural analysis of these laws, errs in assuming that the chicken was pure and untainted.[86] He is reading back later Rabbinic classification, which is not informed by the same concerns as the historical ones of the Torah, into Leviticus.

Israel's task is to maintain the divisions that God created, and by doing so to retain the divine presence in its midst. Because it must shoulder this responsibility, Israel must preserve its own distinctiveness among nations:

> I, the Lord your God, have divided you from the peoples. So you will
> divide between the pure animal and the tainted one, between the tainted

---

[83]Cf. my "Medieval Bible Commentaries," in *Back to the Sources* (see n. 76 above), pp. 213-59, here 246-47.

[84]R. Joseph Bekhor Shor, commentary to Lev. 19:19.

[85]See Mary Douglas, *Purity and Danger* (New York: Praeger, 1966), pp. 41-58; Jean Soler, "The Dietary Prohibitions of the Hebrews," *New York Review of Books*, June 14, 1979, pp. 24-30.

[86]Robert Alter, "A New Theory of Kashrut," *Commentary* 68 (August 1979), pp. 49-52.

fowl and the pure ones, so that you do not pollute yourselves with
animals, fowl, or with anything which creeps on the earth, which I have
divided for you as tainted. So you will be holy to me, for holy am I, the
Lord. I divided you from the peoples to be mine (Lev. 20:24-26; cf.
11:46-47).

The Torah, in this reading, speaks to the exiles and urges them to maintain the
distinctiveness of their practices and their distinctiveness as a people. Unlike the
deportation of the North by Assyria, by whose policy Israelites were transplanted
all over the map, virtually compelling the assimilation that ensued after 722, the
Babylonian Exile left the Judean communities to themselves. The Judeans could
preserve their identity and produce the circumstances in the Diaspora that are
reflected in the Scroll of Esther: "There is one people, diffused and dispersed
among the peoples through all the provinces of your empire; and their laws are
different from every people" (3:8). This is proof positive that the Torah worked.

The Torah may incorporate ancient material; it may remember old concerns.
But the form in which it was finally shaped addressed the particular situation of
the exilic community, the one that first made it Torah (see, e.g., Ezra 7:10;
Nehemiah 8, 10). The typological reading of the Torah is not in itself new, as
the following comment by a nineteenth-century Jewish mystic shows:

> The Torah is eternal; it refers to all times and to every person. It existed
> before the world, and only afterwards took on the form of stories about
> events in time. While the patriarchs Abraham, Isaac, and Jacob lived, the
> Torah took on the stories of their lives. The same should be true of all
> times; Torah is so called because it teaches or points the way.[87]

The Torah remains a sacred book because it can be read within the framework of
current concerns. But it spoke to the Exile first; in form and function it
responded to the catastrophe of 587. The Torah as she is read by contemporary
critical eyes, can mean on different levels simultaneously.

---

[87]Menahem Nahum of Chernobyl, ספר מאור עינים [The Book of the Enlightenment of
the Eyes], trans. Arthur Green (New York: Paulist Press, 1982), p. 249. For a
modern discussion of typologies in the Torah, see Michael Fishbane, "The Sacred
Center" (see Chapter One, n. 95).

Chapter Three

Theory and Argument in Biblical Criticism

"It is the viewpoint that creates the object." – de Saussure.[1]

Israeli archaeologist Gabriel Barkay has recently published a preliminary report and reading of Hebrew inscriptions incised on two thin silver strips.[2] Each has been identified as a version of the so-called priestly benediction that appears in the Massoretic Text in Num. 6:24-26. The larger text is said to contain traces of the three benedictions that we read in the MT. Contrary to what an innocent reader might suppose from any of a number of newspaper accounts of the discovery and deciphering of the texts, the paleographer, Ada Yardeni, did not identify the famous passage by simply reading the ancient Hebrew characters. She had, at first, considerable difficulty in distinguishing the Hebrew letters from other scratches in the silver. She could, however, make out three instances of the tetragrammaton, *YHWH*. She proceeded to identify, decipher, and read additional letters and words only after a friend had suggested that, in view of the three occurrences of *YHWH*, the text might correspond to the threefold priestly benediction.[3] The delicately engraved letters were found to be meaningful only after the paleographer had formed a prior hypothesis about what the text might contain.

Even more to the point: once Yardeni had read three benedictions on the larger silver strip, she realized that one of the instances of *YHWH* that she had earlier noticed was not part of the three benedictions at all. It belonged to another part of the text. In other words, based on partially incorrect data, she tested a hypothesis that proved correct and, as a result, proved that some of the initial data was wrong. I am reminded of a sentence from a murder mystery by Colin Dexter: "[Inspector] Morse, having been put on the right track by the wrong

---

[1]Ferdinand de Saussure, *Course in General Linguistics,* ed. C. Bally and A. Sechehaye with A. Riedlinger, trans. W. Baskin (New York: McGraw-Hill, 1966), p. 8.
[2]Gabriel Barkay, *Ketef Hinnom: A Treasure Facing Jerusalem's Walls* (Jerusalem: The Israel Museum, 1986), esp. pp. 29-31.
[3]Abraham Rabinovich, "Word for Word," *Jerusalem Post Magazine,* July 18, 1986, pp. 10-12, here p. 12.

clues, now finds his judgement almost wholly vindicated."[4] What should be clear from this particular account of Yardeni's decoding the text is that, as philosophers of science and others have long maintained, all observation, be it scientific or of the everyday variety, begins with a theory.[5] Our very observations, and not only our interpretations, are necessarily shaped by whatever presuppositions, hypotheses, and funds of knowledge we possess. As Rawidowicz had said in an extraordinary essay, the most basic perceptions are already "deeply steeped in interpretation."[6] Our theories guide our selection of evidence, and even our construction of evidence.

In the case of Yardeni's reading of the silver engraving, the paleographer brought to her task, we must imagine, a large number of theories or theoretical frameworks within which she examined the inscription. She no doubt made assumptions about how to position the text for reading, about what script the text was written in, about the language of the writing, and – most strikingly – about what the letters might mean. We make assumptions in our work routinely, so much so that we tend to take them for granted. Let us consider a simple illustration.

No one, so far as I know, doubts that a number of chapters of Biblical verse conform to the pattern of an alphabetic acrostic (e.g., Pss. 34, 111, 112, 119, 145; Prov. 31:10-31; Lam. 1-4; and with varying degrees of irregularity Pss. 9-10, 25, 37). Each line or couplet begins with a succeeding letter of the alphabet.

---

[4]Colin Dexter, *The Riddle of the Third Mile* (New York: St. Martin's Press, 1983), p. 127.

[5]Cf., e.g., Stephen C. Pepper, *World Hypotheses: A Study in Evidence* (Berkeley: University of California Press, 1948); Michael Polanyi, *Personal Knowledge* (see Preface, n. 5, above); *Knowing and Being*, ed. M. Grene (Chicago: University of Chicago Press, 1969); Thomas S. Kuhn, The *Structure of Scientific Revolutions*, 2nd ed. (Chicago: University of Chicago Press, 1970); Paul Feyerabend, *Against Method* (London: Verso Press, 1978); Karl R. Popper, *Objective Knowledge*, 2nd ed. (Oxford: Oxford University Press, 1979); Stanley Fish, *Is There a Text in This Class?* (Cambridge, MA: Harvard University Press, 1980); Donald W. Fiske and Richard A. Shweder, eds., *Metatheory in Social Science: Pluralisms and Subjectivities* (Chicago: University of Chicago Press, 1986). Although these and other discussants of theory disagree on many issues, such as the role of evidence in supporting a theory and the necessity of conducting tests for possible falsification of a theory, they agree on this. For a summary discussion, see Ian Barbour, *Myths, Models, and Paradigms* (New York: Harper & Row, 1974). Barbour pays proper attention to types of models (esp. pp. 29-33) and to criteria for evaluating competing models or theories (esp. pp. 112-18). While these are two issues that deserve special treatment in a wider discussion of the role of theory in Biblical criticism, I confine myself to arguing the more limited, prior claim that Biblical studies unavoidably draws on undemonstrable presuppositions and beliefs, even at the stage of defining the evidence. On this point, cf. Barbour's concise discussion on pp. 94-98.

[6]Simon Rawidowicz, "On Interpretation," *Proceedings of the American Academy for Jewish Research 26* (1957), pp. 83-126, here p. 84.

Everyone, I suppose, will agree that the alphabetic acrostic was a convention of ancient Israelite verse. That conclusion, with which I concur, rests upon a number of assumptions that can be posited axiomatically but cannot be proved or deduced from unassumed premises. To begin, one discovers the acrostic in the first place only after one already has a prior concept of what an acrostic is. We match our concept of the acrostic with the pattern that we find in the Biblical text. But in order to find the pattern one must first apply some theory for defining the lines of verse and divide the text into lines. One must then decide that the initial letter of every line or every other line belongs not to a random pattern but to a meaningful design. In the case of the alphabetic acrostic, the meaningful design is the Hebrew alphabet. Without knowing what an acrostic is, one could not discover the alphabet in the pattern; and without knowing the Hebrew alphabet, one could not have found the acrostic pattern in the text. The two identifications are twin components of a single construct.

To claim that the alphabetic acrostic was a convention of Israelite verse demands that we make additional assumptions: that the ancient bard intended to pattern his lines according to an alphabetic acrostic, and, further, that the Israelites had an alphabet. Since we are not "empirical" observers of the Biblical world and its historical setting, even the existence of an ancient Hebrew alphabet rests on theory.[7] To prove that the Hebrews had an alphabet we cannot use the very acrostics we are discussing to document the existence of the alphabet. That would be arguing in too obvious a circle. One can, of course, adduce the Izbet Sarta inscription, part of which more or less corresponds to our idea of the Hebrew alphabet; and one can go farther afield and identify cognate alphabets in Ugaritic and ancient Aramaic and Ammonite epigraphs.[8] But without a prior notion of what an alphabet looks like one could not have found alphabets in these extra-Biblical texts either. To use our identification of the alphabet in one place to prove its existence in another is merely, borrowing a phrase from Nabokov's *Lolita*, "like a conjurer explaining one trick by performing another."

---

[7] As I shall claim below, even had we lived in Biblical times, our observations, like all observation, would remain hypothetical. The term "empirical" is used to deny the necessary "subjective" features of all observation. In opposition to the "empirical" tradition in philosophy, students of perception have found not only that the senses are unreliable but "that there are vast and still largely mysterious jumps – intelligent leaps of the mind, which may land on error – between the sensation and the perception of an object"; Richard L. Gregory, "Perception," The *Oxford Companion to the Mind*, ed. idem (Oxford: Oxford University Press, 1987), pp. 598-601, here p. 599a. On the physiologically demonstrable gap between visual sensation and perception, cf. Oliver Sacks and Robert Wasserman, "The Case of the Colorblind Painter," *New York Review of Books*, Nov. 19, 1987, pp. 25-34.
[8] See Aaron Demsky, "A Proto-Canaanite Abededary dating from the Period of the Judges and Its Implications for the History of the Alphabet," *Tel Aviv* 4 (1977), pp. 14-27; and André Lemaire, "Fragments from the Book of Balaam Found at Deir Alla," *BARev* 11/5 (1985), pp. 26-39, esp. 39.

Rather, in identifying the alphabet in extra-Biblical texts and in discovering alphabetic acrostics in the Bible we follow a certain set of assumptions or beliefs – our theory of the alphabet and its use. The theory entails the assumptions that an ancient Israelite verse-maker and his audience knew the alphabet and that the use of the alphabet in an acrostic was a convention of ancient Hebrew verse. On the basis of this set of premises, we make deductions concerning the structure of various Biblical psalms and elegies.

My intention is not to cast doubt on the reality of alphabetic acrostics in the Bible. It is rather to avow that whenever we make literary or any other kind of observations on the Bible, or on any other texts, we have no choice but to use the models with which we are familiar to identify and classify that which we observe.[9] We find parallelism, chiasm, meter, even metaphor in Biblical verse only after we have a theory of what those literary forms are. The theory adopts or develops methods for identifying those forms.

One cannot simply "infer," as Alter suggests, the conventions of the literature "by a careful inspection of the texts."[10] Alter himself has implicitly acknowledged this point elsewhere, where he admits that a "scholar from another planet" without any training in Elizabethan poetry would fail to discover even the most evident patterns in Shakespeare's sonnets.[11] One cannot in unmediated fashion "elicit...the innate conventions and literary formations of a piece of ancient literature."[12] It is impossible, as Fish and others have contended at length,[13] to "curb all temptations to impose [our] antecedent judgments on the text."[14] The process of perceiving, even at the most physical level, is not

---

[9]See Luis Alonso Schökel, "Of Methods and Models," *SVT* 36 (Leiden: E. J. Brill, 1985), pp. 3-13; and cf. James L. Kugel, *The Idea of Biblical Poetry* (New Haven: Yale University Press, 1981), p. 302; Jonathan Magonet, "The Structure of Isaiah 6," *Proceedings of the Ninth World Congress of Jewish Studies* (Jerusalem: World Union of Jewish Studies, 1986), Division A, pp. 91-97, here p. 91.

[10]Robert Alter, "How Convention Helps Us Read: The Case of the Bible's Annunciation Type-Scene," *Prooftexts* 3 (1983), pp. 115-30, here p. 118. Cf. the critique of Alter's notion that texts speak for themselves in Stephen A. Geller, "Some Pitfalls in the 'Literary Approach' to Biblical Narrative," *JQR* 74 (1984), pp. 408-15. The objectification of the personified text has been assumed by many general critics, such as E. D. Hirsch, *Validity in Interpretation* (New Haven: Yale University Press, 1967); cf., e.g., p. 210: "The point which needs to be grasped clearly by the critic is that a text cannot be made to speak to us until *what it says* [my emphasis] has been understood."

[11]Robert Alter, *The Art of Biblical Poetry* (New York: Basic Books, 1985), pp. 205-6.

[12]Moshe Greenberg, *Ezekiel 1-20*, AB 22 (Garden City, NY: Doubleday, 1983), p. 21.

[13]Fish, *Is There a Text in This Class?;* and cf. W. J. T. Mitchell, ed., *Against Theory: Literary Studies and the New Pragmatism* (Chicago: University of Chicago Press, 1985).

[14]Greenberg, *Ezekiel 1-20*, p. 21.

merely a matter of receiving and storing stimuli.[15] "It is now...fairly generally accepted that stored knowledge and assumptions *actively* affect even the simplest perceptions."[16] Perception is itself an interpretive faculty, an active, though largely automatic, implementation of our prior models, presuppositions, and analytic strategies. It is useful to become aware of our assumptions so that we may subject them to criticism and reconsider our reliance on them.[17] But even when we do not notice them, they are there.

The most exact science begins with deductions from hypothetical foundations. Consider this description of physics by Albert Einstein:

> Physics constitutes a logical system of thought which is in a state of evolution, and whose basis cannot be obtained through distillation by any inductive method from the experiences lived through, but which can only be attained by free invention.[18]

As Einstein had already characterized the project of physics in 1918: "The supreme task...is to arrive at those elementary laws from which the cosmos can be built up *by pure deduction* [my emphasis]."[19] The root of the laws lies in the model in the thinker's imagination:

> Man tries to make for himself in the fashion that suits him best a simplified and intelligible picture of the world. He then tries to some extent to substitute this cosmos of his for the world of experience, and thus to overcome it.[20]

What has been acknowledged for physics applies as well to the social sciences and humanities[21] and has been recognized by some for the specific field of Biblical studies.[22]

---

[15]Cf., e.g., Julian E. Hochberg, *Perception*, 2nd ed. (Englewood Cliffs, NJ: Prentice-Hall, 1978), p. 88.

[16]Gregory, "Perception," p. 601a; cf. Rudolf Arnheim, *Visual Thinking* (Berkeley: University of California Press, 1969), p. 13: "the cognitive operations called thinking are not the privilege of mental processes above and beyond perception but the essential ingredients of perception itself."

[17]Cf. Chapter Four, Part Two (review of Gibson).

[18]Albert Einstein, *Out of My Later Years* (New York: Philosophical Library, 1950), p. 96.

[19]Quoted in Robert M. Pirsig, *Zen and the Art of Motorcycle Maintenance* (New York: Bantam Books, 1975), p. 99.

[20]Loc. cit. The father of phenomenology, Edmund Husserl, too, has contended that physics applies its own principles of logic in order to create a "hypothetical substructure" of "thing-realities"; *Ideas: General Introduction to Pure Phenomenology*, trans. W. R. B. Gibson (New York: Collier Books, 1962; first published, 1931), p. 147.

[21]Cf., e.g., Robert Scholes and Robert Kellogg, *The Nature of Narrative* (New York: Oxford University Press, 1966), esp. pp. 276, 278; Noam Chomsky, *Problems of Knowledge and Freedom* (New York: Vintage Books, 1972); Jonathan

The best known instance of applying a model in Biblical studies involves source criticism in general and the Documentary Hypothesis in particular.[23] Tsevat has challenged Biblical critics to state their underlying assumptions, their "first principles," and subject them to models that are familiar to us from other sources.[24] Tigay has suggested that his own and others' source critical analyses of other ancient Near Eastern texts might serve as an appropriate model for reconstructing the composition of the Torah.[25] This is a perfectly valid proposal. What is mistaken is the concomitant claim that such analyses are somehow "empirical." An empirical observation purports to examine directly the actual historical composition of the texts in question. George Steiner has stated the counterclaim succinctly: "To all past events, as to all present intake, the observer brings a specific mental set."[26] The so-called "empirical" observation of concrete "evidence" is mediated by theory just as all observation is. What Tigay and others produce are theories concerning the historical relationships of ancient Near Eastern texts. They, too, are informed by a number of presupposed principles.

For example, Tigay assumes that documents that are found to have affinities to earlier documents are related through some history of written composition. His evidence for relations in writing can also be explained by assuming that the

---

Culler, *Structuralist Poetics* (Ithaca: Cornell University Press, 1975); and Fiske and Shweder, *Metatheory in Social Science*.

[22]Cf., e.g., Robert Polzin, *Biblical Structuralism* (Missoula/Philadelphia: Scholars Press/Fortress Press, 1977); Arthur Gibson, *Biblical Semantic Logic* (New York: St. Martin's Press, 1981); John Barton, *Reading the Old Testament* (Philadelphia: Westminster Press, 1984); Alonso Schökel, "Of Methods and Models".

[23]Cf., e.g., Alonso Schökel, "Of Methods and Models," pp. 5-6.

[24]Matitiahu Tsevat, "Common Sense in Old Testament Study," *SVT* 28 (1975), pp. 217-30.

[25]Jeffrey H. Tigay, ed., *Empirical Models for Biblical Criticism* (Philadelphia: University of Pennsylvania Press, 1985); cf. Adele Berlin, *Poetics and Interpretation of Biblical Narrative* (Sheffield: Almond Press, 1983), esp. pp. 129ff. For a critique of Berlin, see Chapter Four, Part One. Michael Fishbane, too, somewhat analogously seeks to distinguish different types of ancient scribal explication of the Biblical text on the basis of whether "formulaic indicators" of such explication are evident; *Biblical Interpretation in Ancient Israel* (Oxford: Oxford University Press, 1985). Such indicators, says Fishbane (p. 56), "permit a relatively objective identification of the scribal comments involved." However, Fishbane seems to overlook that it is only through his own, or someone else's, exegesis that certain words or phrases in the Hebrew are taken to be "formulaic indicators" of "scribal comments." There is nothing even "relatively objective" about such exegesis. Although Fishbane himself may feel more sanguine about his determination of explicit scribal annotations than about his determination of implicit ones, both kinds of determination are products of his own analysis. Indeed, without going into details here, I find some of his identifications of "unmarked" explications more convincing than some of his identifications of "formulaically indicated" ones.

[26]George Steiner, *After Babel* (New York: Oxford University Press, 1975), p. 137.

written texts reflect different orally performed versions of the text at hand.[27] Tigay dismisses this alternative by asserting that he distrusts the hypothesis of oral prototypes.[28] He may be correct, but we can never know that because by definition oral performances, until recently, have gone unrecorded. One may not make a virtue out of a necessity and bar unattested and unattestable material from our hypotheses. In more extreme fashion Van Seters virtually disqualifies all "prior versions" of a Biblical text from a hypothesis concerning the historical development of that text.[29] Precisely because no one has direct access to the history of ancient literature, one will always be in the position of imagining, or hypothesizing, the history of the text.[30]

This, in fact, is always the case with history. The history is not in the data but in the analysis. It is worth repeating here the well-known remarks of Carr:

> The belief in a hard core of historical facts existing objectively and independently of the interpretation of the historian is a preposterous fallacy, but one which it is very hard to eradicate.[31]

The role of a theoretical model behind the historian writing the story of ancient Israelite history has been cleverly illustrated by Sasson in his contrast of the American and German schools of modern Biblical historiography.[32] He argues, in a highly suggestive manner, that scholars have imagined – and reconstructed – the origins of the Israelite tribal union according to the way in which their own nations confederated. America was colonized by waves of immigrants who eventually formed a union of states, and so have W. F. Albright, John Bright, and others conceived of the formation of ancient Israel. Germany was unified only through the later confederation of a number of originally autonomous local states – a model that has been translated by A. Alt and M. Noth to the early history of Israel. Indeed, the academic controversy concerning the emergence of Israel has turned more and more explicitly into a discussion of competing models.[33] Rendtorff puts it this way:

> Each of the models is based on particular presuppositions which often seem more important in the discussion than the reconstruction itself,

---

[27]See, e.g., Jeffrey H. Tigay, *The Evolution of the Gilgamesh Epic* (Philadelphia: University of Pennsylvania Press, 1982), pp. 58-59, 61ff., 82ff., and passim.
[28]Ibid., pp. 102-3.
[29]John Van Seters, *Abraham in History and Tradition* (New Haven: Yale University Press, 1975), pp. 155-56.
[30]See also Chapters One and Two above.
[31]E. H. Carr, *What Is History?* (New York: Vintage Books, 1961), p. 10; cf. Baruch Kurzweil, במאבק על ערכי היהדות [In the Struggle over Jewish Values] (Jerusalem: Schocken Books, 1970), Part 2.
[32]Jack M. Sasson, "On Choosing Models for Recreating Israelite Pre-Monarchic History," *JSOT* 21 (1981), pp. 3-24.
[33]For a summary of the models, see Norman K. Gottwald, *The Hebrew Bible: A Socio-Literary Introduction* (Philadelphia: Fortress Press, 1985), pp. 261-88.

since they involve methodological, historical, and theological questions of principle, all at the same time.[34]

It would therefore seem useful in academic discourse among scholars taking divergent theoretical stances to acknowledge the differences in first principles or beliefs that divide us before proceeding to examine the argumentation or logic of the other person's positions. Greenberg points out the axiomatic first steps of scholarship when he speaks of the "a prioris, an array of unproved (and unprovable) modern assumptions and conventions that confirm themselves through the results obtained by forcing them on the text...."[35] Greenberg has in mind those Biblicists who assume that the earlier and more original the material is, the simpler and more thematically uniform it is. By isolating small passages that display simplicity and inner coherence, such scholars believe that they are identifying the historically earlier units of a given text. Greenberg, however, refers to the assumptions of these critics as "prejudices," as though one could choose to be neutral and unprejudiced. But, as Rorty[36] and others (notably Fish) have demonstrated, we all begin with beliefs or assumptions that guide us in our observations and analyses. Greenberg reveals his own premises in the following pages: that the text at hand is to be taken as a whole; that one should "look...for design and for integrating elements" in order to find patterns; and that discontinuities in the text constitute variations on the pattern rather than indications of disparate sources.[37] This set of assumptions or first principles belongs to a coherent theory. It is not an argument of theory versus no theory, or subjectivity versus neutrality. It is an argument between a theory of multiple composition and a theory of single or homogeneous composition.[38]

One finds an analogous opposition of initial premises in the area of textual criticism.[39] The position that regards textual emendation with suspicion has been clearly articulated by Gordis: "the given text is a datum and the emended, deleted or transposed text is a hypothesis."[40] In fact the restructured text is

---

[34]Rolf Rendtorff, *The Old Testament: An Introduction* (Philadelphia: Fortress Press, 1986), p. 22.

[35]Greenberg, *Ezekiel 1-20*, p. 20.

[36]Richard Rorty, *Consequences of Pragmatism* (Minneapolis: University of Minnesota Press, 1982); idem, "Deconstruction and Circumvention," *Critical Inquiry* 11/1 (1984), pp. 1-23.

[37]Greenberg, *Ezekiel 1-20*, pp. 25-26.

[38]Cf. W. B. Barrick, who, in his review of Greenberg's *Ezekiel 1-20* in *JBL* 105 (1986), pp. 142-44, observes that "Greenberg operates in an entirely different mode" from typical historical critics. For further discussion of the general issue, see Chapter Four, Part One.

[39]See further Emanuel Tov, "קריטריונים להערכת גרסאות טכסטואליות – ההגבלות של כללים קבועים" [Criteria for Evaluating Textual Versions – The Limitations on Fixed Principles]," *Beth Mikra* 30 (1984/85), pp. 112-32.

[40]Robert Gordis, "Traumatic Surgery in Biblical Scholarship: A Note on Methodology," *JJSt* 32 (1982), pp. 195-99, here p. 198.

hypothetical. The acceptance of the received text, based on whatever beliefs, is also hypothetical, though. One cannot know that the received text is more original, or "better" in any other way. Gordis employs the metaphor of the text as a body in need of medical repair (cf. his title: "Traumatic Surgery in Biblical Scholarship"). Surgery might be a last resort if the body could be mended by less "traumatic" means. But if a scholar judges that a text is dismembered, only surgery can bind the parts together into an organic whole. It is the initial assumption or hypothesis of the physician, as it is of the philologist, to decide whether one should work with the corpus as it stands or to rebuild the corpus into a unity.

Returning to the higher criticism of the Torah, the debate over the composition of the Pentateuch often represents itself as an argument about logic, methodology, and data. As I see it, however, the contest is often between theories or models of composition. Each theory, as Rendtorff has explained,[41] applies the procedures of analysis or exegesis that serve its ends. As Carr has written of professional historians, "By and large, the historian will get the kind of facts he wants."[42] The analyst ascertains what facts are significant and in what manner to arrange them. This is not meant to disparage historiography; it is meant to describe the only way, under the best of circumstances, that any scientific, as well as humanistic, inquiry can operate. If the source critic assumes that every shift in style or topic conveys special significance, one will never discover diverse sources in the Torah. Applying the tools of source critical analysis, one will perforce disintegrate the text. Because the very tools that a critic uses will perform the task that the critic envisions at the outset, one cannot legitimately use the methods and conclusions of one theory in criticizing another. Each theory's methods select and interpret evidence in order to support or lend substance to the arguments that hold up the theory. One may prefer a house of bricks to a house of wood. But one should not fault the mason for using bricks and mortar instead of boards and nails.

When, for example, Segal attacked the Documentary Hypothesis, he was correct in describing the regnant source theory of his day as follows:

> The principal assertions of the [Documentary Theory's] system, originally nothing more than pure suppositions, have now matured with age and with constant repetition into axiomatic truths, which control the thinking of scholars and direct their approach to biblical problems.[43]

His remarks have been recently echoed by Rendtorff:

---

[41]Rolf Rendtorff, "The Future of Pentateuchal Criticism," *Henoch* 6 (1984), pp. 1-14, esp. p. 11.
[42]Carr, *What Is History?*, p. 26.
[43]M. H. Segal, *The Pentateuch. Its Composition and Its Authorship, and Other Biblical Studies* (Jerusalem: Magnes Press, 1967), p. 2.

> The documentary hypothesis was a dogma and every scholar who wanted to be accepted by the establishment of Old Testament scholarship had to submit to this theory in order to demonstrate that he was able to handle the established method.[44]

What they describe happens in the growth of any discipline or science. Once a number of workers in the field become convinced of a hypothesis or model, they accept it as an axiom and proceed from there.[45] They make deductions from their shared axioms. Segal opposed the Documentary Hypothesis and its source analytical procedures because they conflicted with his own model of a singly authored text, supplemented with occasional additions. Accordingly, he criticized source criticism for its method of "wrench[ing]...passage[s] out of [their] context[s]...and interpret[ing them] as independent of what precedes...and what follows...."[46]

Applying the tools of his own theory of unitary composition, Segal performed often idiosyncratic exegesis so that the theory he espoused would seem impregnable. He interpreted Exod. 3:13, מה שמו, for example, to mean not "What is his name?" but rather "What *meaneth* his name? What is its import and its significance?"[47] In Segal's view, of course, the Hebrews would already have known the tetragrammaton, as it was used throughout Genesis. The common enough Hebrew phrase must, according to his approach, have a sense that differs from its ordinary one. His theory affects, or colors, his reading of Exodus. Because for Segal the Torah is "a continuous whole," the interpreter should "seek out the Theme which guides its successive events and the aim to which they are leading."[48] He claimed that this approach to the text was the one the text itself called for because the text as we now have it is, and has been preserved as, a single piece. This circular argument cannot be accepted by anyone who would conceive of a model of composition other than that of single authorship.

The reasoning of Segal resembles that of those, cited above, who discount the hypothesis of written sources or oral traditions because they do not exist (now). If one believes in a theory of composition that involves the positing of oral sources, one's beliefs cannot be shaken by pointing out that those sources do not exist anymore. An archaeologist does not confine oneself to existing potsherds in diagramming an ancient jug. One imagines that a hypothetical jug possessed the missing pieces, the ones that may have been lost forever, in making one's reconstruction. The literary historian, as another hypothesis builder, must imagine the complete model of a text consisting of all the pieces that one believes once existed.

---

[44]Rendtorff, "The Future of Pentateuchal Criticism," p. 2.
[45]See, e.g., Kuhn, *The Structure of Scientific Revolutions,* and Feyerabend, *Against Method.*
[46]Segal, *The Pentateuch,* p. 5.
[47]Loc. cit.
[48]Ibid., p. 22.

While many scholars are aware that we have conflicting models of the Torah's composition among us, few of us, in our public discussion of rival theories, act on that awareness. In order to illustrate my claim, and distinguish between differences in belief or model and differences in logic and argumentation, I shall draw on my reading of twelve professional reviews – many of them lengthy – of Van Seters' book, *Abraham in History and Tradition*, published in 1975. Van Seters challenged the Graf-Wellhasuen Documentary Hypothesis as it was developed by Noth. According to that theory, as summarized for example in the *Interpreter's Dictionary of the Bible*, [49] the written sources J and E adapted a common tradition, G, that was either oral or written. J and E were redacted into a single edition. Van Seters, on the other hand, following the lead of his teacher F. V. Winnett[50] and anticipated by such nineteenth century scholars as H. Ewald,[51] described a different theory. Before proceeding to delineate that theory it will be useful to consider the reasons that Winnett and Van Seters sought an alternative to the modified Documentary Hypothesis. Few of Van Seters' reviewers considered this.

First, the scholarly consensus on the Graf-Wellhausen theory had been deteriorating for decades.[52] Second, Winnett and Van Seters felt that source analytical procedures fragmented what looked to them like "unified stories and episodes."[53] Third, the E source is notoriously difficult to document except in the so-called "doublets," stories that are told twice or more. Fourth, Winnett and Van Seters recognized that the hypothesis of a common source for J and E, a *Grundlage*, and the assumption of a series of redactors were necessitated only by dint of the prior hypothesis of discrete written sources, J and E.[54]

A fifth, and so far as I know unstated reason for the alternate theory, is simply that Winnett and Van Seters imagined a different possibility for explaining the Torah's composition. It is true that new theories are often advanced in response to a crisis: the old theory would not solve a nagging problem. It is also true, however, that new theories have frequently been introduced when most scholars were content with the old ones.[55] New theories

---

[49]David N. Freedman, "Documents," *Interpreter's Dictionary of the Bible*, ed. G. A. Buttrick et al. (Nashville: Abingdon Press, 1962), s.v.

[50]Frederick V. Winnett, "Re-examining the Foundations," *JBL* 84 (1965), pp. 1-19.

[51]Cf. Albert de Pury, Review of *The Historicity of the Patriarchal Narratives* by T. L. Thompson and *Abraham in History and Tradition* by J. Van Seters, *RB* 85 (1978), pp. 589-618, here p. 604 with n. 39.

[52]Cf. Joseph Blenkinsopp, "The Documentary Hypothesis in Trouble," *BR* 1/4 (Winter 1985), pp. 22-32.

[53]Van Seters, *Abraham*, p. 127; cf. Winnett, "Re-examining the Foundations," pp. 6, 10.

[54]Van Seters, *Abraham*, pp. 125-29.

[55]Cf., e.g., Kuhn, *The Structure of Scientific Revolutions*. One could go even further and note that not only are new theories proposed when old ones can handle the available evidence, but old theories are often maintained after they have been

need not emerge over the rubble of a shattered older theory. To insist that they do is to commit what Pepper has called "the fallacy of clearing the ground."[56] Nor need a new theory explain the presently known evidence better than the older theory. New theories will define new issues and may restructure the current data into different evidence altogether. Because, as I have argued above, theory informs observation, too, new theories will yield new evidence.[57]

Van Seters' work interests us because he in fact shares most of the assumptions and methods of other historical critics.[58] He marshals them toward a different conclusion, however. In our discussion of his work we shall focus not on his dating of the patriarchal narratives but on his, and Winnett's, model of how the Pentateuch was composed. Briefly put, this model views the text's composition not as a redaction of parallel documents but as an agglomeration of successive revisions. It sees a series of writers taking older documents and composing new material to supplement and rewrite those documents. Certain explicit presuppositions guide Van Seters' work. First, as I have noted above, is his disbelief in a background of oral traditions behind the written text.[59] Put positively, he places a premium on the written evidence at hand. Second, he asserts that the same writer would not write the same story twice. This, it should be remarked, is consistent with his first premise, as we ordinarily associate different versions of the same story with oral narration. Third, only gross discontinuities in the text betray signs of diverse sources.[60] Now let us see what the critics have done with Van Seters.

In general, critics admired his work, even when dissenting from his conclusions. A number[61] either neglected or paid little attention to his literary analysis, which is clearly the more significant, as well as the larger, part of his book.[62] Some opposed Van Seters' theory because it rejected the oral background of the narratives that so many came to believe unquestioningly.[63] In

---

contradicted by substantial data; cf., e.g., Kenneth J. Gergen, "Correspondence versus Autonomy in the Language of Understanding Human Action," in Fiske and Shweder, *Metatheory in Social Science,* pp. 136-62, esp. 136-37.

[56]Pepper, *World Hypotheses,* p. 100.

[57]Cf. esp. Feyerabend, *Against Method.*

[58]Cf. Thomas L. Thompson, "A New Attempt to Date the Patriarchal Narratives," *JAOS* 98 (1978), pp. 76-84, here p. 77.

[59]See now also John Van Seters, *In Search of History* (New Haven: Yale University Press, 1983). For some discussion, see Chapter One.

[60]Van Seters, *Abraham,* pp. 154-56.

[61]E.g., Ronald E. Clements, Review of *Abraham in History and Tradition, JSS* 22 (1977), pp. 90-92; Anson F. Rainey, Review of *Abraham in History and Tradition, IEJ* 28 (1978), pp. 131-32; Nahum M. Sarna, "Abraham in History," *BARev* 3/4 (1977), pp. 5-9.

[62]So Van Seters, "Dating the Patriarchal Stories," *BARev* 4/4 (1978), pp. 6-8, here p. 6.

[63]E.g., Sean E. McEvenue, Review of *Abraham in History and Tradition, Biblica* 58 (1977), pp. 573-77; E. W. Nicholson, Review of *Abraham in History and*

and of itself this is legitimate – one may demur. But it is no criticism. The absence of oral tradition fits in perfectly well with Van Seters' model, in which, for the most part, writers rewrite writers.[64] Thompson, in what is otherwise the most sophisticated discussion of Van Seters, faults him for his "methodological tendentiousness."[65] Every method is, in a sense, tendentious, though, as it drives toward a specific, foreseen goal. The type of argument and rhetoric that one uses in the service of a theory, as well as the evidence one adduces in support of the argument, would never have been exercised had they not sustained the theory. That is why, as Fish says, "theories always work and they will always produce exactly the results they predict."[66] And that is what Gertrude Stein explains by writing, "A bed is always comfortable if it is made so."[67]

Some reviewers attacked Van Seters' literary analysis by applying different methods to his texts and by showing that the different methods yield results in line with an alternate theory.[68] That is, however, as it must be. One cannot prove anything by criticizing one theory with the tools of another one, as I have said above; recall the analogy of the mason and the carpenter. Van Selms, for example, agreed with Van Seters that the author of Genesis 21 (the banishment of Hagar) knew the text of Genesis 16 (Hagar's flight).[69] In Van Seters' theory that is because the author of Genesis 21 was rewriting chapter 16; in the reviewer's theory that is because the same author wrote both. Others, assuming the independence of an E source and the work of a redactor,[70] performed variant interpretations of Van Seters' texts with the methods of the Documentary Hypothesis. Van Seters was well aware of source critical alternatives before he began.

Tradition, JTS 30 (1979), pp. 220-34; de Pury, Review (see n. 51 above); Sarna, "Abraham in History"; A. van Selms, Review of *Abraham in History and Tradition, BiOr* 34 (1977), pp. 204-5.

[64]When, however, Van Seters (*In Search of History*, pp. 18ff., 226-27) criticizes the argument for an early oral epic behind the Pentateuchal narrative, he does not answer the arguments adduced from what look like verse fragments, taken to be excerpts from an earlier epic, within the present text. Aside from Frank Moore Cross, *Canaanite Myth and Hebrew Epic* (Cambridge, MA: Harvard University Press, 1973), see especially Umberto Cassuto, "The Israelite Epic," *Biblical and Oriental Studies*, trans. I. Abrahams (Jerusalem: Magnes Press, 1975; first published 1943), vol. 2, pp. 69-109.

[65]Thompson, "A New Attempt," p. 80.

[66]Fish, *Is There a Text*, p. 68.

[67]Gertrude Stein, *Blood on the Dining-Room Floor* (Berkeley: Creative Arts, 1982), p. 80.

[68]E.g., Henri Cazelles, Review of *Abraham in History and Tradition, VT* 28 (1978), pp. 241-55; McEvenue, Review; de Pury, Review.

[69]Van Selms, Review.

[70]E.g., McEvenue, Review; cf. idem, "The Elohist at Work," *ZAW* 96 (1984), pp. 315-32.

Gen. 21:8, for example, refers not expressly to Isaac but to הילד, "the boy." Since "the boy" presupposes Isaac, Van Seters contends that this verse must be an integral part of the preceding passage.[71] A source critic could argue, in opposition, that when the passage containing verse 8 was joined to the preceding one, the redactor replaced "Isaac" with "the boy." Similarly, Hagar's expectation of inheritance rights in chapter 21 presupposes the situation at the beginning of chapter 16. For Van Seters this proves that the author of chapter 21 depended on a preexisting chapter 16.[72] But one could counter that chapter 21 once contained similar information which was omitted in the process of redaction as an unnecessary duplication. All I am saying is that proponents of different theories will perform different analyses. One cannot further discussion by criticizing a theory through the conceptual framework and methods of another theory.

Nicholson has challenged Van Seters' model by asking why an author would write a different story in order to revise one he did not like.[73] Why not simply replace the earlier story with a new one? One could ask the same thing of the hypothetical redactor. But raising the question – rather than imagining an answer – reflects a failure to realize that one is judging Van Seters' by one's own methods. Winnett had a decade earlier provided an answer: the author customarily added new material to old while conserving the old. One may not believe that this is what happened; but it is perfectly plausible that it did. At bottom, debates over compositional history, as over all our other concerns, boil down to conflicts of presuppositions, first principles, beliefs.

Finally, some reviewers dismissed Van Seters' reconstruction because it took account of Genesis alone, and only part of Genesis at that.[74] They implied that such a theory might not be able to explain the composition of the entire Torah, or of at least the Tetrateuch. Again, such critics did not look beyond the Documentary Hypothesis to entertain the possibilities of another theory. The Documentary Theory begins with the assumption of large parallel sources, overlapping in their coverage of a long stretch of Israelite tradition. Adherents of this theory would naturally consider it essential to examine the whole before drawing any conclusions. But Van Seters' theory assumes a stratified model, adding layer to layer. It makes sense within this model to begin with a limited block of material, and the research of Rendtorff on later parts of the Torah can be invoked in support of the promise of Van Seters' theory.[75] Source critics should remember, too, how in the eighteenth century of our era a French physician

---

[71]Van Seters, *Abraham*, p. 196.
[72]Ibid., p. 197.
[73]Nicholson, Review, p. 231.
[74]E.g., Cazelles, Review; Dennis Pardee, Review of *Abraham in History and Tradition, JNES* 38 (1979), pp. 146-48; J. J. M. Roberts, Review of *Abraham in History and Tradition, JBL* 96 (1977), pp. 109-13.
[75]Cf. Rolf Rendtorff, *Das überlieferungsgeschichtliche Problem der Pentateuch* (Berlin: W. de Gruyter, 1977); idem, "The Future of Pentateuchal Criticism."

named Astruc used variations of the divine name in Genesis alone as a basis for identifying sources in the Pentateuch. The Documentary Hypothesis also started small.

We can further appreciate the role that our presuppositions play in our argumentation and rhetoric by examining, or deconstructing, the language we use in our criticism. To take one example from the Van Seters literature, at least four reviewers contended with Van Seters by asserting that the evidence actually "points" in a different direction.[76] Van Seters has himself used this expression in his reply to criticism.[77] Using language that places the truth in the power of the evidence gives the impression that it is not we who rely on our own force of logic or persuasion but that some external, "objective" standard articulates the truth for us. "Pointing" evidence, of course, is actually a metaphor, a personification of the data that *we* have found, structured, and adduced. We interpret the evidence, and we point it. By acknowledging our role behind the evidence we become more aware of our principles and models, and of those of the other person.

To conclude, I return to the silver inscriptions with which we began. According to all reports, the larger text contains three benedictions, similar to those in Num. 6:24-26. The shorter one presents two benedictions. Barkay reads it as follows: יאר יהוה] [אל]יך פניו וׁישׂ[ם לך שלום "May YHWH shine his face toward you, and may he grant you peace."[78] Is this shorter benediction a literary (intentional) conflation of the latter two blessings in the longer version? Barkay seems to think so, as he compares the benediction in Ps. 67:2, which resembles parts of the first two blessings in Numbers 6.[79] It is also possible that the scribe skipped from the first half of the second blessing to the second half of the third, as the first half of each ends with the same phrase, פניו אליך, "his face toward you." It would then be a case of homoioteleuton, one of the commonest of copyist errors.

Which is more likely? There is no method that can dictate an answer. As in all academic questions, the method or approach we take already incorporates some standard of judgment. One can in our case either explain the text as it stands, or restore the text to its perfect form depending upon our view of the inscription and how we imagine the scribe who wrote it. Was he careless? Was he cramped by the short space? Was he underpaid? Was he interested in conveying a shorter text? Was he attempting to be creative? We cannot know. We will take a stand, if we choose to do so, in accordance with other assumptions that we have made, or theories that we hold dear. Whether we see a

---

[76]Clements, Review, p. 91; Rainey, Review, p. 132; Roberts, Review, p. 109; Sarna, "Abraham in History," p. 9.
[77]Van Seters, "Dating the Patriarchal Stories," pp. 6-7.
[78]Barkay, *Ketef Hinnom*, p. 30.
[79]Loc. cit.

whole text or a defective one involves a range of predispositions or beliefs. To engage in Biblical criticism means we must exercise our beliefs.

Does this mean that we cannot appeal to a standard, to a higher authority? Within the academic community – or any other – we share common assumptions with other people, conventions that enable us to communicate with each other.[80] When the community (or one of the communities) to which we belong, or choose to belong, accepts a set of assumptions as "facts," we then take them for granted and build our arguments upon them.[81] The various "methods" in which Biblicists are trained, from comparative Semitic philology to structural poetics to pottery sequence dating, constitute systems of such "facts." In Biblical studies, we have been passing through a period in which many of the old "facts" have been challenged, or at least revealed to represent the objectification of earlier hypotheses. One therefore may facilitate discussion and understanding by laying bare our assumptions and sorting out those of the arguments we criticize. We might then discover that our arguments over method are fundamentally differences in assumptions, principles, or beliefs.

---

[80]See esp. Fish, *Is There a Text*. Fish's concept of interpretive communities has been widely criticized, and misinterpreted; cf., e.g., some of the essays in Mitchell, *Against Theory*. Robert Scholes misses Fish's point that it is a community – whichever community (since language and semiotic codes in general are never strictly solipsistic) – that creates the code for interpreting even so apparently factual a datum as a punctuation mark; *Textual Power* (New Haven: Yale University Press, 1984), pp. 129-65. William E. Cain chides Fish for his deficient "political self-awareness"; *The Crisis in Criticism: Theory, Literature, and Reform in English Studies* (Baltimore: Johns Hopkins University Press, 1984), p. 61; cf. pp. 51-64 and 195-200. In other words, Fish, in Cain's mind, does not confront the political aspects of conflict between interpretive communities. But this criticism does not challenge the fact of overlapping interpretive communities, possessing different reading strategies for different objectives of whatever sort. Most critics misread Fish by failing to realize that he is describing how he thinks we read or interpret evidence rather than prescribing how we ought to do so. In this sense, Fish is, as Cain (p. 61) says, "notably pluralistic and restrained." Further, when Fish asserts that we write what we read he means that the reader must take full responsibility for one's readings, which are not the unmediated product of what the text says but of what one makes of the text.

In expressing my sympathy with Fish's views I do not indicate here the more radical aspects of his position. I confine myself to the major themes of the essay: that theory precedes observation and that so much controversy in Biblical studies boils down to differences over competing theories or fundamental beliefs. It is worth noting, too, that I would formulate much of my own writing on Bible differently were I to start over according to my current thinking. In general I nowadays speak more carefully of what I read than of what the text "says." Nevertheless, there is no harm in personifying, and of objectifying, "the text" so long as one is aware and makes others aware of what one is doing.

[81]Cf. Pepper, *World Hypotheses*.

Chapter Four

How Theory Matters: Four Reviews

We all work within theoretical frameworks. In the preceding chapter I attempted to demonstrate that prior theories and presuppositions govern the adoption and application of whatever methods we use. Awareness of our theoretical assumptions can affect our practice in various ways. The balance of the present chapter consists of four parts, each a book review in a different area of Biblical studies. Each review deals with some way(s) in which theory matters in our work. Part One treats the issue of how a scholar's commitment to a particular theoretical approach predetermines one's criteria for evaluating an argument. Part Two shows how difficult it is to become conscious of all one's assumptions by indicating that even a critic who is attuned to matters of theory is apt to "suppress" some of one's own premises. Part Three illustrates the point made in the preceding chapter that one's objectives guide one's formulation of hypotheses, and those hypotheses in turn affect one's criteria for selecting and interpreting evidence. Part Four highlights a theme that is raised to some degree in each of the other reviews and in Chapters One and Two as well: that different models of analysis – the historical/comparative and the synchronic/structural, in particular – will produce different kinds of meaning. How we work shapes what we find, and find significant.

Part One: Poetics and Interpretation of Biblical Narrative *by Adele Berlin*

The datedness of Berlin's *Poetics*[1] is belied by the relative belatedness of this review. The subsequent appearance (in English) of Meir Sternberg's *The Poetics of Biblical Narrative,* which far more thoroughly and deeply delineates a structural poetics of the Bible, would make virtually any prior treatment seem elementary and superfluous for the serious reader. Our growing sophistication concerning questions of academic presupposition and methodology also affects our reading of Berlin, leaving this reader, at least, with a more negative impression than one might have earlier had. The book is of interest, however, precisely because it directly confronts issues of theory and practice in the analysis of Biblical narrative. Like many other critical readers, Berlin displays far

---

[1]Adele Berlin, *Poetics and Interpretation of Biblical Narrative* (Sheffield: Almond Press, 1983).

keener awareness of the other person's theoretical assumptions than of her own; and the manner in which she attempts to critique contrary positions is rather typical of academic discourse, at least in the field of Biblical studies. Before proceeding to discuss the philosophical matters that interest us, however, let us summarize the program of Berlin's book.

Berlin endeavors to begin writing a "poetics" of Biblical narrative. Working within the assorted conventions of New Criticism, Russian semiotics, and western structuralism, she seeks to describe "how [the Hebrew Bible] tells its stories" (p. 15). She maintains that she can compose a descriptive poetics of Biblical narrative before entering into the interpretation of the text. Poetics, the "science of literature," analyzes the way that literature functions just as linguistics analyzes a language (loc. cit.). A linguist, however, cannot write a grammar without first understanding, i.e., interpreting, the object language. For this reason, Berlin's analogy fails and crucially spoils her enterprise. She had wanted to assert the priority of "poetics" over any other form of analysis by isolating it altogether from the notoriously subjective act of interpretation (cf. the critique by Joel Rosenberg in *Prooftexts* 5 [1985], 287-95). To appreciate the significance of her error, consider the analogy she goes on to make. Literature is like a cake, poetics is the recipe for the cake, and interpretation tells how the cake tastes. This set of analogies suffers a number of difficulties. First, literature, by Berlin's own definition, is a semiotic product; a cake is not. The recipe is followed by the author, while tasting is done by the reader. Berlin, however, urges the reader to study the recipe (i.e., narrative poetics) in order to do better tasting (i.e., interpreting). This does not follow at all. Were the analogy to hold, the cake should not have any taste until the consumer has learned the recipe! Berlin tries to have her cake and eat it, too. Realizing later (pp. 16-17) that to "induce" the poetic conventions from the texts themselves involves a measure of interpretation, she cites the structural poeticist T. Todorov on the "complementarity" of poetics and interpretation.

Berlin develops her poetics chiefly in two areas, the means by which characterization is achieved, and the manipulation of narratival point of view. The three types of characters Berlin identifies in Biblical narrative, the story of David in particular, follow from her readings, thus undermining her earlier claim that poetics precedes interpretation. Her notions of point of view in Biblical narrative derive directly and explicitly from general literary theory, thereby countervening her purported effort to induce the narrative conventions directly from the texts. The chapter on character is rich in exegetical insight, and the chapter on point of view reveals a highly complex system. It is in the latter chapter that professional Biblicists will likely learn most, as Berlin opens our eyes to often subtle indications of diverse perspectives within a narrative. A chapter on "poetics in the Book of Ruth" is meant to apply the poetics outlined in the preceding chapters. In fact, it more often introduces further areas of narratological study such as the uses of names and epithets and the analysis of plot structure.

Berlin's *Poetics* might have ended there, but she has a larger agenda. She, like Robert Alter and certain other literary critics of the Bible, wants to use synchronic, poetic analysis in order to dispute the arguments and conclusions of historical, i.e., diachronic analysis. For example, Berlin, at the end of her chapter on Ruth, observes that many narratives only draw to a close with a "coda" that "takes the audience out of the time frame of the story and brings them back to real time" (p. 107). Although she only adduces two other story types as evidence, she confidently concludes that "we are dealing here with a universal poetic principle." Because the genealogy at the end of Ruth places the foregoing story in the narrative sequence from Genesis through Kings, Berlin makes the *historical* contention that the genealogy is not only apt but original to the book (pp. 109-10).

In her chapter on "Poetic Interpretation and Historical-Critical Methods" and on many previous occasions Berlin argues for the priority of poetic over historical analysis. The contradictions that pervade her argument, however, reveal that her argument is little more than a tissue of presuppositions. Her major thesis is that synchronic, poetic analysis has a critical role to play in Biblical studies by acting as a check on historical analysis. "At the very least," she writes (p. 112), "it can prevent historical-criticism from mistaking as proof of earlier sources those features which can be *better explained* as compositional or rhetorical features of the present text" (my emphasis). The apparent inconsistencies in the episode of the sale of Joseph in Genesis 37, for example, may result from narratival shifts in point of view rather than from the interweaving of different sources. That is what Berlin demonstrates, and if that were all she claimed, she might be right. But she claims much more than that. She contends that the poetic explanation of diverse perspectives within the narrative must take precedence over any historical explanation. She hypostatizes what she has contended is a possibility into what *must* be the case. Berlin would have come to recognize this faulty reasoning had she paid more careful attention to her own cautions.

In her discussion of the psychology of art and narrative interpretation in her final chapter, she notes that it is in the nature of perception that "we see what we expect to see" (p. 136). With regard to academic analysis, she observes that "Proponents of each methodology seem to end up proving the assumption with which they began" (p. 112). More disarming, she acknowledges that "those who view the text as a unity find textual support for their view....Synchronic literary approaches view the present text as a unity" (loc. cit.). Berlin is saying here that those who take the synchronic, poeticist approach begin with the prior assumption that the text is unified. As a partisan of the poeticist position, Berlin will predictably find a synchronic explanation "better" than a historical one. Yet she appears unconscious of this evident bias. Consider the following statement:

> It has been noticed by many scholars that the problem with traditional
> source criticism is that it begins with the assumption that the text is
> composed of a number of sources, and then proceeds to find them.
> Methodologically speaking, it is *more correct* [my emphasis] to begin
> with the text, and find sources only if a careful reading so indicates
> (p. 116).

After acknowledging that both synchronic and diachronic methodologies begin with theoretical presuppositions, Berlin here axiomatically posits the proposition that the synchronic viewpoint, which regards the unified text as a given, is "more correct" than the diachronic one. She further states: "It remains a methodological question whether, having explained a piece of evidence synchronically, we can then use the same piece of evidence for a diachronic reconstruction" (pp. 125-26). Although Berlin is trying to maintain theoretical neutrality by speaking of "a methodological question" as though there were a universally accepted, "objective" methodology, she is clearly biasing the case in favor of her synchronic propensity. A historical critic might well reverse Berlin's statement by asking whether one could legitimately consider a synchronic explanation once one had in hand a diachronic one.

In opposing the source critical analysis of Genesis 37 by D. B. Redford, Berlin presents her own "poetic" exegesis. She attempts to camouflage her synchronic bias by claiming to allow the text to "speak for itself" (p. 117). But in the very next sentence she writes: "I will present here my reading of the text...." That is indeed what she does and does well. The ingenuity as well as the occasional idiosyncrasy of Berlin's reading shows quite clearly that the text has no mouth and does not speak. It has been made to speak by a ventriloquist – an insightful and sensitive reader.

Part Two: Biblical Semantic Logic: A Preliminary Analysis *by Arthur Gibson*

As philosophers such as Karl Popper have repeatedly demonstrated, all scientific observation follows lines of inquiry generated by the assumptions and expectations of the observer, and all argumentation rests upon premises which are necessarily posited and cannot themselves be proved. The Biblical philologist, like other scholars, labors in a field in which certain assumptions are presupposed by all and the theoretical biases entailed by certain methods are taken for granted and are not explicitly acknowledged. By remaining unconscious of our premises and the theoretical underpinnings of our methods, we cannot criticize and reconsider our principles. Perhaps our arguments depend upon presuppositions which we ourselves do not hold.

In *Biblical Semantic Logic*[2] Arthur Gibson, a disciple of the logician P. T. Geach and the Biblicist James Barr, has undertaken to expose some of the questionable premises and logical errors that, he avers, characterize Biblical

---

[2]Arthur Gibson, *Biblical Semantic Logic: A Preliminary Analysis* (New York: St. Martin's Press, 1981).

(Hebrew and Greek) philology to an "alarming" degree. Before we may advance in "descriptive semantics and conceptual analysis" in Biblical studies, Gibson would have us clear the area of typical mistakes. With mean spirit he treats specific methodological errors committed by an array of Biblicists, among them W. F. Albright, F. M. Cross, and R. Bultmann. He has chosen to point the way by indicating false steps taken rather than by showing the direction we should take.

Most of the lessons in Gibson's book are well worth learning: that one tends to "suppress" the non-empirical premises that color one's observations and descriptions; that one cannot predict the meaning of a Semitic word merely by knowing its "root"; that a word's "sense" and its "reference" are, with G. Frege, distinct; that what may be cannot be hypostasized as what is; that different words cannot be unqualifiedly "equivalent" or "synonymous"; that one should not attribute psychological implications to linguistic phenomena; that we need a stricter definition of "idiom"; that we must determine meaning at the level of the sentence, not the word.

Unfortunately, Gibson is not a very congenial teacher. While in a few places his examples involve important questions, such as the meaning of YHWH's name (pp. 151-64) and the limitations of form criticism (pp. 90-91), most of his cases are minor and some of the errors he uncovers are, too. His writing is characteristically difficult and pedantic. One might learn the major lessons more sympathetically from such works as Stephen C. Pepper's *World Hypotheses: A Study in Evidence*, Karl R. Popper's *Objective Knowledge*, Stanley Fish's *Is There a Text in This Class?*, especially part two, and Robert Polzin's *Biblical Structuralism*, especially part one.[3]

For a work devoted to fault-finding, Gibson's book displays rather serious errors, both in evidence and argumentation. For example, following A. Goetze, few Semitists today regard the D-stem as primarily an intensive (so p. 21); Hebrew does not have a "future tense," nor do prefixed-*t* verbs in Ugaritic represent a "past" tense (so p. 25); the YQTL form of the Hebrew verb is not a "conjugation" (so p. 122); Ugaritic *šm* 'name' is misquoted as *sm* no fewer than seven times; the Qumran Damascus Document (7:8-9) is not "quoting" Num. 30:17 (so p. 51), as it diverges significantly; כסא in Ps. 89:37 means 'throne', not 'moon' (pp. 179-80); the Akkadian personal name *Ibašši-ilum* means "the god is," not "the god continually *shows* himself" (so p. 137).

Ironically, Gibson suppresses some premises of his own. For example, he challenges the Sargon legend as a source for the Moses birth-story because the earliest exemplar of the former is Neo-Assyrian (p. 147). I was not aware that we

---

[3]For complete bibliographic citations and other references, see Chapter Three, nn. 5 and 22.

had texts of Exodus that antedate the Common Era, much less the Neo-Assyrian period.[4]

In the end, scholars such as W. F. Albright and his students, who are impressed by the similarities between the Bible and other ancient Near Eastern literatures, begin with different assumptions from those who, like Gibson and James Barr, are not similarly impressed. Gibson may criticize lapses in logic by the comparativist, but he may no more than demur from the comparativist's presuppositions.[5]

Part Three: Hapax Legomena in Biblical Hebrew *by Frederick E. Greenspahn*

Does the Hebrew Bible have more than its share of *hapax legomena?* What significance does the amount of *hapax legomena* have? Those are the main questions that this revised 1977 dissertation, written at Brandeis under the direction of Nahum Sarna, addresses.[6] Defining *hapax legomena* as "those words which occur only once [in a corpus] and seem unrelated to otherwise attested roots" (p. 23), Frederick Greenspahn examines 289 verbs that meet his definition and draws the following conclusions: the Hebrew Bible is unexpectedly low in *hapax legomena* in comparison with other literatures; *hapax legomena* are more concentrated in Biblical poetry than in prose; and rare diction would seem to serve as a stylistic device in the Bible.

Greenspahn wants to offset what he asserts is the modern notion that *hapax legomena* are particularly difficult to interpret. He does not document this alleged modern attitude very well, citing only a single encyclopedia article from 1930 as evidence (p. 13, n. 47). Nevertheless, a happy feature of this study is that *hapax legomena* are not privileged as a special class of words from a philological standpoint. The ways that scholars from ancient to modern times have tackled these words are the same as the ways they have tackled other words. Greenspahn makes the point that modern scholars have not developed any new methods for interpreting *hapax legomena*. He underscores "the limits of modern methodology" (p. 120).

Those are fighting words, and one of the fights he picks is with an earlier SBL Dissertation, Harold R. (Chaim) Cohen's *Biblical Hapax Legomena in the*

---

[4]Because this is a critical point, allow me to elaborate. Many Biblicists hold extra-Biblical documents to much stricter tests of antiquity and authenticity than they do Biblical materials. Despite the fact that our earliest manuscripts of the Hebrew Bible are late, the original sources are assumed to be centuries earlier. Gibson, in positing the antiquity of the material in Exodus 2, betrays the commonly held assumption. I do not necessarily dispute this premise, but it is nothing more than a currently unprovable hypothesis. Gibson's suppression of this premise is exactly the sort of "error" for which he takes others to task.
[5]For further discussion of this point, see Chapter Three above.
[6]Frederick E. Greenspahn, *Hapax Legomena in Biblical Hebrew: A Study of the Phenomenon and Its Treatment Since Antiquity with Special Reference to Verbal Forms,* SBLDS 74 (Chico, CA: Scholars Press, 1984).

Light of Akkadian and Ugaritic (1978). I tend to agree with Greenspahn that Cohen unduly confines *hapax legomena* to words that occur in only one context and restricts any possible Semitic cognates to words that occur in that context alone. But Greenspahn does not properly understand Cohen's approach.[7] Cohen does not, for example, adduce semantic parallels elsewhere in Semitic for nothing. If one finds, as Cohen does, that various Semitic words mean both 'anger' and 'foam', it does not prove that a word like Hebrew קצף means both 'anger' and 'foam'. But it certainly raises this as a possibility to be tested in context. When Cohen compares Hebrew תשורה 'gift' to Akkadian *tāmartu* 'gift' and explains that both derive from verbs meaning 'to see' (שור and *'amāru*, respectively), he is not merely "supplying...an etymology," as Greenspahn asserts (p. 14). He is lending analogical corroboration from a parallel semantic pattern or development within Semitic.

In his discussion of his 289 *hapax legomena*, Greenspahn surveys modern scholarship and negotiates between the etymological approach to meaning and the so-called inductive or contextual one. At bottom, context can be the only real guide. When one seeks an etymology, one searches the Semitic languages for words that sound right phonologically and suit the sense that one desires.[8] Greenspahn indicates as much when he says things like "Whatever [this word's] etymology, there is no question that this word means..." (p. 156). Yet, one of the disappointments of this study is that Greenspahn frequently reaches no conclusion on the meaning of a word; he rarely analyzes a case in depth and often takes no stand.

His decisions, when he makes them, follow certain conservative principles and jibe with his anti-modern bias. He eschews emendation unless there is ancient manuscript support, or a root does not conform to the phonological parameters of Semitic.[9] He assumes the high antiquity of the Pentateuch and, as a corollary of sorts, argues against Aramaic influence in nearly all cases. These stands often lead Greenspahn to peculiar results. On the one hand he will claim that there are "many...Aramaisms...in early Hebrew texts" (p. 104), while on the other he will posit that Genesis was written before Aramaic could have influenced Hebrew (p. 154). What he does with the pure Aramaic in Gen. 31:47 I don't know. Rather than allow an Aramaism in Exod. 32:16, Greenspahn would contend, on the basis of ad hoc conjecture, that חרת is a "dialectical [he means 'dialectal'] variant" (p. 117).

After evaluating his data on the basis of these principles, it is no wonder that Greenspahn concludes that there are "no more than two...loan words" (p. 180) and that there are very few convincing instances of textual corruption (p.

---

[7]Cf. now Cohen's review of Greenspahn's book in *JBL* 105 (1986), pp. 702-4.

[8]As I contend in Chapter Three, this is the nature of all scientific investigation: one does not so much discover as look for.

[9]Cf. the discussion of diverse approaches to textual criticism and their conflicting presuppositions above in Chapter Three.

181). His criteria have determined his conclusions. Yet, in order to lend his principles the force of logic, Greenspahn attempts to argue in a pseudo-syllogistic manner. For example, he sets forth the following series of propositions (pp. 32-33; cf. p. 172): statistically, *hapax legomena* comprise over a third of the vocabulary in any textual corpus. *Hapax legomena* comprise less than a third of the Biblical corpus. Therefore, a Biblical word's authenticity cannot be doubted on the grounds that it is a *hapax legomenon*. The third proposition, or conclusion, does not follow from the preceding two. Using the same pseudo-logic, one might conclude that a large number of Biblical words are corrupted *hapax legomena!* Greenspahn could have avoided this problem by establishing his principles or evaluative criteria at the beginning and confining his conclusions to the results of his examination.[10]

Part Four: The Torah: A Modern Commentary, *edited by W. Gunther Plaut*

A good commentary should "psyche out" its audience. It should articulate the questions its readers would ask, respond to the difficulties its readers feel, and spell out the text's implications for its readers' lives. It should lead its audience to see significance it might otherwise miss, to hear a message it might not otherwise grasp, and to confront issues it might prefer to avert or suppress. It takes a measure of academic competence to write a good commentary. To write a great commentary takes, in addition, a profound sensitivity to the "voice" of the text and to the mind of the audience. But a great, not merely good, commentary can be written only for a good audience, one that is ready to plumb the depths of the text together with its guide. Great literature is not written for the unsophisticated, nor is a great commentary composed for an ordinary audience. A great commentary, like great art, makes high demands.

The Torah: A Modern Commentary[11] aims at a synagogue audience with little or no understanding of the Hebrew original. The Hebrew word-associations that it chooses to highlight are of the simplest sort – אדם and אדמה, for example. W. Gunther Plaut, the learned rabbi who is responsible for most of the commentary, concedes that "in the end the full quality of the Biblical text can be appreciated only in Hebrew" (p. 6). Despite this admission, the commentary does little to lead its readers to the original. It adopts the New Jewish Version (of the

---

[10]There is a necessary circularity in any discipline, for one's conclusions always follow from postulated first principles as well as certain rules of argumentation (or rhetoric). When, however, one's conclusions themselves amount to principles or aspects of "methodology," one can avert such obvious circularity by stating one's principles at the outset and then applying them. What results is then the analysis itself rather than an uninteresting restatement of one's initial principles. Note, for example, in Part One of this chapter that Berlin concludes that the ending of the Book of Ruth is integral to the work after having postulated at the outset that the book is a unit.

[11]W. Gunther Plaut, ed., *The Torah: A Modern Commentary* (New York: Union of American Hebrew Congregations, 1982).

Jewish Publication Society) as its translation, a rendering which is philologically superb but reads so smoothly in a contemporary idiom that one may not detect the faint cries of the Hebrew that lies behind it. By contrast, the German rendition of Martin Buber and Franz Rosenzweig – forged in a German that bears the linguistic, stylistic, and conceptual earmarks of the original – constantly reminds us that the Biblical voice is coming through an interpreter. The Buber-Rosenzweig reproduction of verbal repetition and other features of the Hebrew also facilitates our perception of literary associations and the stimuli of rabbinic midrash, both of which depend on nuances of Biblical Hebrew.[12]

Because it assumes Hebrew illiteracy, the commentary rarely takes note of peculiarities, ambiguities, and other stylistic elements that abound in and contribute crucially to the richness of the Torah. Consequently, the commentary cannot put questions to the text itself and search it for meaning, as traditional exegesis has done.

This is doubly unfortunate because the commentary encourages pluralism in interpretation and views this process as "open-ended" (p. xx). Yet instead of setting a model of inquiry by producing a commentary that asks probing questions for the audience to ponder, the commentary more often than not provides answers, explanations, and dissertations.[13] The commentary is geared for brief encounters and limited brushes with the text, such as one might enjoy during an abbreviated reading of the Torah in the synagogue. It may suit this purpose very well, but it does not lend itself to more intensive textual study.

The commentary does fill a basic need in modern Jewish life: it raises basic theological issues and suggests contemporary responses. In what sense is the Torah revealed? "The Torah is a book about humanity's understanding of an experience with God" (p. xviii). "How can natural events be understood as judgments of God?" (pp. 61-62). Modern minds tend to attribute historical catastrophe to human sinfulness, but natural disasters are not purposeful divine acts. "Did God in fact speak to Abraham and make the promise reported in this chapter?" "Abraham acted on his comprehension of the Divine..." (p. 93). In this commentary theology incorporates the fruits of historical criticism, which understands the Bible as ancient Israel's formulation of its perceptions of God.

The commentary is not organized like the pluralistic Rabbinic Bible – מקראות גדולות – in which the text is surrounded by a number of different commentaries, each with its own sensibility and voice. It has a form somewhat reminiscent of Gersonides' fourteenth century commentary, which had three parts: explication of difficult words and phrases; paraphrastic interpretation of the passage at hand; and lessons to be learned from the passage. The *Modern Commentary* has three similar parts: a running explication of terms and

---

[12]See further Chapter Five.

[13]A welcome exception may be found, for example, on p. 39b, where various interpretations of the Garden story are discussed.

concepts; introductions, which are cut with homily; and more extensive discussion of selected motifs and themes. It features a fourth component as well: anthologies or "gleanings" of pertinent excerpts from ancient to contemporary times, with special – and deserved – advantage given to rabbinic midrash.

The Torah, with the midrash, may have seventy faces; but they are not equally handsome. Thus the commentary is necessarily selective in choosing topics and interpretations for its attentions. There may be seventy ways to interpret the Torah, but they do not all produce the same degree of significance.

An important characteristic of the *Modern Commentary* is that it seeks to expose the meaning of the text through the comparative method. This approach saw its heyday in the first half of this century and reached something of a plateau in E. A. Speiser's Anchor Bible commentary on Genesis and Nahum Sarna's *Understanding Genesis*.[14] Comparativism rests on an epistemological assumption holding that I can know x best by showing how it is similar to and different from things that bear an apparent resemblance to x . Such analysis endeavors to delineate x's most distinctive traits. The approach is epitomized in the following excerpt from the commentary on the Tower of Babel story:

> While there is a Sumerian story of the confounding of tongues, no parallel account has so far been found in Near Eastern records that would afford us the kind of comparison and contrast through which the Biblical purpose of the Flood tale is seen in high relief (p. 79).

Moreover, in accord with this method, each book of the Torah is introduced with an essay by a historian of the ancient Near East, William W. Hallo, whose observations on the transmission and standardization of ancient literature are particularly valuable.

The commentary regularly adduces comparative material, especially from Mesopotamia. There are a number of points at which extra-Biblical Canaanite (mainly Ugaritic) literature could have been considered. To give one example: in Exod. 19:18, in the description of the Sinai theophany, the commentary notes that where the Massoretic Text (and the Samaritan) have *the whole mountain trembled,* "the Septuagint and some manuscripts have 'the whole *people* trembled'" (p. 523). The fact is that when the Canaanite storm-god, Baal, appears amid thunder and lightning, as does YHWH here, the earth reacts by trembling (cf. also Ps. 18:8). Therefore, the Septuagint's variant is most likely a contamination of our verse by v. 16.

The commentary's penchant for comparison is often carried to the point of a fetish, when literary parallels are cited that do nothing to elucidate the Biblical text. *On Gen. 2:10:* "This concept [of a primeval river branching into four] occurs also in other cultures, notably in India and China"; *on Adam's choice:* "The 'Adapa' tale also deals with man being offered life but choosing death";

---

[14]See the beginning of Chapter Two.

"Esau resembles the uncivilized man of 'Gilgamesh', Enkidu, who has shaggy hair and lives in open spaces"; *on Gen. 6:2:* "Hurrian, Phoenician, and Greek myths told of Titans, supermen of great stature and strength, who were supposedly the offspring of unions between gods and men"; and so on.

Building on Susan Sontag's thesis in the title essay of *Against Interpretation* that interpretation as an enterprise seeks to "tame" art, I find implicit in the commentary an assumption that readers will somehow appreciate or accept the Biblical text so long as its components are familiar from elsewhere. The Torah will find acceptance if it is not perceived as strange. But rather than comfort the audience by demystifying the Torah, the commentary might have been more aggressive in lowering its readers' guard and encouraging them to become more aroused, intrigued, and even disturbed by the text.

The "General Introduction to the Torah" by Rabbi Plaut adopts in principle the perspective of Buber and Rosenzweig – as well as that of more recent literary critics of the Bible[15] – that the Torah must be studied as it comes to us, in its final edited form. For this reason it is dismaying that the commentary does not employ a compatible, essentially synchronic, approach to the text, rather than a comparative, historical one. A synchronic method views the text as a system in which numerous components interact at various levels, from the less conscious "gut" concerns of the deeper levels to the more didactic and narrational discourse at the surface. The diverse meanings are understood to be coded in the text, and through intensive analysis of the structure and idiosyncracies of the text, it is decoded. Buber and Rosenzweig acknowledged this and consequently devoted themselves to elucidating the integration of form and content in the Torah.

A synchronic exegesis operates on the analogy of the Freudian analysis of dreams. Just as dreams are interpreted through an internal analysis of the patterns and recurrent motifs of an individual's dreamwork, so is the text interpreted through attention to its own features and structures – and not by comparing an ancient Israelite text to a foreign one. After all, the import of your dreams can hardly be identified by comparing them to mine, even if we are both dreaming on the same subject.

Two expressions of the synchronic method, literary criticism and structural anthropology, have come to regard the Biblical narrative as myth – that is, as a society's articulation in story form of how it perceives the different parts of the world to be interrelated.[16] The *Modern Commentary's* outdated definition,

---

[15]See Chapter Two.

[16]For a fundamental discussion of myth as it pertains to the Bible, with bibliography, see Eduardo Rauch, "Toward an Understanding of the Forgotten World of Myth – An Essay in Definition," *The Melton Journal* 13 (Winter 1982), pp. 4, 18-19. See also Northrop Frye, *The Great Code: The Bible and Literature* (New York: Harcourt Brace Jovanovich, 1982). For fine examples of the structural method illuminating underlying themes of the Torah, see the studies by Mary Douglas, Alan W. Miller, and Nathaniel Wander, discussed above in Chapter Two.

however, characterizes myth as "a tale involving human beings and divine powers, a tale which was meant and understood as having happened and which by its existence expressed, explained, or validated important aspects of existence" (p. xx). Myths can be just about people. The themes embedded in the Biblical narrative reflect the many issues that exercised the psyche of the Israelites over the centuries, and the Torah's materials were conserved and organized as they were because they mediated those concerns.

There are at least two major reasons why the *Modern Commentary* might eschew the synchronic method. For one thing, such analysis demands intensive textual study and discussion of many passages at once. It is not easily adapted to weekly reading in the synagogue. Second, the commentary invests heavily in the historicity of the main events in the Torah's story: the election of Abraham, the Exodus, and the revelation at Sinai (see, e.g., p. 517). Analysis of the Bible as myth detracts from the significance of the Torah as history.[17]

The commentary insists that the validity of the Torah's religious truth somehow depends upon the text's historical claim that the Hebrews as a community experienced a "public" revelation at Sinai (p. 516). Phenomenologically, however, this is only to say that the Sinai revelation was so profound that the individual members of the Israelite group each came away with a similar experience. Consider the insight of the Kabbalist Isaac Luria, that the 600,000 (male) souls present at Sinai each perceived a different aspect of the divine.[18] This assumes that the Israelites actually gathered at the mountain after the Exodus. But is the enduring religious value of the Torah to be left to the uncertainties of historical reconstruction? Doesn't the truth of the Torah depend upon the independent convictions of each person who will give it a hearing and engage in its study? Can one not embrace the Torah's concerns without accounting the narrative as historical fact?

The commentary is extremely rich, and one could entertain its ideas and contributions at very great length. But let me confine my closing remarks to correcting a few unfortunate notions that the commentary perpetuates.

The word תהום "the deep," in Gen. 1:2 is poetic diction for "sea" in both Ugaritic and Hebrew, and would not likely have suggested the Mesopotamian goddess Ti'amat to an Israelite, who heard the latter as *ti'áwat*.

"Let us make man" (Gen. 1:26) does not represent a "plural of majesty" because ancient Near Eastern and Israelite kings referred to themselves as "I," not "we."

---

[17]We may recall the observation in Chapter One that frustration in reconstructing the history of ancient Israel seems to be one factor behind the attraction of many Biblicists to synchronic perspectives.

[18]References and discussion in Gershom Scholem, *On the Kabbalah and Its Symbolism* (New York: Schocken Books, 1965), pp. 64-65.

כעת היה in Gen. 18:10 means "at this time next year," as Gen. 17:21 and a semantically equivalent idiom in Akkadian – *ana balāṭ* – demonstrate.

In discussing Gen. 12:10, Nahmanides says that Abraham sinned by bringing his wife into a dangerous situation, not, as the commentary implies (p. 100), by trying to save himself at her expense – which is approved by traditional *halakha* (see the commentary of David Zvi Hoffmann).[19]

It is about time to lay to rest E. A. Speiser's theory about an alleged "wife-sister" status in Nuzi and in the Bible. Speiser's argument was circular to begin with[20] and hinges on very uncertain textual connections.[21]

Last, but hardly least, I do not see why the commentary must consistently refer to the human being as "man," even though the Bible generally does. In Genesis 1, male and female are created together and share the name אדם (v. 27), which must mean here "human" or, as the commentary itself proposes, "earthling." The sexist bias of the Torah should be mitigated to a degree by the remarks of Phyllis Trible, quoted in the "gleanings" on p. 33. Moreover, by not calling attention to the coeval creation of man and woman in Genesis 1, the commentary fails to prepare the reader for the midrash cited on p. 32 that boldly suggests that the human being was first created androgynous.

---

[19]Cf. now David Berger, "On the Morality of the Patriarchs in Jewish Polemic and Exegesis," in Clemens Thoma and Michael Wyschogrod, eds., *Understanding Scripture* (New York: Paulist Press, 1988), pp. 49-62.

[20]The "wife-sister" situation is created by reading Nuzi details (and misreadings) into the Bible and Biblical details (and misreadings) into Nuzi documents.

[21]For critiques, see David Freedman, " A New Approach to the Nuzi Sistership Contract," *JANES* 2/2 (Summer 1970), pp. 77-85; Thomas L. Thompson, *The Historicity of the Patriarchal Narratives* (Berlin: W. de Gruyter, 1974), pp. 234-48; John Van Seters, *Abraham in History and Tradition* (New Haven: Yale University Press, 1975), pp. 71-76; and Samuel Greengus, "Sisterhood Adoption at Nuzi and the 'Wife-Sister' in Genesis," *HUCA* 46 (1975), pp. 5-31.

Part Two

THEORY AND METHOD IN BIBLE TRANSLATION

Chapter Five

Theories of Modern Bible Translation

The Sumerians saw it as a nasty prank by a trickster god.[1] The Israelites took it as the Creator's defense against the threat of human collaboration.[2] It has been derogated by some as a barrier to human fellowship and lauded by others as an instrument for widening our perceptions. One mind, many languages – the universality of the human faculty for language, the diversity of human speech. Those who want to know what the other person is saying must learn that one's language or get a translation. The vast majority of those who want to hear what the Biblical God is saying take the latter alternative. The Hebrew Bible, or portions thereof, has been rendered into nearly two thousand languages, and in English alone Bible translation proliferates in hundreds of versions.[3] To some degree this trend may correlate with a growing impatience to learn a foreign language, especially a classical one. But far more important seems the effort to capture a greater measure of truth. Different translations bring various funds of knowledge and insight to bear on the interpretation of the Bible, its meaning. Each may offer a different slice of the truth. As everyone knows, each version of translation means something different. Not only different understandings of the text, but different methods of translating change the face of Scripture.

In the early 1960s Harry Orlinsky, the chief editor of the Jewish Publication Society's new rendering of the Torah (the New Jewish Version or NJV), wrote of a new "rage to translate – really to retranslate – the Bible."[4] As it happened in the Romantic period, when a surge in translating (the classics especially) was accompanied by considerable attention to the art and nature of translation as an enterprise,[5] the recent wave of Bible translation has been joined by its proper

---

[1]See Samuel N. Kramer, "The 'Babel of Tongues': A Sumerian Version," *JAOS* 88 (1968), pp. 108-11.

[2]This is only one aspect of the Tower of Babel story (Gen. 11:1-9).

[3]Cf., e.g, Sakae Kubo and Walter F. Specht, *So Many Versions: 20th Century English Versions of the Bible*, rev. ed. (Grand Rapids: Academie Books, 1983).

[4]Harry M. Orlinsky, "The New Jewish Version of the Torah: Toward a New Philosophy of Bible Translation," *Essays in Biblical Culture and Bible Translation* (New York: Ktav, 1974), pp. 396-417 [first published in 1963].

[5]Cf. A. Leslie Willson, "Introduction," in idem, ed., *German Romantic Criticism* (New York: Continuum, 1982), esp. pp. xv-xvi.

companion and critic: the study of the theory of Bible translation. The subtitle of Orlinsky's essay, "Toward a New Philosophy of Bible Translation," is only one of many indicators of the self-consciousness that modern Bible translators bring to their task. The merit of any translation rests not only on the skill of the translator, but even more fundamentally upon the philosophy that underpins it. Different styles of translating manifest divergent theories of translation.

It is customary to speak of translation types in terms of the polar opposition of two styles. Such tidy categorizing oversimplifies a variety of overlapping yet distinctive positions. The most widely used taxonomy pits the *literal* mode – typically understood as a mechanical word-for-word reproduction – against the *idiomatic* – or sense-for-sense. The first to articulate this opposition, and the father of the idiomatic style,[6] was Jerome, who translated the Bible into Latin around the turn of the fifth century C.E. From Jerome on it has been characteristic of those who classify translation types to choose sides and advocate one over the other. The reasons that various proponents give often generate, or are capable of generating, more finely shaded categories of translation style.

Some favor the literal mode as an earnest overture of love for words. The words themselves must somehow be gingerly transferred from text to translation. Notable among the advocates of relative literality are certain authors, who belong naturally to a class most apt to be enamored of words; and if one views literature as the art of using words, one could with some justice refer to the more literal type of translation as the more literary. The novelist Vladimir Nabokov, for example, translated Pushkin "into a rigorously literal and consequently rather ugly English version" because he felt that only in this manner could one lead the reader to the poem itself.[7] John Berryman, the lyric poet, employed a fairly literal style of rendering the Book of Job into English, contending that such a translation would be "truer."[8] Indeed, the literal mode of rendering served a number of great Romantic writer-translators. The early twentieth-century German poet, Rainer Maria Rilke, expressed a clear preference for a more literal translation of the Mesopotamian Gilgamesh Epic over a more recent but less literal one.[9] It is hardly coincidental that many Biblicists, as well as some serious amateurs, who devote themselves to the literary analysis of Scripture tend toward the more literal styles of translation.[10]

---

[6]Cf., e.g., Chaim Rabin, "The Translation Process and the Character of the Septuagint," *Textus* 6 (1968), p. 16; James Barr, *The Typology of Literalism in Ancient Biblical Translations,* Mitteilungen des Septuaginta-Unternehmens 15 (Göttingen, 1979), pp. 39-40. Jerome is discussed further in Chapter Seven.
[7]Joel Agee, "Pony or Pegasus," *Harper's* 263/1576 (September 1981), p. 76.
[8]For references and discussion, see Chapter Six.
[9]William L. Moran, "Rilke and the Gilgamesh Epic," *JCS* 32 (1980), pp. 208-10.
[10]Cf., e.g., Gabriël H. Cohn, *Das Buch Jona in der Lichte der biblischen Erzählkunst* (Assen, 1969); Hans Walter Wolff's translation of Jonah in his *Studien zum Jonabuch* (Neukirchen-Vluyn: Neukirchner, 1965), pp. 84-89; Edward F. Campbell, Jr., *Ruth,* AB 7 (Garden City, NY: Doubleday, 1975); J. Cheryl

A work of literary art is essentially an arrangement of words, as music comprises tones and silences and as sculpture comprises matter and space. If one loses the words, one loses the art, just as one loses the music if one loses the tones or the silences.[11] But aside from a purist's devotion to words, there are two other foundations supporting more literal translation. The one is stylistic. The meaning of a Biblical passage may hinge on the repetition of a word or an allusion. For example, in 2 Samuel 7 the word בית "house," interweaves three themes: King David had already established his kingship and was dwelling in a royal *house;* the Lord, his God, was then dwelling in a tent-shrine, not in a stationary *house;* David will build for the Lord a *house,* and the Lord will assure the enduring prosperity of David's *dynasty,* which is expressed in Hebrew by בית, "house."[12] The more literal rendering of the King James (or Authorized) Version (KJV) of 1611 translates בית consistently as "house" so that the literary device of verbal repetition reaches the English reader.[13] The more idiomatic rendering of the British New English Bible (NEB) of 1970 translates *bayit* as "house" when it refers to the king's palace or the future temple but as "family" when it refers to David's dynasty. The superidiomatic Today's English Version (TEV, entitled the *Good News Bible*) of the American Bible Society (1976) renders בית as "palace," "temple," and "dynasty" in its respective references, completely obliterating the thematic connections of the original.[14]

Exum, "Literary Patterns in the Samson Saga: An Investigation of Rhetorical Style in Biblical Prose" (Ph.D. diss., Columbia University, 1976); Michael Fishbane, *Text and Texture* (New York: Schocken, 1979), more so in prose texts than verse; Evelyn Strouse and Bezalel Porten, "A Reading of Ruth," *Commentary* 67/2 (February 1979), pp. 63-67; Phyllis Trible, *Texts of Terror: Literary-Feminist Readings of Biblical Narratives* (Philadelphia: Fortress Press, 1984); to a degree, Robert Alter, *The Art of Biblical Narrative* (New York: Basic Books, 1981) and *The Art of Biblical Poetry* (New York: Basic Books, 1985); and cf. my "An Equivocal Reading of the Sale of Joseph," in Kenneth R. R. Gros Louis with James S. Ackerman, eds., *Literary Interpretations of Biblical Narratives, Volume II* (Nashville: Abingdon Press, 1982), esp. pp. 124-25. I am omitting here the works of Martin Buber and Franz Rosnezweig, Everett Fox, and Reynolds Price because I shall be discussing them below.

[11]I shall take up the problem of whether the words of one language can be replaced by equivalent words in the other below.

[12]Cf., e.g., Shimeon Bar-Efrat, העיצוב האמנותי של הסיפור במקרא [The Artful Shaping of Biblical Narrative] (Tel Aviv: Sifriat Poalim, 1979), p. 19.

[13]For an appreciation of the type of literalism represented in the KJV and Renaissance Bible translations generally, see now Gerald Hammond, "English Translations of the Bible," in Robert Alter and Frank Kermode, eds., *The Literary Guide to the Bible* (Cambridge, MA: Harvard University Press, 1987), pp. 647-66.

[14]The TEV is discussed further below and in Chapter Seven.

Moshe Greenberg argues similarly that בני ישראל must be rendered "sons of Israel" and not "Israelites" in Ezek. 2:3 in order to reproduce its correlation with the stubborn בנים, "sons," of the following verse; "The Use of the Ancient Versions for Interpreting the Hebrew Text: A Sampling from Ezekiel ii 1-iii 11," *SVT* 29 (1978), pp. 135-36; for another example, see ibid., p. 137.

Before continuing the argument from style, we pause to note that this argument dovetails with another of the oppositional classes of translation styles, the *form-oriented* versus the *content-oriented*. It is necessary to state the obvious: this opposition is recognized only by those, such as the idiomatic translators of the American Bible Society,[15] who see a dichotomy between form and content in literature. The dean of American Bible Society translation, Eugene Nida, speaks of an old-fashioned but, in his view, wrong-headed "delight in being able to reproduce stylistic specialties, e.g., rhythms, rhymes, plays on words, chiasmus, parallelism, and unusual grammatical structures."[16] Although Nida acknowledges that in a literary work style makes a significant contribution to the "impact" of a text,[17] he holds fast to the principle that "the meaning must have priority over the stylistic forms."[18] Style, literary form, are in this view somehow distinct from "meaning."

In diametrical (theoretical) opposition to this posture is the modern concept of art as the total assimilation of form and sense. This understanding had been comfortably ensconced in early Romantic criticism, as the following statement by Wilhelm von Humboldt, the nineteenth-century linguistic philosopher, attests:

> The work of art is fully a whole; it depicts an idea to us through a particular form. Yet form and idea are so intimately united that they can no longer be separated....In art, *form* is what is essential.[19]

Meaning in literature entails tone, mood, attitude, feeling, the voice of a speaker, not merely information. "Style," as an eighteenth-century French naturalist put

---

[15]E.g., Eugene H. Glassman, *The Translation Debate: What Makes a Bible Translation Good* (Downers Grove, IL: Intervarsity Press, 1981), who contrasts "form-oriented" and "content-oriented" translation styles as the "two ways of translating"; esp. pp. 47-67.

[16]Eugene A. Nida and Charles R. Taber, *The Theory and Practice of Translation* (Leiden: E. J. Brill, 1974), p. 1. Nida's more recent writing has shown greater appreciation of the more rhetorical features of discourse; see now Jan de Waard and Eugene A. Nida, *From One Language to Another: Functional Equivalence in Bible Translating* (Nashville: Thomas Nelson, 1986).

[17]Cited in Glassman, *The Translation Debate*, p. 17.

[18]Cited in ibid., p. 57. Cf. Barry Hoberman, "Translating the Bible," *The Atlantic Monthly*, February 1985, pp. 43-58, esp. 55: "The point is that this definition of *translation* centers on the concept of meaning; no importance has been attached to reproducing the original text's sentence structure, word order, grammatical features, and so on."

[19]Wilhelm von Humboldt, "On the Imagination," trans. R. R. Read III, in Willson, ed., *German Romantic Criticism*, pp. 139, 152. Cf. the remarks of Ernst Behler in the "Foreword" to this book (p. vii): "the early Romantic critics...saw the poetic unity of a literary work as an inner conformity with itself."

it, "is the man."[20] In contemporary criticism the style is the art.[21] It imparts meaning to the whole by infusing the parts with thematic coherence. Psalm 19, as Fishbane has shown,[22] develops the motif of *speaking* in each of its three segments.[23] The motif is introduced in the very first verse:

> The sky *relates* the glory of God,
> of the work of his hands the vault *tells*.

The TEV buries the motif in its "idiomatic" rendering:

> How clearly the sky *reveals* God's glory!
> How plainly it *shows* what he has done!

The inseparability of form and content informed above all the translation method of Martin Buber and Franz Rosenzweig, who began to render the Hebrew Bible into German in 1925, and it accounts in part for what at first blush has appeared to many as a literal, word-for-word version. In their essays on Bible translation, both Buber and Rosenzweig exploded the false division between content and form.[24]

That style constitutes an essential component of the text is nowhere more apparent than in repetitive patterns in which it is the fact and manner of repetition, not the semantic content – which remains the same – that is the point. With Gertrude Stein we may concede that "there is no such thing as repetition,"[25] for a stimulus has a different effect each time it is presented. For example, a unique pattern in Biblical (and Ugaritic) prosody is the so-called "staircase," a three- (or more) line figure in which the material of the first line is

---

[20]Georges de Buffon, cited in Alphonse M. de Lamartine, *Cours familier de littérature* (Paris: Privately printed, 1856), vol. 2, p. 135; cf. pp. 137-39.

[21]Cf., e.g., Susan Sontag, "On Style," *Against Interpretation* (New York: Delta, 1966), pp. 15-36. For a dissent, see, e.g., E. D. Hirsch, Jr., "Stylistics and Synonymity," *Critical Inquiry* 1/3 (March 1975), pp. 559-79, who argues that to say that style conveys meaning begs the question because one would first have to know the meaning. The argument fails for its lack of understanding that in the process of making sense one can hardly but consider phenomena that we conventionally characterize as style.

[22]Fishbane, *Text and Texture*, pp. 84-90.

[23]Fishbane's analysis would be even stronger would he realize that Heb. הגיון לב in Ps. 19:15 means "utterance of the throat," not "thoughts of the mind"; see H. L. Ginsberg, "Lexicographical Notes," *SVT* 16 (1967), p. 80.

[24]See Martin Buber and Franz Rosenzweig, *Die Schrift und ihre Verdeutschung* (Berlin: Schocken, 1936), esp. pp. 56, 113, 137. Cf. Everett Fox, "Technical Aspects of the Translation of Genesis of Martin Buber and Franz Rosenzweig" (Ph.D. diss., Brandeis University, 1974), p. 21. One wishes that Fox had been careful not to dichotomize form and content in his review of the NJV *Nevi'im (Prophets)*, "Former Prophets or Formerly Prophets," *genesis 2*, March 1979, p. 10.

[25]Gertrude Stein, *Lectures in America* (New York: Vintage Books, 1975), pp. 166-67.

interrupted, then repeated and completed or extended in the second line.[26] It is the suspense-producing interruption of the first line, in its position just prior to the repeated material, that creates the effect. Consider the famous example in Ps. 92:10. The classic, more "literal" KJV renders:

> For lo, thine enemies, O Lord
> For lo, thine enemies shall perish;
> all the workers of iniquity shall be scattered.

The "idiomatic" versions of the NEB and TEV render:

> Thy foes will surely perish,
> all evildoers will be scattered.

> We know that your enemies will die,
> and all the wicked will be defeated.[27]

They dissolve the pattern altogether.

A second basis supporting the literal mode of translation, in addition to the stylistic, is anthropological. Instead of telling us how we would say it, a literal translation tells us how they would say it. Reynolds Price, an American novelist who has produced conscientiously literal, direct renderings of some stories from the Hebrew and Christian Scriptures, renderings reminiscent of the Buber-Rosenzweig effort, stresses the importance of conveying in translation the physicality, the sensuousness, of the original's language. "Failure to convey that reality is failure to tell the story."[28] Yet, the idiomatic camp would point to its own work as the truly anthropological. A preeminent ancient Near East scholar, A. Leo Oppenheim, contended that:

> ...scholars [who] translate...texts in a more or less 'oriental style' (often imitating typical Biblical styles) in which the picturesque idiom does not sound out of place and even adds 'color' to the alleged style of the text...are simply wrong.[29]

He reasoned further that:

---

[26]I have analyzed the form and psychological effects of this pattern in "Two Variations of Grammatical Parallelism in Canaanite Poetry and Their Psycholinguistic Background," *JANES* 6 (1974), esp. pp. 96-105; and "One More Step on the Staircase," *UF* 9 (1977), pp. 77-86.

[27]In contrast to the more "literal" translations of Ugaritic verse by H. L. Ginsberg in James B. Pritchard, ed., *Ancient Near Eastern Texts Relating to the Old Testament,* 3rd ed. (Princeton: Princeton University Press, 1969), see the more "idiomatic" renderings of Michael David Coogan, *Stories from Ancient Canaan* (Philadelphia: Westminster Press, 1978).

[28]Reynolds Price, *A Palpable God: Thirty Stories Translated from the Bible with an Essay on the Origins and Life of Narrative* (New York: Atheneum, 1978), p. 53.

[29]A. Leo Oppenheim, "Idiomatic Accadian," *JAOS* 61 (1941), p. 252a.

...by resorting to literal translations, the translator indicates his own refusal to accept the existence of a gap between the two languages and, with it, of the gap between the two civilizations.[30]

It may be true that idiomatic translation can bridge the common ground among cultures; but it is the more literal mode that brings out the distinctive topography.[31] A remarkably effective idiomatic translator, J. B. Phillips, converts the literary conventions of Amos (1:3) into contemporary English expression:

> This is what the Lord says:
> Because of outrage after outrage committed by Damascus
> I will not relent!
> For they have battered Gilead,
> They have threshed her with iron-studded sledges.[32]

But *An American Translation,* or the "Chicago Bible," which tends toward literality, reproduces Amos' own idiom:

> Thus says the Lord,
> "For three transgressions of Damascus,
> and for four, I will not turn back;
> Because they have threshed Gilead
> With threshing-tools of iron.[33]

We wouldn't say it that way, but Amos more or less did.

A more literal reproduction of imagery can often shed light on the realia of an alien society.[34] Consider the following case, in which even the KJV simplifies, and blurs, the realia of the imagery in Lam. 2:4a:

> He [the Lord] hath bent his bow like an enemy;
> he stood with his right hand as an adversary.[35]

---

[30]Oppenheim, "Can These Dry Bones Live? – An Essay on Translating Akkadian Texts," *Letters from Mesopotamia* (Chicago: University of Chicago Press, 1967), p. 59. Cf. p. 58, where Oppenheim refers to his own perspective as "the anthropological."

[31]See further Chapter Seven.

[32]J. B. Phillips, Four Prophets: *A Translation into Modern English* (New York: Macmillan, 1969), p. 5. For a discussion of Phillips' method, see, e.g., E. H. Robertson, *The New Translations of the Bible* (Naperville, IL: Alec R. Allenson, 1959), pp. 102-18; and Phillips' own "Translator's Preface" in *Four Prophets,* pp. vii-xxi.

[33]Edgar J. Goodspeed and J. M. Powis Smith, *The Short Bible: An American Translation* (New York: Modern Library, 1933), p. 4. For a discussion of the philosophy and method of this translation, see, e.g., Robertson, *The New Translations,* pp. 88-101.

[34]Cf., e.g., Chaim Raphael, "The Prophets in Modern Idiom," *Commentary* 67/3 (March 1979), p. 71.

[35]Cf., e.g., the NJV; contrast the NEB, which alters the image: "In enmity he strung his bow...."

The Hebrew says דרך קשׁתו, "he stepped on his bow," which depicts the ancient technique of grasping the longbow with one's left hand, securing it at bottom with one's foot, and pulling the arrow back in the bowstring with one's right hand.[36] It is the "picturesque," *contra* Oppenheim, that actually represents "the anthropological side."[37]

The issue of anthropological authenticity has resurfaced most conspicuously of late in the debate over sexism in Biblical translation. The imminent publication of a revised Revised Standard Version by the National Council of Churches has engaged controversy and anticipation in its reported efforts to eliminate unnecessary male-oriented language in the Bible.[38] Despite the uncontested denotation of Hebrew אישׁ as "man," it is maintained that the word merely refers to "a human being" in verses in which gender is not at stake.[39] A parade example is Ps. 1:1. The KJV had rendered:

Blessed is the *man* that walketh not in the counsel of the ungodly...

The TEV circumvents gender here by translating:

Happy are *those*
    who reject the advice of evil men...

In principle the TEV opposes "any attempt to modernize the text,"[40] but it seems certain that the male-oriented language of the Hebrew Bible honestly reflects the cultural perspective of those who first transmitted it. The concept of "person," devoid of gender connotations, may not have been part of ancient Israel's mindset, just as the concept of an integrated "universe," which the TEV posits in Gen. 1:1, was not.[41] The question once raised by a very popular idiomatic Bible translator, James Moffatt, abides: "How far is a translator justified in modernizing an Oriental book?"[42]

---

[36]For an ancient description, see Xenophon's *Anabasis*, Book 4, ii = *The March Up Country*, trans. W. H. D. Rouse (Ann Arbor: Ann Arbor Paperbacks, 1964), p. 89.

[37]See above with notes 29-30.

[38]Cf., e.g., "Unmanning the Holy Bible," *Time*, Dec. 8, 1980, p. 128; "Plans for a 'Sexless' Bible Denied by National Council of Churches," *New York Times*, March 22, 1981; "New Editions of Bible Provoke Controversy," *New York Times*, November 29, 1981; for discussion, cf. Hoberman, "Translating the Bible," pp. 57-58.

[39]Cf., e.g., Harry M. Orlinsky's lectures on "Male Oriented Language in Bible Translation," reported in *The Baltimore Sun*, Nov. 15, 1977, and in *Johns Hopkins Magazine*, March 1978, pp. 47-48; I heard versions of this lecture at New York University, Feb. 21, 1980, and on subsequent occasions.

[40]"Preface" to the *Good News Bible* (New York: American Bible Society, 1976), no page.

[41]See further Chapter Seven.

[42]Cited in Robertson, *The New Translations*, p. 74.

If the literal mode is taken to be the more literary type of translating, then the idiomatic might be perceived as a "philological" style.[43] The nature of philology is to try to recover the basic sense of a foreign text and fix its meaning as precisely as possible, usually for the sake of reconstructing ancient history and a particular cultural milieu. The philological approach understands a text primarily as a medium of information, and it seeks to transmit that information through an accurate, contemporary equivalent in the language of the translation. Scientific discourse, or simply expository prose, nearly always favors for both accuracy and efficiency an idiomatic translation mode.

We may oppose to this the "literary" approach, which views the text as a medium of sensibility. An outstanding representative of this school, Walter Benjamin (d. 1940), in his "unequalled"[44] essay on "The Task of the Translator,"[45] insisted that "a literary work" does not in any essential way tell anything or impart information.[46] It does, it is. In the "literary" view it is perhaps more crucial to convey the rhetorical features of the text and the manifold connotations of its words than it is to convey the denoted or ideational message of the text. Philological translation endeavors to pin down meaning while literary translation seeks, as in literary analysis, to proliferate meaning.[47]

Ironically, one of the sharpest examples of philological Bible translation is the recent rendering of Ruth by Jack Sasson,[48] whose commentary abounds in fine literary observations.[49] His method is almost point-for-point antithetical to the literary translation style par excellence of Buber-Rosenzweig (see below). He uses different English words to translate the same Hebrew word (e.g., ותשאר in 1:3 is rendered "was left alone" but in 1:5 "survived"). He uses the same English word for different Hebrew words (e.g., "was left" renders ותשאר in 1:3 while "left" renders ותצא in 1:7). Combinations of words in the Hebrew are translated by a single expression in English (e.g., וילך...לגור in 1:1 is rendered "[he] migrated"). He rearranges verbal, even clausal, sequence for the sake of English idiom. Yet, Sasson's commentary constantly betrays signs of his chiefly philological

---

[43]De Waard and Nida, *From One Language to the Other,* pp. 182-83, describe a "philological" approach with respect to literalism, in attention to formal elements of the source – what I call here the "literary" mode.

[44]George Steiner, "A Friendship and Its Flaws (A Review of *Walter Benjamin-Gershom Scholem Briefwechsel...*)," *The [London] Times Literary Supplement* No. 4031 (June 27, 1980), p. 723. It should be noted, though, that Benjamin was standing on the shoulders of Schleiermacher, Humboldt, and others; see below.

[45]Walter Benjamin, "The Task of the Translator," *Illuminations,* ed. Hannah Arendt, trans. Harry Zohn (New York: Schocken, 1969), pp. 69-82.

[46]Ibid., esp. p. 69.

[47]Cf., e.g., the theory and practice evinced in Roland Barthes, *S/Z* (New York: Hill & Wang, 1974), esp. p. 7.

[48]Jack M. Sasson, *Ruth: A New Translation with a Philological Commentary and a Formalist-Folklorist Interpretation* (Baltimore: Johns Hopkins University Press, 1979).

[49]See my review in "Biblical Narratology," *Prooftexts* 1 (1981), pp. 201-8.

interest. Through minute philological details Sasson makes a noble attempt to recreate, even visually if possible, the specific sociological circumstances of the Ruth narrative. He tries to paint in the background and disambiguate the language. In both these efforts Sasson may be working at cross-purposes with the story itself. But in any event the philological style of his translation coordinates with the method of his commentary.[50]

Now, although I have appropriated the label "literary" for the more literal mode of translation, there are others who would argue the reverse: the most literal method produces the least literary translation – using "literary" to refer to a translation that itself amounts to literature.[51] The translation should employ its own idiom to produce an "effect,"[52] or "response,"[53] or "reaction"[54] equivalent to what the translator judges the original to produce. A literal version might yield effects quite different from those in the source. Among the more recent idiomatic Bible translators, seeking to reproduce the Hebrew's impact, are three American Jewish poets, Stephen Mitchell – who has rendered Job,[55] David Rosenberg – who has done Psalms, Job, and Isaiah,[56] and Marcia Falk – who has rendered the Song of Songs.[57] Consider, for example, Falk's translation of Song 1:1-2, which "aim[s]...to uncover resonances" of the Hebrew that is "lost in other translations"[58]:

> Oh for your kiss! For your love
> More enticing than wine,
> For your scent and sweet name –
> For all this they love you.
>
> Take me away to your room,
> Like a king to his rooms –
> We'll rejoice there with wine.
> No wonder they love you.

---

[50]Contrast Sasson's remarks on Marvin H. Pope's translation of the Song of Songs in *Maarav* 1 (1978/79), pp. 177-96, esp. 181.

[51]Cf., e.g., Herbert G. May, Review of the *Good News Bible, Interpretation* 32 (1978), p. 189, who employs the opposition literal vs. literary. For a sophisticated discussion, see André Lefevere, "Programmatic Second Thoughts on 'Literary' and 'Translation'," *Poetics Today* 2/4 (Summer/Autumn, 1981), pp. 39-50. See further the discussion of K. Chukovsky's *The Art of Translation* in Chapter Seven.

[52]Cf. H. L. Ginsberg, "The New Jewish Publication Society Translation of the Torah," *Journal of Bible and Religion* 31 (1963), esp. p. 188.

[53]Nida and Taber, *Theory and Practice*, pp. 1, 22-28.

[54]Glassman, *The Translation Debate*, p. 52.

[55]See Chapter Six.

[56]David Rosenberg, *Blues of the Sky* (New York: Harper & Row, 1976); *Job Speaks* (New York: Harper & Row, 1977); *Lightworks* (San Francisco: Harper & Row, 1978).

[57]Marcia L. Falk, *Love Lyrics from the Bible* (Sheffield: Almond Press, 1982). An earlier version was published in 1977.

[58]Falk, *Love Lyrics*, p. 6.

One cannot deny the contemporary sensuality of Falk's verse. In order to achieve it she was compelled to deviate from the Hebrew linguistic structure in a number of ways. She changed third person to second person address; she introduced enjambement; she replaced the feminine noun "young-girls" with the coy "they"; and she performed several semantic alterations. The original is literature; she clearly feels the translation should be, too. The translator must compensate in some artful way for the losses suffered in conversion from source to translation.[59]

The literary-idiomatic translator, however, perpetrates an act of deception. Translation is a cunning way of transforming a work of art. For while it turns the work into something other than itself, it gives the semblance of having changed the original barely at all. Conversions of art from one form into another are familiar: poems and paintings into music, novels into films, films into novelizations, even the plastic (a Grecian urn, say) into poetry.[60] Music has been transcribed from a piano arrangement into an orchestral score, and vice versa. We even tolerate the reproduction of polychromatic paintings in black-and-white in a textbook. But in each of these examples the transfer from one form to the other is obvious; we are made aware of the fact that each conversion creates a different work – or a pale replica, a xerox – of the earlier one. In the translation of a work from language to language the metamorphosis is disguised, an impersonation. An idiomatic translation does not switch the medium of representation. Since most readers of translation are not conversant with the source language, they cannot measure the gap between the original and its surrogate. This is not so with respect to the other types of artistic conversion, from medium to medium. The difference between a performance by piano and one by full orchestra is clear even to the tone-deaf. The distinction between a painting and a photograph is evident even to the blind (who can by touch alone feel the difference). In such conversions the perceiver either has a continual sense of experiencing a transfer or reproduction or realizes that he or she is experiencing a different work of art. But the experience of reading, or hearing, a text is similar, whatever the language – especially if the translation of a poem, say, consists in another poem. In considering this fact, Serge Gavronsky has termed idiomatic/literary translation "cannibalism." He explains:

---

[59]See George Steiner, *After Babel: Aspects of Language and Translation* (London: Oxford University Press, 1975), esp. pp. 395-413; cf. Falk, *Love Lyrics*, p. 54.

[60]By citing such conversions I do not mean to imply that they produce equivalence. I am sympathetic to the following remarks of Myles naGopaleen (pseudonym of the novelist Flann O'Brien, pen-name of Brian O'Nolan): "There can be a *fusion* of artistic activities directed towards the communication of a single artistic concept. Example: a song – a poem sung to an air. But is artistic function interchangeable? Can a play be made a novel? Some people are chronically incapable of appreciating a thing in terms of itself"; *The Best of Myles*, ed. Kevin O'Nolan (New York: Penguin Books, 1983), pp. 38-39.

> The use of this term emphasizes the disappearance of the slightest trace
> of the "original" qua original, and the presentation of what the
> "innocent" reader might consider as a perfect text in itself, and not as an
> Introduction-text, through which one can still reform the semantic,
> syntactical and grammatical structure of the departure [i.e., source]
> tongue.[61]

Idiomatic translation wishes to serve the audience with a poem that it can
experience as a poem. In fact, one can recast the opposition between literal and
idiomatic translation style as that betweeen *author-oriented* and *audience-oriented*
translation. As the German Romantic Friedrich Schleiermacher put it, in his
epoch-making essay "On the Different Methods of Translation": "Either the
translator leaves the author in peace, as much as possible, and moves the reader
towards him; or he leaves the reader in peace, as much as possible, and moves
the author towards him."[62] The author-oriented translator will produce a version
that is liable to appear slavishly literal as one attempts to copy each linguistic
and literary maneuver of one's source. The Buber-Rosenzweig rendering, for
example, has been lambasted as "unspeakable,"[63] erecting "a barrier between the
reader and the meaning of the text."[64] The idiomatic, audience-oriented translator
recoils from the "unnatural"[65] output of literality. The American Bible Society
worries over "discourag[ing] the reader from attempting to comprehend the
content of the message" because the translation presents it in a difficult form.[66]
"The new focus," they say, "has shifted from the form of the message to the
response of the receptor."[67] In such a view, the task of the Biblical translator "is
to communicate the truth of the Biblical message in the idiom of *his* language"
[emphasis mine].[68] The alternative, to retool the audience to learn to interpret
the translation and become better acquainted with the style and idiom of the
source, places burdens on both translator and audience. The translator must
forsake one's literary freedom and remain shackled to the idiom of the other's
voice. The audience can negotiate a literal rendering only through efforts greater
than those required by texts of comparable complexity in its own language.
Buber and Rosenzweig, whose first collaboration began in opening a center for

---

[61] Serge Gavronsky, "The Translator: From Piety to Cannibalism," *Sub-Stance* No.
16 (1977), pp. 53-62; here, p. 59.
[62] Friedrich Schleiermacher, "On the Different Methods of Translation," trans. A.
Lefevere, in Willson, ed., *German Romantic Criticism*, pp. 1-30; here, p. 9; cf.
Rosenzweig, in *Die Schrift*, p. 89.
[63] Cf. Falk, *Love Lyrics*, p. 60.
[64] Ralph P. Kingsley, "The Buber-Rosenzweig Translation of the Bible," *CCAR
Journal* 11/4 (January 1964), p. 22.
[65] H. L. Ginsberg, "The New Translation of the Torah, II. In the Path of True
Scholarship," *Midstream* 9/2 (June 1963), pp. 75-86, esp. 76.
[66] Nida and Taber, *Theory and Practice*, p. 2.
[67] Ibid., p. 1.
[68] A. C. Partridge, *English Biblical Translation* (London: André Deutsch, 1973), p.
1.

adult Jewish education, wished to transform the audience, to lead them to the text.[69] In an extreme posture, one which Buber and Rosenzweig would never have respected, Walter Benjamin held that "no poem is intended for the reader," so audience-oriented translation would make no sense at all.[70]

The audience-oriented, idiomatic translators have two chief, intertwined concerns. They believe in the purity not necessarily of Language but of particular languages. Translations must read well and sound well.[71] A German translation must be in good German, an English one in good, contemporary English. After a text like the Bible has been rendered into another language repeatedly, as in the case of the ancient Greek translations of the Hebrew Scriptures, a specialized language for translating the text develops, a "translation language."[72] Translation languages of the Bible inevitably pick up linguistic and stylistic features of the Hebrew, acquiring a Hebraic character. It happened to the English of the Tyndale[73] and King James versions[74]; it happened to the German of Martin Luther's Bible translation.[75] Idiomatic translators seek to crack the brittle crust of Hebraic style, of barbarism, to achieve a flawless native-looking veneer.[76] Older English Bible translations, and the RSV of 1950,[77] for example, imitate Hebrew word order and syntax to a degree that makes them sound classical – or "quaint."[78] The valuable literary effect of such literalism is

---

[69]Cf. Fox, "Technical Aspects," p. 21. For a fine recommendation of the author-oriented approach, see Agee, "Pony or Pegasus" (see n. 7 above).

[70]Benjamin, "The Task of the Translator," esp. pp. 69-70.

[71]Cf., e.g., the preface to The Bible: An American Translation, cited in Robertson, The New Translations, p. 95; the first principle of the NEB, cited in F. F. Bruce, History of the Bible in English, 3rd ed. (New York: Oxford University Press, 1978), p. 237; Charles R. Taber, "Translation as Interpretation," Interpretation 32 (1978), p. 131; de Waard and Nida, From One Language to Another, p. 39.

[72]Cf. Rabin, "The Translation Process" (see n. 6), esp. p. 8.

[73]Cf., e.g., George Steiner, "The Book," Language and Silence (New York: Atheneum, 1977), esp. pp. 189-90.

[74]Cf., e.g., Bruce, History of the Bible in English, p. 121. C. H. Sisson puts it more broadly: "[The local tradition of the Bible translation and Prayer Book] is...the funnel through which foreign influences, Latin, Greek, Hebrew, French, Spanish, Italian and German, have played upon those who have written in English in [Great Britain]"; "The Prayer Book Controversy: An Insular View," in Michael P. O'Connor and David N. Freedman, eds., Backgrounds for the Bible (Winona Lake, IN: Eisenbrauns, 1987), pp. 497-98.

[75]Cf., e.g., Rosenzweig's brilliant essay, "Die Schrift und Luther," Die Schrift, pp. 88-129.

[76]Cf., e.g, Ginsberg, "The New Jewish Publication Society Translation," esp. pp. 187-90; Bruce, History of the Bible in English, pp. xi, 15-16; Glassman, The Translation Debate, p. 57; Falk, Love Lyrics, pp. 57-58.

[77]Cf., e.g., Millar Burrows, "The Revised Standard Version of the Old Testament," SVT 7 (1960), esp. p. 210; Keith R. Crim, "Old Testament Translations and Interpretation," Interpretation 32 (1978), p. 145.

[78]Cf., e.g., Ginsberg, "The New Translation of the Torah," esp. p. 83.

to present the audience with images and concepts in their original sequence.[79] (Imagine reversing the notes of a melody or the frames of a film.) The NJV,[80] and most other recent English translations, abandon any adherence to Hebrew word order because in their view an English translation must employ English sequence.

Implicit, and sometimes explicit, in the idiomatic/audience-oriented approach is that such a method serves the author best, too. The thinking runs: this is how the author would have said it had he said it in English, say, and not in Hebrew. An exponent of the idiomatic method views translation as "an equivalence of thought which happens to be expressed verbally in a variety of ways."[81] This assumption should not be taken as a given. The great author-oriented philosopher, Schleiermacher, argued the contrary: language articulates thought. If one language expresses something different from the idiom of another language, the concepts being expressed in the different languages are also different. One cannot say the same thing in the other language using the foreign idiom of that language.[82] It is becoming apparent that, as George Steiner has definitively demonstrated in *After Babel*, different translation styles rest upon divergent philosophies of language.[83] We shall expand on this topic below. We shall see that in opposition to the stance committed to linguistic purity is a philosophy that insists on warping the language of a translation in conformity to the contours of the source and thereby enhance its expressibility.

Besides linguistic purity, the idiomatic/audience-oriented approach betrays a second, related concern: evangelism. The Word of God must speak every language. Practically all idiomatic translations enunciate this purpose.[84] The American Bible Society seeks not only to make the Scriptures "intelligible to Christians" but also "to non-Christians" so that "the translation of the Bible" can serve "as an [effective] instrument of evangelism."[85] Herb and Judy

---

[79]Cf. Price, *A Palpable God*, pp. 56-57.
[80]Cf., e.g., Jeffrey H. Tigay, "On Translating the Torah," *Conservative Judaism* 26/2 (Winter 1972), esp. pp. 15-16.
[81]Glassman, *The Translation Debate*, p. 75; cf., e.g., Nida and Taber, *Theory and Practice*, pp. 4-5.
[82]Schleiermacher, "Different Methods," esp. p. 20. Cf. the view that every translation of literature produces a new literary work; see, e.g., José Lambert, "Literary Contacts and Translation: Theoretical *vs*. Descriptive Studies," *Hasifrut* 25 (1977), p. 30 [in Hebrew].
[83]See esp. Steiner, *After Babel*, p. 47: "A study of translation is a study of language." The entire monumental book serves to elaborate on that remark.
[84]Cf., e.g., the Preface to the NJV *Torah;* the first memorandum circulated to the NEB committee, cited in Robertson, *The New Translations*, p. 177; the Preface to Taylor's *Living Bible*, cited in Robert G. Bratcher, "One Bible in Many Translations," *Interpretation* 32 (1978), p. 124; the Preface to the revised KJV published by Thomas Nelson Inc. (Nashville, 1979), p. iii; Glassman, *The Translation Debate*, p. 51 and passim.
[85]Nida and Taber, *Theory and Practice*, p. 31.

Zimmerman of the Evangelical Free Church of America will have spent over twenty years to produce a Bible translation in a north Canadian Indian language for a community of only 2,500.[86] It is hard to avoid the impression that Christian evangelical translators view what they call the "new," idiomatic method of translating as the supplanter of the "old," literal, Hebrew-laden style much as the Church understood the ascendancy of the "New" over the "Old" (read: antiquated) Testament. It is better, truer, an irreversible advance.[87] The "new" method attempts "to reformulate [the] message [of Scripture] within a completely new linguistic, historical, and sociocultural environment."[88]

In one of his essays on Bible translation Martin Buber drew a similar connection between the surrender of Hebraic constructions and the various efforts to adapt the text to a new audience.[89] Buber, of course, waxed ecstatic over the "diction, sentence structure, and rhythmic cadence" of the Bible's Hebrew and, with Rosenzweig, sought to restore an audience to the Hebrew voice of the text. They could reasonably only contemplate a Jewish audience. Throughout history the Christian church has always heard its Scriptures in translation while the Jewish synagogue has chanted its Bible in Hebrew.[90] Rosenzweig feared "that the Germans won't stomach [Buber-Rosenzweig's] extremely un-Christian Bible."[91] Indeed, it might not be too drastic a simplification to label the Hebrew-literal style of translation *Jewish* in contrast to the idiomatic, evangelical, *Christian* mode.[92]

---

[86]Reported in the *New York Times*, Feb. 1, 1981, p. A14.

[87]I feel convinced of this perception even though Harry Orlinsky of the NJV committee likewise hails the "new" approach to translating; see references in notes 4 and 39. Cf., e.g., the following dismissal of Jewish literalism as no less than "idolatry" in an excerpt from a recent United Bible Societies publication, prefaced approvingly by Eugene Nida: "[The belief that God sought to communicate with the Israelites verbally] gave rise to Israel's strong reverence for and devotion toward the Word of God, the sacred Scriptures – an attachment that unfortunately later developed (under the strict instruction of Jewish sects such as the Pharisees) into what amounted to an attitude of idolatry. Thus the literal form of the Word was transformed into an object of worship [*sic!*], while its meaning was lost in the process (Matthew 15:6-9)"; Ernst R. Wendland, *The Cultural Factor in Bible Translation* (London: United Bible Societies, 1987), p. 12.

[88]Wendland, ibid., p. 31.

[89]See Buber's "Über die Wortwahl in einer Verdeutschung der Schrift," *Die Schrift*, esp. pp. 137-38.

[90]Cf. David Stern, "Translating the Ancients," *Commentary* 59/6 (June 1975), esp. p. 45. De Waard and Nida, *From One Language to Another*, p. 23, imply that this practice has authoritative early Christian precedent: "For New Testament writers the Septuagint translation of the Old Testament was regarded as valid as the Hebrew."

[91]Rosenzweig, cited in Nahum N. Glatzer, *Franz Rosenzweig: His Life and Thought*, 2nd ed. (New York: Schocken, 1961), p. 153.

[92]Cf. also Buber, "Biblical Humanism," *On the Bible*, ed. Nahum N. Glatzer (New York: Schocken, 1968), pp. 211-16. Cf. also Robertson, *The New Translations*,

After all, Jewish exegesis of Scripture has traditionally found great significance not only in the *sense* of the text but quite as importantly in its configurations of Hebrew phrases, words, even letters. For classical midrashic interpreters the text was read not as a continuous semantic message, which could be grasped only in chunks of sense, but was decoded according to atomized units of various sizes, sometimes as small as the shape of a letter.[93] The midrashic premium on the sacred significance of every letter of Scripture had its parallel in the ancient Jewish translations.[94] The ancient rabbis displayed an understandable antipathy to any sort of Bible translation. But the translations that were produced – and the Greek one by the proselyte Aquila in particular[95] – endeavored to transfer word for word, particle for particle, each meaningful component of the original. Partly this resulted from the translators' uncertainties in interpreting Hebrew expressions. Rather than parse a difficult form or explain an unfamiliar idiom, they would noncommittally render element for element, leaving it to the reader to figure out the sense of the whole.[96] Mostly, though, they took pains to preserve every potential signifier in the text, every *nota accusativi* (את particle) for example,[97] because it is all crucial to the divine revelation. For Aquila, "the Hebrew text represents a mosaic which must be left unchanged, except for the

---

pp. 165-75, esp. p. 170, on Hugh Schonfield's "Jewish flavor" in rendering the Christian Scriptures. I do not mean to imply that a tendency to literalism was exclusively Jewish in the ancient world. In opposition to the classical trend to render idiomatically, or sense-for-sense, there was another tradition of rendering word-for-word, especially when dealing with sacred texts; see Sebastian Brock, "Aspects of Translation Technique in Antiquity," *Greek, Roman, and Byzantine Studies* 29 (1979), pp. 69-87. Nor do I deny that Jewish scholars, especially in Medieval Spain, opted for the sense-for-sense translation mode (under Arabic influence? see Brock, pp. 74-75). Cf., e.g., these remarks of Moses ibn Ezra: "If you come to translate anything from Arabic to Hebrew, take only the idea and the intent and do not translate word for word, for all languages are similar to one another...You would do well to convey the idea of the source with more apt words than you will find in the language of the translation"; *Shirat Yisra'el*, trans. from the Arabic by Ben-Zion Halper (Leipzig: Stybel Publishing, 1924), p. 132.

For the Christian approach to translation as characteristically evangelical, cf. de Waard and Nida, *From One Language to Another*, p. 20.

[93]Cf., e.g., Yitshaq Heinemann, דרכי האגדה [The Ways of Midrash], 3rd ed. (Jerusalem: Magnes Press, 1970), pp. 100-7.

[94]Cf., e.g., ibid., pp. 169-72; Nechama Leibowitz, *Die Übersetzungstechnik der jüdisch-deutschen Bibelübersetzungen des 15. und 16. Jahrhunderts dargestellt an den Psalmen* (Halle, 1931), pp. 1-2.

[95]See esp. Dominique Barthélemy, *Les devanciers d'Aquila*, SVT 10 (1963), pp. 3-30 ("L'herméneutique d'Aqiba et son influence sur Aquila"); cf. also Barr, *The Typology of Literalism;* Leibowitz, *Die Übersetzungstechnik*, pp. 9-11.

[96]Cf. Barr, *The Typology of Literalism*, esp. p. 42; Rabin, "The Translation Process," pp. 23-24; Harry M. Orlinsky, "The Septuagint as Holy Writ and the Philosophy of the Translators," *HUCA* 46 (1975), esp. p. 104.

[97]See esp. Barthélemy, *Les devanciers d'Aquila*, pp. 11-15.

replacement of its Hebrew 'stones' by Greek ones."[98] Since the revealed text encodes its meanings in the merest elements, every characteristic of the Hebrew must find a corresponding one in the translation.[99] That such attention to the text's Hebraic properties is distinctively (though not exclusively) Jewish has been recognized by Barr: "The sort of devotion to the forms and patterns of an original language implied by it was such that it was not likely to become much developed except among Jews."[100] Indeed, it is doubtfully a coincidence that the first to render the Bible idiomatically was the great Church father, Jerome.[101] I do not mean to imply that Christian translations of the Bible have not been literalistic.[102] Early English translations, notably those influenced by John Wycliffe, were extremely literal – but Latinate, not Hebraic.[103] They were based on Jerome's *Vulgate*. When I speak of "literal" in this regard, therefore, I mean "Hebrew-literal."

The rigidly literal method of Jewish translation, in which each element of the Hebrew is somehow conferred, probably harks back to the oral, simultaneous procedure of translation in the ancient synagogue.[104] Simultaneous translation tends to follow a mechanical stimulus-response, one-for-one correspondence model. This pattern of element-by-element rendering continued in use by Jewish schools of the traditional type right up through our century.[105] The first Jewish translation to break the pattern was the important late eighteenth century rendering by Moses Mendelssohn, who wanted to provide German Jews with a Bible in fluent, idiomatic German, to launch them into the stream of secular culture.[106] The literal mode did not resurface among Jews in any meaningful way until Buber and Rosenzweig. Their literalism has with some justice been compared to the word-for-word methods of the ancient literal versions.[107]

---

[98]Katz, cited in Barr, *The Typology of Literalism*, p. 37. For classical Greek antecedents of such a practice, see Brock, "Aspects of Translation Technique," pp. 81-82.

[99]Cf. Leibowitz, *Die Übersetzungstechnik*, p. 1; Orlinsky, "The Septuagint as Holy Writ," p. 103; Carr, *The Typology of Literalism*, pp. 31-32.

[100]Ibid., p. 46.

[101]For some ambivalence about idiomatic/literal translation among the Septuagint translators, see Brock, "Aspects of Translation Technique," pp. 71-72.

[102]Cf. Hammond, "English Translations of the Bible" (n. 13 above).

[103]Cf. Bruce, *History of the Bible in English*, pp. 12-23, esp. p. 15.

[104]Cf. Rabin, "The Translation Process," p. 18; Avigdor Shinan, "Live Translation: On the Nature of the Aramaic Targums to the Pentateuch," *Prooftexts* 3 (1983), pp. 41-49. Brock, "Aspects of Translation Technique," explains the word-for-word translation style as a result of concern to render legal detail. It is possible, of course, that both factors affected the development of the more literal mode of translation.

[105]Cf. Leibowitz, *Die Übersetzungstechnik*, pp. 11-16.

[106]Cf. ibid., p. 17; S. Billigheimer, "On Jewish Translations of the Bible in Germany," *Abr-Nahrain* 7 (1967-68), p. 3.

[107]Cf. Leibowitz, *Die Übersetzungstechnik* pp. 9-11; Barr, *The Typology of Literalism*, pp. 8-9.

However, as the following pages will make clear, Buber and Rosenzweig's methods were not of the same literalism as that of their ancient and medieval predecessors. And, more important, their methods derived from literary and linguistic philosophies that were of a different nature from the traditional, theological rationale.

Before turning to the relations of translational styles to distinctive philosophies of language, let us sum up our discussion of the various permutations of the literal vs. idiomatic opposition. Alternative modes of translation do different things and serve different functions.[108] More literal translations can cover a wider spectrum of literary features; idiomatic renderings can depict the historical denotations of the text with greater clarity. While the idiomatic style can present a culture to us in familiar terms, a literal rendering can disclose the more idiosyncratic aspects of that culture. One may liken the idiomatic mode to the clear voice of a speaker reciting someone else's message in one's own language. The literal translation resembles the voice of the author, but muffled. The author's sense may be difficult to discern, but the reader who wishes to hear it will make the requisite efforts.

> Rabbi Judah says: "He who translates a verse according to its form – this one is a fabricator. And he who adds to it – this one deforms and diminishes it."[109]

Of the modern Bible translations, only two sets are grounded in developed philosophies of language and translation: those of the American Bible Society (ABS), such as the superidiomatic TEV, and the Hebraic renditions of Buber and Rosenzweig. Both share a general philosophy of language holding that the human mind universally possesses a common apparatus of thought and a common linguistic structure. Different languages transform that basic underlying structure's meaning into various surface forms. This broad position – within which is a kaleidoscope of diversity – contrasts with another, represented most famously by Nietzsche,[110] maintaining that the structures of language constrict

---

[108]Cf., e.g., the admirable discussion of the problems of translation in John Bright, *Jeremiah,* AB (Garden City, NY: Doubleday, 1965), pp. cxixff.

[109]Tosefta *Megilla* 4:41. For variety in ancient Jewish Bible translation, see, e.g., Barr, *The Typology of Literalism;* and Michael L. Klein, "Converse Translation: A Targumic Technique," *Biblica* 57 (1976), pp. 515-37.

[110]Cf., e.g., Arthur Danto, *Nietzsche as Philosopher* (New York: Columbia University Press, 1965), pp. 12, 83-89, 96-97, 106, 123-24; George Steiner, "Silence and the Poet," *Language and Silence* (n. 73 above), pp. 36-54, esp. 44. See, e.g., Friedrich Nietzsche, "On Truth and Lie in an Extra-Moral Sense," in Mark C. Taylor, *Deconstruction in Context: Literature & Philosophy* (Chicago: University of Chicago Press, 1986), pp. 216-19; see also *Basic Writings of Nietzsche,* trans. and ed. Walter Kaufmann (New York: Modern Library, 1968), pp. 406-7.

the processes of perception and thought.[111] One issue at stake between the two positions is the problem of privacy in language: How do I know that what I mean by saying x and what the other person means by x are really the same thing?[112] How do I know the answer to the question posed by Jorge Luis Borges: "You who read me, are you sure you understand my language?"[113] Both the ABS linguists and Buber and Rosenzweig believe in the possibilities of true communication. But their philosophical differences led them to antithetical views of translation.

The simpler theory is that of the ABS. They hold that languages are essentially alike, that any language can in some way express that which any other language can express, that the synbols of language suffice to verbalize experience and thought, and that the underlying linguistic structure of an utterance corresponds directly to the speaker's concept.[114] It is a modified version of Noam Chomsky's transformational-generative grammar.[115] Based on these philosophical assumptions, the procedure for translating that Nida and Taber describe is, concisely, as follows.[116] The translator analyzes the source-text with respect to its semantic and grammatical relations. Then one transfers the decoded message into one's own mind. Finally, the translator must restructure the message in the forms of the translation-language.

---

[111]On this bipolar contrast of linguistic philosophies, cf. Steiner, *After Babel*, pp. 73-74.

[112]For a would-be solution to this problem, see Willard V. Quine, "Meaning and Translation," in Jerry A. Fodor and J. J. Katz, eds., *The Structure of Language: Readings in the Philosophy of Language* (Englewood Cliffs: Prentice-Hall, 1964), pp. 460-78. There are a number of problems with Quine's argument. One is that he deals only with certifying whether two speakers are denoting the same thing; sameness in connotation is not verifiable by his procedure. A second is: even if we could verify that my statement refers to the same thing as yours does, how do we know that our language directly represents our thoughts? For a mentalist's critique of Quine, cf. Jay F. Rosenberg, *Linguistic Representation* (Boston: D. Reidel, 1974), pp. 49-71.

[113]Jorge Luis Borges, "The Library of Babel," *Ficciones*, ed. Anthony Kerrigan (New York: Grove Press, 1962), p. 87.

[114]Cf. Nida and Taber, *Theory and Practice*, pp. 4-5, 19-20, 23 and passim; Taber, "Translation as Interpretation," esp. pp. 140-42; Glassman, *The Translation Debate*, p. 48.

[115]See esp. Noam Chomsky, *Aspects of the Theory of Syntax* (Cambridge, MA: MIT Press, 1965). Introductory presentations may be found in D. Terence Langendoen, *The Study of Syntax* (New York: Holt Rinehart and Winston, 1969); Ronald W. Langacker, *Language and Its Structure*, 2nd rev. ed. (New York: , 1969); Robert P. Stockwell, *Foundations of Syntactic Theory* (Englewood Cliffs: Prentice-Hall, 1977). For the philosophical implications and roots of this theory, see Jerrold J. Katz, *The Underlying Reality of Language and Its Philosophical Import* (New York: Harper Torchbooks, 1971).

[116]Nida and Taber, *Theory and Practice*, p. 33 and passim.

The philosophy of language upon which the ABS bases itself stretches the theory from which it derives in critical ways and, as a consequence, cannot rely on the theory it marshals in its support. Chomsky's theory does not actually identify the level of conceptualization and the deep-structure of language.[117] The deep-structure of a language encodes the ideas of a speaker, but there is no certainty that thought and language are commensurate. Moreover, although Chomsky posits a finite repertoire of linguistic structures for all languages, he does not claim that the *substantive* aspects of language – e.g., tenses and moods of the verb, lexical denotations and connotations – are universal, only their *formal* representation.[118] Nida and Taber seem to acknowledge this when they allow that "each language has its own genius" and that different languages segment reality differently.[119] By saying this they edge themselves philosophically over toward the linguistic theory of Humboldt and others, a position taken by Franz Rosenzweig, too (see below). Indeed, they appear to lose the ground beneath their method. They compensate only inadequately by disparaging the stylistic nuances and connotations of particular linguistic forms. Their assertion that "anything that can be said in one language can be said in another" is compromised by a crucial subordinate clause: "unless the form is an essential element of the message."[120] As we saw above, however, form is not separable from meaning. "To preserve the content of the message," they say, "the form must be changed."[121] To make any sort of translation, they are right – form must be changed. But it is only their wishful profession that in translation the message remains the same. It does not.

Behind the Buber-Rosenzweig renderings a battery of discrete, self-sufficient rationales – literary, linguistic, and theological – is arrayed. Because the basis of their translational mode is so multifacted, would-be critics would have to attack it on all sides, not only on one. In fact, though, most discussion of the Buber-Rosenzweig translation, pro and con, has limited itself to the literary aspect.[122]

---

[117]Cf. Steiner, *After Babel*, pp. 100ff.

[118]Cf. P. F. Strawson, "Take the B Train," *New York Review of Books* 26/6 (April 19, 1979), p. 36.

[119]Nida and Taber, *Theory and Practice*, pp. 3-4, 20-22.

[120]Ibid., pp. 4-5. As noted above, Nida seems to have become more sensitive to the more rhetorical and connotative features of language in the more recent exposition, de Waard and Nida, *From One Language to Another*. Yet, even here it is "form" that is blamed for obstruction in translation: "The loss of meaning in translation is largely proportionate to the extent that a meaning is carried by the form" (p. 44). Form must always make a difference in meaning. Despite de Waard and Nida's increased attention to form, it is still important to examine the earlier formulation of Nida's linguistic philosophy because it is that theory that undergirds the TEV translation, which is the subject of discussion both in this chapter and in Chapter Seven.

[121]Ibid., pp. 5-6.

[122]This is so, for example of Walter Kaufmann, "Buber's Religious Significance," in Paul A. Schilpp and Maurice Friedman, eds., *The Philosophy of Martin Buber*

This is not hard to understand. Not only does this side appear most pronounced and intelligible, it is the one that most motivated Buber, the better known of the two partners. If one compares the respective essays in *Die Schrift* by Buber on the one hand and by Rosenzweig on the other, and then examines the correspondence between the two on their collaborative translation, which Everett Fox has brought to light,[123] one gains the impression that Buber's interest was chiefly literary while Rosenzweig's was philosophical, and that Buber may have only superficially grasped the linguistic-philosophical background that Rosenzweig brought to their project. I do not mean to fault Buber for this; he urged Rosenzweig to work with him precisely on account of the latter's expertise in the theory and practice of translation. It is just that in order to appreciate the difficult, sometimes disconcerting mode in which Buber and Rosenzweig translated, one must also attend to Rosenzweig's philosophy of language.[124] It was Rosenzweig's theory of language that decisively shaped the joint translation.[125]

Knowing that a translator cannot duplicate all the linguistic and stylistic features of a text, Schleiermacher had advised the traducer to select for special treatment those features that strike him as most expressive and significant.[126] Buber and Rosenzweig followed this program. For them the most outstanding quality of the Hebrew Bible was its intention to be declaimed, its "spokenness."[127] Buber and Rosenzweig sought to confect a translation that would by its very nature be voiced. Historical and anthropological thinking from the eighteenth century on had come to recognize that ancient literature in general was designed for oral performance. "Read Homer as if he were singing in the

---

(LaSalle, IL: Open Court, 1967), esp. pp. 670-77; Tigay, "On Translating the Torah," esp. p. 18; Shemaryahu Talmon, "Martin Buber's Ways of Interpreting the Bible," *JJSt* 27 (1976), pp. 195-209; Michael Fishbane, "Martin Buber as an Interpreter of the Bible," *Judaism* 27/2 (Spring 1978), pp. 184-95; and the several essays of Everett Fox, e.g., "Technical Aspects," and "A Buber-Rosenzweig Bible in English," *Amsterdamse cahiers voor exegese en Bijbelse theologie* 2 (1981), pp. 9-22.

[123]Fox, "Technical Aspects."

[124]Cf., e.g., Rivka G. Horwitz, "Franz Rosenzweig on Language," *Judaism* 13 (1964), pp. 393-406; Billigheimer, "On Jewish Translations," p. 17.

[125]Cf. Fox, "Technical Aspects," esp. pp. 153-54.

[126]Schleiermacher, "On the Different Methods," p. 13.

[127]See Buber, *Die Schrift*, e.g., pp. 56ff., 140; Rosenzweig, ibid., e.g., pp. 76-87, 124; cf. Everett Fox, "We Mean the Voice: The Buber-Rosenzweig Translation of the Bible," *Response* 12 (Winter 1971-72), pp. 29-42; idem, *In the Beginning: An English Rendition of the Book of Genesis = Response* 14 (Summer 1972), pp. 143-59 [cf. now the introduction to *In the Beginning* (New York: Schocken, 1983)]; idem, "Technical Aspects," pp. 10-11 and passim; idem, "The Samson Cycle in an Oral Setting," *alcheringa* 4/1 (1978), pp. 51-68, esp. p. 51; Kingsley, "The Buber-Rosenzweig Translation," p. 17; Billigheimer, "On Jewish Translations," p. 18; Talmon, "Martin Buber's Ways," pp. 202-3; Fishbane, "Martin Buber," pp. 185-86, 189-90.

streets," said Herder in the late eighteenth century.[128] Nietzsche saw "a rebirth of the art of hearing" in the nineteenth century,[129] and this regained faculty made an indelible impress on the study of Biblical poetry, too.[130] Today, the oral character of the Hebrew Bible is axiomatic in most quarters,[131] and its adherents include the American Bible Society.[132] For Buber, to achieve a speaking rendering of Scripture serves a second, Jewish purpose: it sustains the tradition of reading the text aloud.[133] For both Buber and Rosenzweig, though, the most important reason for spokenness was theological: the divine voice speaks through the words of the text. A voice is best heard, not visualized in print. The Biblical narrator must be furnished the means of immediately affecting his hearer, to "address him and make his ears prick up in his full spiritual and living present."[134]

To imbue their translation with spokenness, Buber divided the text into breath-lengths, corresponding to the natural punctuation of discourse by breathing.[135] It had been assumed, at least since the writing of the French epistemologist Condillac in the early eighteenth century, that language itself originates in breath-long, primal utterances – an idea that in the Romantic period crystallized in the widespread principle that rhythm is the most elemental ingredient of poetry and that rhythm, as the immediate capsule of perception, enables poetry to recapitulate the most primitive sensations of natural man and woman.[136] The theory often holds, too, that ancient verse was recited as part of

---

[128]Cited in Francis B. Gummere, *The Beginnings of Poetry* (New York: Macmillan, 1901), p. 52. On Herder and his relation to Vico, see Isaiah Berlin, *Vico and Herder* (New York: Viking, 1976).

[129]Friedrich Nietzsche, *On the Genealogy of Morals and Ecce Homo*, trans. Walter Kaufmann (New York: Vintage Books, 1969), p. 295.

[130]Cf., e.g., Johann G. von Herder, *The Spirit of Hebrew Poetry*, trans. J. Marsh (Burlington: Edward Smith, 1833). For Herder's contributions to Biblical studies, see Thomas Willi, *Herders Beitrag zum Verstehen des alten Testaments* (Tübingen: J. C. B. Mohr, 1971).

[131]Cf., e.g., Theodor H. Gaster, *Myth, Legend, and Custom in the Old Testament* (New York: Harper & Row, 1969), p. xlvii: "Popular literature is *heard*, rather than *read*, and the influence of recitation is present everywhere in the Old Testament."

[132]Cf., e.g., Nida and Taber, *Theory and Practice*, pp. 28-31.

[133]Buber, *Die Schrift*, p. 141.

[134]Rosenzweig, *Die Schrift*, p. 245.

[135]Cf., e.g., Fox, "Technical Aspects," p. 32; idem, "The Samson Cycle," p. 52a. Rosenzweig accredits this technique to Buber in *Die Schrift*, pp. 80-81; cf. Fox, "A Buber-Rosenzweig Bible in English," p. 21, n. 8; see there, pp. 10-11, for an excellent illustration of how the division of the text into breath-lengths highlights the text's ironic use of language. Note also Rosenzweig, *The Star of Redemption*, trans. William W. Hallo (Boston: Beacon Press, 1972), p. 197.

[136]See Hans Aarsleff, *From Locke to Saussure* (Minneapolis: University of Minnesota Press, 1982), esp. p. 288. Cf. Richard Wallaschek, *Primitive Music* (London, 1893), e.g., p. 234: "The power exerted over us by any rhythmical movement lies in its being adjusted to the form in which ideas and feelings succeed each other in our mind." Cf. esp. "Rhythm as the Essential Fact of Poetry"

a dance-like ritual in which the participants – the bard and his cohort – worked up a loud, pulsating rhythm of breathing.[137] By means of reproducing the Bible's rhythms, Buber and Rosenzweig hoped not only to resuscitate the cultural context of Scripture but above all simply to translate faithfully. "Every language has its own peculiarities of rhythm, for prose as well as for poetry," as Schleiermacher had said,[138] and it is the responsibility of the translator to imitate the cadences of Hebrew.[139]

In a similar vein, Buber and Rosenzweig sought to somehow duplicate the pervasive assonance and wordplay of the Bible in German.[140] The Bible, they perceived, communicates not only through semantics but also through sound, as speech transmits sense through tone of voice. This technique has been successfully assimilated by Buber-Rosenzweig's American heir, Everett Fox. In the following two instances Fox has captured two Hebrew wordplays that Buber himself failed to convey in the Book of Jonah:

> But HE hurled a great wind upon the sea,
> and a great storm was on the sea,
> so that the ship was on the *brink* of *breaking* up. (1:4)

> Now Yona *had gone* down...
> and *had gone* to sleep. (1:5)[141]

But the by far more significant kind of repetition that Buber and Rosenzweig found in the text was that of words and word-stems, the well-known "leading-words," *Leitwörter*, which by their recurrence function to underscore a theme or motif or associate disparate verses or passages.[142] In order to convey these

---

in Gummere, *The Beginnings of Poetry*, pp. 30-115. Note in particular Gummere's citation of the Biblicist, Karl Budde, on p. 62.

[137]See Gummere, ibid., p. 100, n. 3; cf. Fox, "We Mean the Voice," p. 31.

[138]Schleiermacher, "On the Different Methods," p. 27.

[139]Cf., e.g, Buber, *Die Schrift*, p. 57. For a slightly later appeal by a Biblicist to attempt to reproduce the text's rhythm in translation, cf. R. Tournay, "Poésie biblique et traduction française, un essai: le psaume XI," *RB* 53 (1946), pp. 349-64, esp. 352-53. See also Henri Meschonnic, "Translating Biblical Rhythm," in David H. Hirsch and N. Aschkenasy, eds., *Biblical Patterns in Modern Literature* (Chico, CA: Scholars Press, 1984), pp. 227-40.

[140]E.g., Buber, *Die Schrift*, pp. 152ff.; cf. Fox, "Technical Aspects," e.g., pp. 39, 45-46. For an appreciation of the importance of capturing assonance in translation, cf. Robert Martin-Achard, "An Exegete Confronting Genesis 32:23-33," in Roland Barthes et al., *Structural Analysis and Biblical Exegesis* (Pittsburgh: Pickwick Press, 1974), esp. p. 39.

[141]E. Fox, "Yona: An English Rendition," *Response* 22 (Summer 1974), pp. 7-17, here p. 7.

[142]See esp. Buber's essay, "Leitwortstil in der Erzählung des Pentateuchs," *Die Schrift*, pp. 211-38; a Hebrew version appears in Buber's דרכו של מקרא [The Bible's Way] (Jerusalem: Mossad Bialik, 1964), pp. 284-99. Cf., e.g., Fox, "Technical Aspects," pp. 48-67; Nahum N. Glatzer, "Buber as an Interpreter of the Bible," in Schilpp and Friedman, eds., *The Philosophy of Martin Buber*, esp. pp. 362-68;

meaningful repetitions Buber and Rosenzweig, for the most part, rendered Hebrew stems by the same German stem even in contexts where the German word was partly inapposite. It is this word-for-word, "concordant" translation technique that most disturbs the ABS and other idiomatic translators.[143] We have observed one of the battlegrounds (in 2 Samuel 7) above. In this the ABS follows an innovation of the KJV, which imposed on the Hebrew text its own stylistic predilection for variety in diction.[144] Idiomatic translators have honorably felt the need to carry on the fight against the medieval conception of language that gave rise to concordant rendering. That conception places the origins of speech in the mouth of Adam and views all subsequent linguistic history as a development – or degeneration – of the pure, primal, God-given Hebrew.[145] Even in the twentieth century an English rendering entitled *The Concordant Version* bases itself on just that idea.[146] Each Hebrew word must be given a corresponding, fixed English one lest the primal linguistic structure be lost. However, as we shall see, Rosenzweig had philosophical views similar to yet crucially different from the Adamic perspective, and these views help to underpin the "concordant" style of the Buber-Rosenzweig mode beyond its sound literary justifications.

Translating the same word in each of its contexts acontextually, the same way each time, rests upon another cardinal principle of the Buber-Rosenzweig method. To connect distant verses by means of concordant translation presupposes the unity of the text.[147] The conception of literary unity, which, as we saw above, had been articulated by Humboldt,[148] became a basic hermeneutical rule of Buber and Rosenzweig's predecessor, Wilhelm Dilthey,[149] and is the keystone of contemporary structuralism. For Buber and Rosenzweig it was more than a premise or proposition – it was their conclusion. The leading-

---

William W. Hallo, "Notes on Translation," *Eretz Israel* 16 (1982), pp. 99*-105*, esp. 101*-2*. For the adoption of this literary analytical technique by modern Biblicists, see my "Biblical Narratology" (see n. 49), pp. 202-3.

[143]Cf., e.g., Taber, "Translation as Interpretation," and Crim, "Old Testament Translations and Interpretation"; cf. already Friedrich Schlegel, "Dialogue on Poetry," trans. E. Behler and R. Struc, in Willson, ed., *German Romantic Criticism*, p. 121.

[144]Cf. Bruce, *History of the Bible in English*, pp. 104-5.

[145]For discussion of the "Adamic" theory of language and the philosophical war against it, see Aarsleff, *From Locke to Saussure*, pp. 24-25 and passim; cf. also Steiner, *After Babel*, pp. 58-59 and passim.

[146]Cf. Bruce, *History of the Bible in English*, p. 184.

[147]See Rosenzweig, "Die Einheit der Bible," *Die Schrift*, pp. 46-57; Buber, ibid., pp. 139, 168ff., and passim; cf. Fox, "We Mean the Voice," pp. 38-39; idem, "Technical Aspects," p. 65.

[148]See above with n. 19.

[149]Cf. Edgar V. McKnight, *Meaning in Texts: The Historical Shaping of a Narrative Hermeneutic* (Philadelphia: Fortress Press, 1978), esp. p. 28. Dilthey's major statement is *Die Einbildungskraft des Dichters: Bausteine für eine Poetik* (1887).

words are guideposts to the unity that informs the entire text. They do not imagine that the text was composed by a single author in a single period. Buber said that he detected "a variety of voices in the chorus" of sources that stands behind the text.[150] Yet, in its final edited form the text comprises a wide network of associations. A good translation should keep the network intact by highlighting the lexical, and any other, connectors.

Words possess associations not only horizontally – in their connections across a text – but also vertically – in their historical relations. Buber and Rosenzweig acknowledged that a word rarely makes a clean break with its past and for a number of reasons sought to translate words according to their etymological or root meaning. One reason intertwines with the *Leitwort:* only by translating Hebrew words according to the sense of the stem can the repetition of various words built upon the same root appear to the audience.[151] Another reason is anthropological: the root meaning of a Hebrew word often clarifies the psychological or theological impulse behind a term. Buber and Rosenzweig follow the lead of the nineteenth-century German Jewish Orthodox leader, Samson Raphael Hirsch, in rendering קרבן, typically glossed as "sacrifice," as "a bringing nigh," which is what it suggests etymologically.[152] The difference in nuance between the two glosses needs no comment. Buber and Rosenzweig did the same for personal names,[153] which likewise wear their associations on their sleeve, so to speak. In an oft-cited example, the name of Moses, מֹשֶׁה, denotes "one who draws out (water)" despite the fact that when Pharaoh's daughter names him מֹשֶׁה, she says that *she* had drawn *him* out of the water (Exod. 2:10). She saw only a passive, helpless infant; the text in its global scope sees a heroic deliverer.[154] Without the Buber-Rosenzweig technique of providing the audience with the text's etymology of names, such irony would be missed.

Translating etymologically could be construed as a throwback to rabbinic midrash, which often erected linkages using etymological connections, real and fanciful.[155] But Buber and Rosenzweig's more secular rationales find strong

---

[150]Buber, "Abraham the Seer," *On the Bible*, p. 24. Cf. Benno Jacob, *Das erste buch der Tora: Genesis* (Berlin: Schocken, 1934), p. 10 [English translation of part of this passage in Alex Preminger and Edward L. Greenstein, *The Hebrew Bible in Literary Criticism* (New York: Frederick Ungar, 1986), p. 392].

[151]See, e.g., Buber, "Replies to my Critics," in Schilpp and Friedman, eds., The *Philosophy of Martin Buber,* p. 727. For a friendly critique of Buber's etymological translation style, see James Muilenburg, "Buber as an Interpreter of the Bible," in ibid., p. 387.

[152]See, e.g., Buber, *Die Schrift,* pp. 142ff., 157ff.; cf. Billigheimer, "On Jewish Translations," pp. 9, 16-17; Fox, *In the Beginning* (1972), pp. 147-52.

[153]Cf., e.g., Fox, "A Buber-Rosenzweig Bible in English," p. 11.

[154]See Buber, *Moses* (New York: Harper Torchbooks, 1958), pp. 35-36; James S. Ackerman, "The Literary Context of the Moses Birth Story (Exodus 1-2)," in Kenneth R. R. Gros Louis et al., eds., *Literary Interpretations of Biblical Narratives* (Nashville: Abingdon Press, 1974), pp. 94-95.

[155]Cf., e.g., Barr, *The Typology of Literalism,* pp. 44-48.

precedent in German Romantic criticism. For Jacob Grimm, for example, the use of a root meaning points to the "sensual notions" out of which a word emerged,[156] and Schleiermacher, like Buber, urged translators to traduce ideas according to the perceptual and expressive framework of the language of the source.[157] Yet an ideational contact between midrash and the Buber-Rosenzweig method may in fact exist. That contact is less historical or traditional than philosophical. Midrash, like the Adamicists (see above), understands a name to be more than an arbitrary, conventional designation of a thing. A name captures some essential significance concerning that which it denominates. Thus, it is God who gives the names, since it is God who knows the essences.[158] Rosenzweig, in his philosophy of language, tries to pull the two antithetical positions – naming as convention and naming as divine creation – together. As so often in Rosenzweig's thought, the strands that make up the web of the thinking do not reach far enough to make contact on their own. But they course through Rosenzweig's mind like nervous impulses traversing a synapse, powered by his faith in the great enabler, God.

When one seeks out Rosenzweig's rationale for translating as he and Buber did, one finds that his theory of translation rests, as it should, on the wide base of a linguistic philosophy. Thus, in explaining the need for etymological translation Rosenzweig pays little mind to literary devices or anthropological authenticity. He penetrates to the philosophical core, to Language itself: at the root level of languages the diverse languages of the world share a common domain and structure. The translator must probe to this most basic, universal level of language. Only at that level can translation take place.[159] So far, this may sound like the translational philosophy of the American Bible Society. But at this point Rosenzweig and Eugene Nida would surely part company. Language with a capital "L" can, according to Rosenzweig, say whatever is conceived, but – and here is the pivotal point – languages cannot. All languages combined can just about say anything. In collusion they asymptotically approximate Language, the language of God. That doesn't sound like Nida, but it does recall Herder, his teacher Hamann, Humboldt, Schleiermacher, and especially Rosenzweig's younger contemporaries Walter Benjamin, Martin Heidegger, and in many respects Ludwig Wittgenstein. In more recent times Benjamin's outlook has been revived by Jacques Derrida.[160]

---

[156]Jacob Grimm, "On the Origin of Language," in Willson, ed., *German Romantic Criticism*, pp. 281-82; cf. also Herder, *The Spirit of Hebrew Poetry*.

[157]Schleiermacher, "On the Different Methods," pp. 25-26.

[158]Cf. Heinemann, דרכי האגדה, pp. 11-12. For Kabbalistic influence on the seventeenth-century Adamicists, see Aarsleff, *From Locke to Saussure*, pp. 60, 281.

[159]Rosenzweig, *Die Schrift*, p. 125; cf. his *The Star*, p. 126.

[160]Jacques Derrida, *The Ear of the Other*, ed. Christie V. McDonald, trans. Peggy Kamuf (New York: Schocken, 1985), pp. 91-161.

The human is the speaking animal (a notion as old as Hesiod with roots in Kabbala as well, where the human is designated by the term *medabber*, "the speaking-one").[161] Out of one's perceptions of things one utters names, invented not altogether arbitrarily but not capturing the essence of the things either.[162] The true names, embodying universal essences, are known only to God; they are:

> ...the archetypal words [which]...lie hidden under each and every manifest word as secret bases and...rise to the light in it. In a certain sense they are elemental words which constituted the manifest course of speech....In living speech, these inaudible arch-words became audible as real words...real language. Those inaudible elemental words, standing side by side without relationship, were the language of the protocosmos, lying side by side.[163]

This assumption of words more elemental than human words, the words of God, resolves a paradox in Genesis 1, a text that underwent exegesis in the philosophy

---

[161]Cf. Rosenzweig, *The Star*, p. 110: "Man became man when he first spoke." For Hesiod and Aristotle, cf. Steiner, *Language and Silence*, p. 36; for Kabbala, cf. Gershom Scholem, "Kabbala," *Encyclopedia Judaica* (Jerusalem: Keter, 1971), vol. 10, col. 610. For the notion, with a slight twist, in Heidegger, cf. George Steiner, *Martin Heidegger* (New York: Penguin, 1980), esp. pp. 30-31, 50ff.; McKnight, *Meaning in Texts*, pp. 39-53.

[162]Cf. esp. Walter Benjamin, "On Language as Such and on the Language of Man," *Reflections*, ed. P. Demetz, trans. E. Jephcott (New York: Harcourt Brace Jovanovich, 1978), pp. 314-32, esp. 324-25. It is worth noting here that Benjamin's and Rosenzweig's twin theories of language and translation are strikingly similar; see also Benjamin's "The Task of the Translator." Although Benjamin had read Rosenzweig's *The Star* prior to composing the latter essay, and although the two had met once, uneventfully (see Benjamin, *Briefe*, ed. G. Scholem and T. W. Adorno [Frankfurt: Suhrkamp, 1966], vol. 1, pp. 195-96), Benjamin's ideas on translation had been developed by 1916, when he wrote the former essay. Nor was Rosenzweig in *The Star* aware of Benjamin's essay, which remained unpublished until 1955. Rosenzweig and Benjamin drew on the same philosophical sources – Benjamin had studied Wilhelm von Humboldt's linguistic philosophy and had contemplated anthologizing Humboldt's writing on language (cf. G. Scholem, *Walter Benjamin – die Geschichte einer Freundschaft* [Frankfurt: Suhrkamp, 1975], pp. 33, 175; cf. idem, "Two Letters to Walter Benjamin," *On Jews and Judaism in Crisis*, ed. W. J. Dannhauser [New York: Schocken, 1976], p. 241). Perhaps more poignantly, both Rosenzweig and Benjamin, like Kafka, hoped for a redemption through language – through Hebrew even – from their German-Jewish alienation. Cf. George Steiner, "Introduction" to W. Benjamin, *The Origin of German Tragic Drama*, trans. J. Osborne (London: NLB, 1977), p. 13. On Kafka's alienation as Jew and attraction to Hebrew, see Marthe Robert, *As Lonely as Franz Kafka*, trans. R. Manheim (New York: Harcourt Brace Jovanovich, 1982).

For a brief sketch of Benjamin's thinking on language subsequent to the 1916 essay, see Anson Rabinbach, "Introduction to Walter Benjamin's 'Doctrine of the Similar'," *New German Critique* 17 (Spring 1979), pp. 60-64.

[163]Rosenzweig, *The Star*, p. 109.

of both Rosenzweig and Benjamin.[164] When God creates light, he says, "Let there be light," speaking the name, *light,* of something that he had not yet brought into existence. God has the name in hand prior to the existence of that which the name signifies. Heidegger transforms this notion into his idea that things do not become perceptible, they cannot "thing," until they are named. Naming differentiates that which is into discrete, nameable things.[165] But for Rosenzweig the lesson is more blatantly[166] theological: God uses language and through revelation shares this language with humanity:

> The word as heard and as spoken is one and the same. The ways of God are different from the ways of man, but the word of God and the word of man are the same. What man hears in his heart as his own human speech is the very word which comes out of God's mouth.[167]

Human speech begins when one person seeks to do that which is naturally divine and human – to encounter the other and overcome one's isolation by addressing the other, an I to a Thou.[168] Despite the universal foundation of Language, each one's perceptions and linguistic formulation of experience may differ.[169] Different people name things differently because these namings emerge from different encounters. Only God can encounter all the world simultaneously and possess a unified language, a single roster of names. Speech can only arise meaningfully in dialogue, and thought cannot proceed without speech. Thus, Rosenzweig adopted the notion of "speech-thinking" – not that thought and speech are coterminous, but we have no handle on thought unless we speak our

---

[164]Rosenzweig, *The Star*, pp. 151-55; Benjamin, "On Language," pp. 326-30.

[165]Martin Heidegger, *Poetry, Language, Thought,* trans. Alfred Hofstadter (New York: Harper & Row, 1975), pp. 189-210, esp. 198-203.

[166]Steiner discusses the ambiguous theological thrust of Heidegger's philosophy in *Martin Heidegger*, pp. 62-63.

[167]Rosenzweig, *The Star*, p. 151.

[168]Innocent readers should not assume that Rosenzweig acquired the philosophy of I-Thou from its most famous exponent, Martin Buber. The notion has its roots in the poetry of Friedrich Hölderlin at the turn of the nineteenth century and had been formulated fully later in that century by Ludwig Feuerbach. Cf. N. N. Glatzer's "Foreword" to *The Star*, pp. xiv-xv; Richard Unger, *Hölderlin's Major Poetry: The Dialectics of Unity* (Bloomington: Indiana University Press, 1975), p. 15. The social drive behind speech is stressed notably by Hölderlin and Humboldt; cf. Aarsleff, *From Locke To Saussure*, p. 343; N. N. Glatzer, "Introduction," to Franz Rosenzweig, *Understanding the Sick and the Healthy: A View of World, Man, and God* (New York: Noonday, 1953), pp. 16-17.

[169]Cf., e.g., Friedrich von Schiller, *Naive and Sentimental Poetry and On the Sublime,* trans. J. A. Elias (New York: Frederick Ungar, 1966), who delineates in the former essay different types of personality and sensibility; and, more fundamentally, Herder's view that differences in language reflect different shades of experience; see Berlin, *Vico and Herder*, p. 170.

thoughts.[170] We do not, however, merely speak or name. For Heidegger, speaking is an anonymous activity: Language speaks.[171] For Benjamin, naming itself is the purest act of speech, for it produces knowledge. To speak to the other is to debase and exploit language in order to control the other.[172] Rosenzweig understands that we tailor each of our utterances for a particular Thou in a particular meeting.

> Everyone must translate and everyone does translate. Whoever speaks is translating his thoughts for the comprehension he expects from the other.[173]

From a neurological standpoint, the equation of speech and translation was ill-advised; speech and the ability to translate are quite discrete faculties.[174] Nonetheless, as metaphor the equation makes clear that for Rosenzweig we each speak a different language; yet, we strive to bend our language toward our interlocutor.[175]

The function of language to connect with the world stands out by contrasting it with its dysfunction, tragedy. The tragic hero is isolated, and his isolation expresses itself in speechlessness.[176]

---

[170]For discussions of Rosenzweig's "speech-thinking" and its place in his thought, see, e.g., Nahum N. Glatzer, "הלשונות והעברית במיוחד במשנתו של רוזנצוייג" [Languages and Hebrew in Particular in Rosenzweig's Philosophy], in Baruch Kurzweil, ed., יובל שי (S. Y. Agnon Festschrift; Ramat-Gan, 1958), pp. 229-36; Horwitz, "Franz Rosenzweig on Language." Here, too, Benjamin and Heidegger are on the same wavelength. Cf. also the later work of Ludwig Wittgenstein; see Gerd Brand, ed., *The Essential Wittgenstein*, trans. R. E. Innis (New York: Basic Books, 1979), pp. 53-65, esp. p. 53; copntrast the earlier thinking of Wittgenstein in his *Tractatus Logico-Philosophicus*, trans. D. F. Pears and B. F. McGuiness (London: Routledge & Kegan Paul, 1961), p. 19. Rosenzweig opposed especially the philosophy of G. W. F. Hegel, who contended that thinking and speaking are essentially different in nature; cf., e.g., Hegel, *On Art, Religion, and Philosophy*, trans. J. G. Gray (New York: Harper & Row, 1970), pp. 31, 35, 153-54, and passim.

[171]Cf. Heidegger, *Poetry, Language, Thought*, pp. 190-91, 195, 197.

[172]Benjamin, "On Language," esp. pp. 317-18, 327-30. In this regard he follows Nietzsche; cf. Danto, *Nietzsche as Philosopher*, esp. p. 120; Anson Rabinbach, "Critique and Commentary/Alchemy and Chemistry: Some Remarks on Walter Benjamin...," *New German Critique* 17 (Spring 1979), p. 6. For a neo-Nietzschean deprecation of the tendentious use of language, cf. the novelist John Barth: "we converse to convert"; *New York Times Book Review*, May 9, 1982, p. 3.

[173]Rosenzweig, *Die Schrift*, p. 88, as translated in Glatzer, *Franz Rosenzweig*, p. 255.

[174]Cf. Martin L. Albert and Loraine K. Obler, *The Bilingual Brain: Neuropsychological and Neurolinguistic Aspects of Bilingualism* (New York: 1978), pp. 217-20.

[175]Rosenzweig, *The Star*, p. 81; *Understanding the Sick and the Healthy*, p. 59.

[176]Rosenzweig, *The Star*, esp. p. 77; cf. Benjamin, *The Origin of German Tragic Drama*, pp. 107ff., who develops Rosenzweig's concept. Contrast to Rosenzweig's

The languages of individuals each capture fragments of perception and insight. The more people truly communicate, the richer the conversants' language will become.[177] The more that people with something to say say it strikingly, the more language will fulfill its potential to express all that can be expressed.[178] It follows, then, that no language can increase its expressiveness without growing, without incorporating the features of other languages. Language contains within it all languages, and it is the goal of those who desire to attain the greatest expressiveness and knowledge to make of each translation an expansion of the translation language by incorporating features of the source language. Ultimately, all languages will merge into the all-expressive language of God. This is the upshot of the essays on translation by Schleiermacher, Rosenzweig,[179] Benjamin, and – now – Derrida.[180] There can be no real translation, if what is meant is the transfer of what a text says to another language.[181] The words don't match. German *brot* and French *pain*, as Benjamin

---

hopeful vision the tragic one of Franz Kafka; cf. Glatzer's "Introduction" to Rosenzweig, *Understanding the Sick and the Healthy*, pp. 19-20.

[177]Rosenzweig, *Understanding the Sick and the Healthy*, p. 59.

[178]Rosenzweig, in Glatzer, *Franz Rosenzweig*, p. 253; cf. Schleiermacher, "On the Different Methods," p. 6; Schiller, *Naive and Sentimental Poetry*, pp. 98-99.

[179]See esp. Glatzer, *Franz Rosenzweig*, pp. 252-54 from "Nachwort," in Franz Rosenzweig, *Jehuda Halevi* (Berlin: Lambert Schneider, 1927), pp. 153-68.

[180]Derrida, *The Ear of the Other*, esp. pp. 119-24. Cf., e.g., the following excerpt (pp. 122-23):

> Translation augments and modifies the original, which insofar as it is living on, never ceases to be transformed and to grow. It modifies the original even as it also modifies the translating language. This process – transforming the original as well as the translation – is the translation contract between the original and the translating text....Benjamin explains that translation reveals in some way the kinship of languages – a kinship that...is of another order....How, then, can translation assure the growth – what he calls the "hallowed growth" – of languages and the kinship among languages? By trying to fulfill that impossible contract to reconstitute, not the original, but the larger ensemble....This impossible possibility [of translation] nevertheless holds out the promise of the reconciliation of tongues. Hence the messianic character of translation.

[181]Cf. Derrida, ibid., pp. 123-24:

> A translation never succeeds in the pure and absolute sense of the term. Rather, a translation succeeds in promising success, in promising reconciliation....A translation puts us not in the presence but in the presentiment of what "pure language" is, that is, the fact that there is language, that language is language...that there is a plurality of languages which have that kinship with each other coming from their being languages.

points out,[182] both denote "bread," but they do not convey that information from the same perspective. The terms of one language interconnect in a unique system, and that system cannot be found in another language.[183] One translates root meanings because each language's gloss of the more abstract arch-word succeeds in covering at least a part of a concept.

The Bible speaks in Hebrew. The sense of Scripture, then, cannot be conveyed faithfully in any other language. Biblical Hebrew forms a system of unique interconnections, and for Rosenzweig, Hebrew itself becomes a medium of special epxressiveness, the language of the holy.[184] (For the idiomatic translators of the American Bible Society, conveniently, Hebrew is an ordinary language, convertible into any other.)[185] The Biblical translator can therefore take two legitimate tacks: to Hebraize the language of translation and to drive readers of the translation to the original.[186] Rosenzweig had seen the ways in which Hebrew had been insinuated into the German language through Luther's translation.[187] English has been forever changed by the Hebraicisms of the Tyndale and King James Version.[188] He determined to ply modern German into expressing itself, in some respects, not as German had but as German could – by speaking Hebraically.[189] By continuing the translation alone in the post-Nazi period Buber knew that he was offering his gift to the language of Germany's cultural past. Indeed, Pope John Paul II praised the Buber-Rosenzweig translation as a great Jewish contribution to German culture.[190]

---

[182]Benjamin, "The Task of the Translator," p. 74; cf. Wittgenstein, in Cyril Barrett, ed., *Wittgenstein: Lectures and Conversations on Aesthetics, Psychology and Religious Belief* (Berkeley: University of California Press, 1972), p. 29.

[183]Schleiermacher, "On the Different Methods," p. 25; cf. Herder's view in Berlin, *Vico and Herder*, pp. 188-89. Note also the view of modern structural linguists; cf., e.g., William G. Doty, "Linguistics and Biblical Criticism," *JAAR* 41 (1973), pp. 114-21.

[184]Cf., e.g., Rosenzweig, *The Star*, pp. 301-2; idem, in Glatzer, *Franz Rosenzweig*, pp. 263-71. Interestingly, what Hebrew is for Rosenzweig is more or less what Greek is for Heidegger; cf. Steiner, *Martin Heidegger*, pp. 19ff., 45ff.

[185]Cf. Nida and Taber, *Theory and Practice*, pp. 6-7. The later formulation by de Waard and Nida, *From One Language to Another*, does acknowledge that each language comprises a unique set of semantic interrelations.

[186]Cf., e.g., Glatzer, "הלשונות והעבריית," p. 233; Stern, "Translating the Ancients," p. 51b. Note that Rosenzweig prefaces the "Nachwort" to his Yehuda Halevi translations with an epigraph from von Stollberg's translation of the Illiad – bidding the reader to learn the original and destroy the translation.

[187]Rosenzweig, *Die Schrift*, pp. 95-96.

[188]Cf. Steiner, "The Book," *Language and Silence*, p. 189; Bruce, *History of the Bible in English*, p. 121; Richard G. Moulton, *The Modern Study of Literature* (Chicago: University of Chicago Press, 1915), pp. 469-70.

[189]Cf. also Hallo, "Notes on Translation," pp. 100*-101*.

[190]"Pope Meets with West German Jews," *New York Times*, Nov. 18, 1980, p. A16.

Rosenzweig knew they could achieve both objectives – Hebraization of German and dependence on the original – at one deft stroke: through a type of literal translation. "The Holy language demands to be understood, word for word."[191] The literalism would mold the German in Hebraic constructions, and the awkwardness of the result would compel serious readers to look into the Hebrew. What was needed was a literalism that would preserve the Hebrew images and idioms, the root meanings of words, the morphology of the words, the cadences, the syntax. No wonder that John Berryman, as we saw above, esteemed literalism and admired Hebrew. In his own poetry he manipulates English in ways that smack of Hebraic construction. As Hebrew builds both nouns and verbs from the same root, so does Berryman, for whom "to child," "to raven," and "to gourmandize" are verbs, and for whom "the hear" is a noun. Note also his supple, quasi-Hebraic syntax: "Six at a time, or so, built he fires under."[192] English learns to speak in the manner of Hebrew.

Buber and Rosenzweig did not simply traduce word for word. To see that their German is not merely a mechanical literalism, one need only compare their renderings with a truly slavish and artless reproduction such as one finds in the Medieval German Jewish translations.[193] Compare on Gen. 37:5:

Hebrew:	ויחלם יוסף חלום
Medieval:	*un' es traumt Josef ein traum.*
B-R:	*Josef traumte einen traum.*
English:	Joseph dreamed a dream.

Or compare on Gen. 27:34:

Hebrew:	...ויצעק צעקה גדלה
Medieval:	*un' er schrei schreiung gross...*
B-R:	*schrie er einen schrei einen übergrossen...*
English:	he cried a great crying...

The Medieval rendering takes no account of producing some sort of sentence in German; Buber and Rosenzweig do.

---

[191]Rosenzweig, in Glatzer, *Franz Rosenzweig*, p. 268. Cf. Benjamin, "The Task of the Translator," p. 82: "The interlinear [i.e., word-for-word] version of the Scriptures is the prototype or ideal of all translation."

[192]Examples from John Berryman, "Cantatrice," in Theodore Solotaroff, ed., *New American Review #3* (New York: New American Library, 1968), p. 105; idem, *Henry's Fate and Other Poems, 1967-1972* (New York: Farrar, Strauss & Giroux, 1977), pp. 26, 64, 21, 64. For a discussion of Berryman's artful use of language, see Muffy E. A. Siegel, "The Original Crime': John Berryman's Iconic Grammar," *Poetics Today* 2/1a (Autumn 1980), pp. 163-88.

[193]The difference is noted by Leibowitz, *Die Überstzungstechnik*, pp. 65-72. The examples are taken from there, pp. 69-70.

But they want German to do that which Hebrew can. Hebrew can burnish an image by repeating a word, so should German. This, for example, is one of the characteristics of Hebrew that Yiddish melded into German.[194] In Yiddish one can say "a going have I gone" (i.e., "I took a walk" – *geyn bin ikh gegangen*) or "a taking he has taken me" (i.e., "he took me" – *nemen hot er mikh genumen*).[195] Hebrew can, as we noted, construct nouns and verbs from the same stem; Buber and Rosenzweig derived nouns from verbs and verbs from nouns in German; e.g., *Braus*, "a rushing," from *brausen*, "to rush"; *Gespross*, "a sprouting," from *spriessen*, "to sprout"; *fruchten*, "to bear fruit," from *Frucht*, "fruit."[196] Hebrew forms verbs by combining stems with affixes; once combined they are indivisible. In idiomatic German many verbs must separate stem from prefix, but Buber and Rosenzweig will have German, like Hebrew, resist such a violation of unity: *ansag* (not *sag...an*) *den Söhnen Jissraels*, "announce to the sons of Israel"; *augstieg* (not *stieg...auf*) *Mosche zu Gott*, "Moses climbed up to God."[197]

To accommodate the nuances or tone of a Hebrew word Buber and Rosenzweig would often search through the history of German for the right gloss, and so their rendering abounds in archaic diction and constructions: *Und Licht war* for *es werde Licht*, "there was light"; *walten* for "to rule"; *zollen*, "to tender to."[198] When the right word wasn't there, they would invent it: *Sonderschatz*, "special treasure" (Hebrew סגולה); *abhegen*, "to fence in" (Heb. הגביל); *steingesteinigen*, "to stone by stone" (Heb. סקל יסקל).[199] They would even concoct unprecedented German idioms and syntax in order to represent Hebrew deployment of word-order and prepositions. Yet, they were also sensitive to tone, to the proper decorum of relating to God. In Exod. 19:9 Buber-Rosenzweig render הגיד with *melden*, "to report," not with *ansagen*, "to announce," as in verse 3. Why this transgression of their commitment to consistency? The solution is certainly that *ansagen* would not do for Moses' announcing to God because it has the connotation of "commanding," and Moses cannot command God. This example shows, too, the impossibilities of translating even following the Buber-Rosenzweig method. As Rosenzweig had

---

[194]On the question of Yiddish influence in Buber-Rosenzweig's German translation, see Hallo, "Notes on Translation," p. 100*.

[195]Thanks to my informant, David Roskies. John Milton adapted this Hebraic feature in his "Biblical" poem, "Samson Agonistes":

> Dagon,...their god who hath delivered
> Thee, Samson, bound and blind into their [the Philistines'] hands –
> Them out of thine, who *slew'st* them many a *slain* (lines 437-39).

[196]Examples from the Buber-Rosenzweig rendering of Genesis 1 in *Die Schrift* (Berlin: Lambert Schneider, 1926-).

[197]Examples from ibid., on Exodus 19.

[198]Examples from ibid., on Genesis 1 and Psalm 29.

[199]Examples from ibid., on Exodus 19.

written, "Only one who is profoundly convinced of the impossibility of translation can really undertake it."[200]

Since, in this view, translation is a mirage, the transfer of the Bible to another language must serve as no more than an aid to hearing the Biblical text. The Buber-Rosenzweig theory of translation produces language that can be read only with effort – like all great literature and the Bible itself. Walter Benjamin reportedly disliked the Buber-Rosenzweig rendering,[201] recoiling perhaps at its foreignness. But after all, Buber and Rosenzweig had put into effect that which Benjamin, too, had philosophized. It may be that, as Rosenzweig said in another connection, "when one hears one's own ideas uttered by someone else, they suddenly become problematic."[202] True, it is hard to imagine an audience bent on utilizing an unidiomatic rendering such as the Buber-Rosenzweig. Yet, such a style of translation may be especially well suited for those who approach the Bible as holy. When a translation sounds like a translation it constantly reminds one that the translation is but a mask of the sacred text that lies behind it. To read a good rendition in the Buber-Rosenzweig mode is somewhat like Moses standing barefoot before the Burning Bush, perceiving that something other dwells behind the façade. Most people would feel more comfortable in sandals, so to speak, sparing themselves the irritation of the hot sand and rock. But religion requires a shedding of the sandals – of contemporary idiom – to experience the sacred – (in this case) the Hebraic. For Buber and Rosenzweig the Germanizing of the Bible was a spiritual act, peeling away a layer of German idiom so that the faint voice of the Hebrew could become more audible.

---

[200]Cited in Hallo, loc. cit.
[201]G. Scholem, "Walter Benjamin," *On Jews and Judaism*, pp. 193-94.
[202]Rosenzweig, in Glatzer, *Franz Rosenzweig*, p. 242.

Chapter Six

The Job of Translating Job

It is difficult to imagine a more formidable task of translating than that of restating the Hebrew text of Job in other words. The Book of Job is in essence an outpouring of words, words whose power reaches far beyond argument with rhetorical and emotive force. The power is in the words themselves. The Book of Job calls attention to its medium, first, by describing the act of speech in concrete, physical language: "Job committed no error with his *lips*" (2:10); "Job opened his *mouth* and cursed his (birth)day" (3:1); "Is there any distortion on my *tongue?* Can't my *palate* detect vile speech?" (6:30). Second, Job's initial outcry seems all the louder for having shattered a silence kept for seven days, during which "none spoke a word to him" (2:13). Third, each of Job's interlocutors begins his response by specifically referring to words – words of Job that cannot go unanswered, words of their own that cannot be held back (4:2; 8:2; 11:2). Fourth, the first charge that is levelled against Job, by Eliphaz, is that Job had misspoken, and it is this charge that Job counters forthwith, at the end of chapter 6 and elsewhere. Indeed, he accuses his companions of uttering deceit (e.g., 13:4). Job's speech had always been ingenuous, and the Lord tells as much to the companions at the end of the book (42:7).

Stories can to some degree be retold in different words; they can occasionally be transferred to another medium with success. Words, sheer rhetoric, cannot be adequately replaced. Rhetoric mobilizes all the affective aspects of language – sound, rhythm, metaphor, connotation, association – in order to move an audience further than the reasoning embedded in the semantic content can by itself achieve. Yet, it is notoriously these affective aspects of language that pose special problems for the translator.

The authors of the two Job translations I shall discuss[1] show keen awareness of the limitations that their enterprise has by its nature imposed upon

---

[1]*The Book of Job. A New Translation According to the Traditional Hebrew Text*, with introductions by Moshe Greenberg, Jonas C. Greenfield, and Nahum M. Sarna (Philadelphia: The Jewish Publication Society of America, 1980); the translation alone has been incorporated into the Jewish Publication Society's *Tanakh* (1985).

Stephen Mitchell, *Into the Whirlwind. A Translation of the Book of Job* (Garden City, NY: Doubleday, 1979); revised with an introduction as *The Book of Job* (San Francisco: North Point Press, 1987).

them. The New Jewish Version (NJV) translators have expressly committed themselves to rendering the Hebrew of Job in "modern literary English." In doing so, they wittingly abandon any attempt to imitate the peculiar linguistic constructions of the Hebrew in a sort of Hebraicized English, like what Buber and Rosenzweig had done in German.[2] Stephen Mitchell shares this posture, but in sacrificing a number of stylistic elements of the Hebrew, he seeks to preserve two: the rhythm of the lines and their imagery.

Although it is generally considered unfashionable to compose a translation that sounds like a translation, such a version may assume a more authentic tone than an idiomatic rendering.[3] Consider the unfulfilled project of the late American lyric poet John Berryman. In a letter to Saul Bellow Berryman revealed that around 1947 he came to the realization that he "was the man born to translate [the Book of Job] into English verse."[4] Berryman's translation of Job 3-5 was published posthumously in *Poetry* magazine.[5] In theory at least, he advocated a more literal style of translation, one which would as a result be "simpler & more lucid & truer."[6] He studied some Hebrew and produced some lines of Job that command great interest. In certain verses his rendering evinces a clear Hebraic sound: "I fear a fear: it comes. That which I dread comes to me" (3:25); "you stiffened the folding knees" (4:4b); "Lo, happy a man whom God corrects, who Shaddai's training takes; For first He hurts, then heals; wounds, and His hands make whole" (5:17-18).

To their credit, the NJV committee has also paid heed to certain affective aspects of Job's language. They imitate the wordplay in 6:21a with "At the *sight* of misfortune, you take *fright*." They convey the repetition of ...פנו...פנו in 6:28 with "Now be so good as to *face* me; I will not lie to your *face*."

On the whole, the NJV characteristically hews much more closely to the semantics of the Hebrew than the somewhat more poetic versions of Berryman and Mitchell – who is himself a poet and an experienced translator of poetry. Mitchell seeks to duplicate what he judges to be the impact of the original rather than the words *per se*. An example is at 3:3, where the NJV translates "Perish the day on which I was born," but which Mitchell renders "God damn the day I was born." One can argue over whether a translation that replaces the semantics of the *Vorlage* with a somewhat different, yet equally forceful, wording is truly faithful. In fact, when one considers the liberties that both Berryman and Mitchell have taken when they alter, supplant, and add to the images within the Hebrew, one may wonder whether it is possible to translate the poem of Job as a

---

[2]For references and discussion, see Chapter Five.
[3]See further, Chapter Seven.
[4]John Haffenden, "Job, by John Berryman," *Poetry* 136/1 (April 1980), p. 39.
[5]John Berryman, "From Job," *Poetry* 136/1 (April 1980), pp. 35-38. Thanks to Miles Bellamy for bringing this to my notice.
[6]See note 4. Berryman's "Hebraic" style is discussed above, in Chapter Five.

poem at all without departing from the Hebrew time and again.[7] Nevertheless, there are many instances in which Mitchell's rendering both hits the mark semantically and delivers the punch of the Hebrew: "Have you lost all faith in your piety; all hope in your perfect conduct?" (4:6); "For pain doesn't spring from the dust, or sorrow sprout from the soil" (5:6).[8]

Mitchell may not possess the philological experience of Professors Moshe Greenberg, Jonas Greenfield, and Nahum Sarna of the NJV committee, but he has taken his philological task no less seriously. He constantly compares the ancient versions and has steeped himself in the critical commentaries. He has devoted almost a quarter of his pages to philological notes, explaining where he reads the Hebrew differently from the Massoretic Text and why he often interprets in a novel way. In an "Afterword"[9] Mitchell openly discusses the textual difficulties in dealing with Job. When one regards such chapters as the truncated speech of Bildad (25) and the unmoored paean to wisdom (28), not to mention the verse-by-verse problems that pervade the book, one can hardly help but acknowledge that the text of Job had at some point suffered physical damage and is by no means intact. As S. D. Luzzatto indicated programmatically over a century ago, even under the best of circumstances a Biblical exegete must take a critical attitude toward the received text. The NJV, in its various introductions, on the one hand articulates its awareness of the difficulties one finds in "what is preserved in the text" (p. xiv) and yet binds its hands from ever emending it (p. vii), adhering strictly to the Massorah. Many will question the authenticity of the NJV when it renders gibberish written in Hebrew characters into comprehensible English.

Mitchell's solution may appear radical to some, but it bespeaks his concern for authenticity. Where the text seems impossible or seems to consist in a secondary glossation or interpolation, he omits these passages from his translation, advising the reader to consult his list of "verses deleted or omitted" (p. 140).[10] For the most part, however, Mitchell accepts the received text and adopts only small changes in its vocalization and letters. A fortuitous instance is at 4:3, where Mitchell follows N. H. Tur-Sinai and others by reading רְבִים, literally "trembling," for MT's רַבִּים, "many," and translating: "Once you encouraged the timid," which forms an apt parallel to "and filled the frightened with strength."

---

[7]Cf. the criticism of Mitchell's revised edition by Edwin M. Good, "Stephen Mitchell's Job: A Critique," *The World & I*, December 1987, pp. 368-74.

[8]The NJV erroneously renders אוֶן here and in 4:8 as "evil" rather than "misfortune." Mitchell learns from the context here but mistranslates in 4:8. Cf. Ps. 90:10.

[9]In the revised version, it is labelled "A Note on the Text." Mitchell's reconstruction has been criticized by Good, "Stephen Mitchell's Job," and by James L. Crenshaw, "The High Cost of Preserving God's Honor," *The World & I*, December 1987, pp. 375-82, esp. 381-82.

[10]Page 131 in the revised version.

As we would expect, the NJV can be counted on more for philological precision. Thus, in interpreting 3:8, a verse in which Job invokes the demons of Canaanite mythology to exorcise the day of his birth, Mitchell veers widely from the Hebrew when he renders:

> Let Sorcerers make the Serpent
>   to blast it with eternal blight.

The NJV, stretching its strict text-critical parameters to the limit, supplies a footnote according to which we may read ם for ם and render:

> May those who cast spells upon the sea damn it,
>   Those prepared to disable Leviathan.

As Greenfield indicates in his introduction, the NJV takes cognizance of the Canaanite "mythological background of such imagery as the battle with the sea (26:12-13)..." (p. xvi). But the NJV's textual conservatism prevents them from exploiting their sophistication to advantage.[11] A growing number of Biblicists[12] follow Tur-Sinai in slightly redividing and repointing the words of 26:13a in order to produce a line that both makes sense contextually and finds substantial comparative support from ancient Near Eastern parallels, most notably Enuma Elish Tablet IV. Reading בְּרוּחוֹ שָׂם יָם שְׂפָרֹה, "With his wind He put Sea into His net," is, it seems to me, preferable to rendering "By His wind the heavens were calmed" (so NJV), which satisfies neither context nor grammar.

Translations of a text so nettlesome as that of Job will never please the philologian, who will readily find additional difficulties and alternate proposals. Only someone who has seriously grappled with the Hebrew text of Job can properly appreciate the enormity of the challenge. In the end, even the most careful philology may arrive at an ambiguous interpretation. At that point the committed Job student must examine the alternatives, deliberate, and choose, albeit tentatively. Let me raise one final example. The NJV renders 5:26 as follows:

> You will come to the grave in ripe old age,
>   As shocks of grain are taken away in their season.

---

[11]Implicit in this comment is that while this NJV committee and I share the two principles of respecting the given text and reading the Biblical text within a larger Canaanite (and ancient Near Eastern) context, the committee may, in an instance like this, where the two principles may conflict, lean more heavily on the former principle than I might.

[12]Cf., e.g., Marvin H. Pope, *Job*, AB 15, 3rd ed. (Garden City, NY: Doubleday, 1973), p. 181; Michael Fishbane, *Text and Texture* (New York: Schocken, 1979), p. 14; and see my "The Snaring of Sea in the Baal Epic," *Maarav* 3 (1982), pp. 195-216.

Perhaps the intended meaning is, with the NJV, that the pious will grow old and not be harvested by the Grim Reaper before their time. On the other hand, recalling that the Torah admires Moses because he died not only old but in full possession of his faculties (Deut. 34:7), the translation of Mitchell (and Berryman, too)[13] may be more to the point:

> You will die at the height of your powers
>   and be gathered like ripened grain.

---

[13]Berryman: "You shall die unimpaired, & old, as a shock of corn in its season."

Chapter Seven

Assessing a Bible Translation

The act of translating from one language to another may comprise a skill, it may reflect an art. The translator may work within a well-designed method or operate intuitively.[1] But behind the act of translation lie a number of difficult theoretical questions, each of which bears upon our understanding of the translational enterprise and its evaluation.

Translation is a problem because, among other reasons, people hold opposing views on the question of whether translation is truly possible. Can, in the words of Eugene Nida and Charles Taber, mentors of the American Bible Society translations, "anything that can be said in one language...be said in another...?"[2] Can a particular meaning be expressed in virtually any language, or, at the very least, a number of diverse languages? Some say yes, some say no. But before proceeding to discuss that question it is important to note that our answer colors our understanding of the very term "translation." Nearly everyone uses the word "translation" in its descriptive sense. "Translation" is widely employed to refer to a text that is purported to represent a text written in another language. Numerous translations – so called – exist so that no one questions the reality of translation in this sense of the term.

If, however, one wishes to speak of translation as a reproduction of the meaning of one text in another text written in a different language, one plunges into the battle zone, the arena of debate. The strongest version of the belief in

---

[1]For an engaging and insightful analysis of a practicing translator's work, see Robert Bly, "The Eight Stages of Translation," in William Frawley, ed., *Translation: Literary, Linguistic, and Philosophical Perspectives* (London: Associated University Presses, 1984), pp. 67-89. Bly's approach is clearly audience-oriented, in the sense I described in Chapter Five. Nevertheless, he pays acute attention to the more formal elements of poetry. In the end he observes: "We know that we have not captured the original; the best translation resembles a Persian rug seen from the back – the pattern is apparent, but not much more" (p. 89). For a highly useful and richly illustrated analysis of what an idiomatic translator does in linguistic terms, see Joseph L. Malone, *The Science of Linguistics in the Art of Translation* (Albany: State University of New York Press, 1988).

[2]See Chapter Five, n. 120.

translation contends that the entire meaning of a text can be conveyed in another language. It views the ideal of translation as attainable. Few take so strong a position. More typical is, for example, the approach of William Smalley. On the one hand, he states that one can "writ[e] the same thing in a different way."[3] On the other, he acknowledges that "because translation is not a surface phenomenon" – i.e., it operates on the level of deep structure – "it follows that linguistic devices such as puns and plays on words which depend heavily on surface similarities are not usually translatable."[4] In this compromised sense, many understand that the term "translation" refers to something that is ontologically real. Translation – of the essential – is possible. For anyone who challenges the possibility of real translation, however, the term "translation" must carry a tinge of cynicism and suspicion. Translation in such a view will never replicate the source; it will necessarily distort.

Philologists and translators often give the impression that translation across languages is possible by posing their questions onomasiologically – by asking, "How does one say *x* in a given language?" That manner of posing the question presupposes that the concept *x* already exists in that particular language. Rather than admitting that *x* is not represented precisely in the language, one looks for (and finds) an "equivalent." We shall examine a case in point below, but let me suggest an illustration briefly here. In Chapter Five we noted that Harry Orlinsky (and others) maintain that Hebrew אִישׁ can be used to refer to a person regardless of gender. That claim proceeds onomasiologically. It asks, "How does one say 'person' in Biblical Hebrew?" – assuming that there must be a way to say it. But if one were to begin at the other end and ask, semasiologically, "What does אִישׁ mean?" one might find that אִישׁ refers in all contexts to a man. The Hebrew Bible may, historically speaking, simply not have had the concept of a genderless person. It is true that אִישׁ may be used to represent all people, but it is significant anthropologically that only a word for "man" could stand for the species.[5]

The argument about the possibility of translation hovers above an even more fundamental problem, the question of the extent to which a language – any language – can convey one's thoughts and feelings. Many follow Nietzsche in holding that language cannot itself translate what we really think and feel.[6] The novelist Italo Calvino, for example, writes "I do not believe totality can be

---

[3]William A. Smalley, "Restructuring Translations of the Psalms," in *On Language, Culture, and Religion: In Honor of Eugene A. Nida,* ed. Matthew Black and W. A. Smalley (The Hague: Mouton, 1974), p. 340.
[4]Ibid., p. 356.
[5]Cf., e.g., de Waard and Nida, *From One Language to Another* (above, Chapter Five, n. 16), p. 24.
[6]For references, see Chapter Five, n. 110.

contained in language."[7] "Beneath every word there is nothingness."[8] Or consider this excerpt from a novel satirizing philosophy:

> There is a level of thought where words have no part to play. Words are made for a certain exactness of thought, as tears are for a certain degree of pain. What is least distinct cannot be named; what is clearest is unutterable.[9]

Language cannot express vague thoughts, only precise ones. Some would say that that is because precise thoughts are nothing but the products of language. In Derrida's writing, language is always prior to thought.[10] It makes sense, then, in Derrida's thought, that signifiers (the expressive aspect of the sign) and signifieds (the referential aspect of the sign) must always be out of sync. At the very basis of meaning, translation must operate: "translation practices the difference between signified and signifier."[11] When, however, translation from language to language is considered, the transformation is much more substantial – "for the notion of translation we would have to substitute the notion of *transformation:* a regulated transformation of one language by another, of one text by another."[12]

In any case, if one must needs fall short of translating ideas and sensations into linguistic expression, one can hardly expect someone to translate fully across languages. Each language, in this view, grasps only fragments of what is felt and conceived. Another language may capture different fragments of that perceived reality. Recall the linguistic philosophies of Benjamin and Rosenzweig, discussed above in Chapter Five, for example. If different languages do not align in their representations of reality, even in trying to say the same thing they will say something different.

The writer Anthony Burgess, in an essay entitled "Is Translation Possible?", explains that the translator must seek to render the entire world-view of the culture in which the source-text originates.[13] This, he claims on the basis of his own trials, is unachievable. In light of the philosophy that finds language to be

---

[7] Italo Calvino, *If on a Winter's Night a Traveler,* trans. William Weaver (New York: Harcourt Brace Jovanovich, 1981), p. 181.

[8] Ibid., p. 83. Cf. Hayyim Nahman Bialik, "The Explicit and the Allusive in Language," trans. and annotated Avraham Holtz, in *Literature East and West* 15 (1973), pp. 498-508.

[9] René Daumal, *A Night of Serious Drinking,* trans. David Coward and E. A. Lovatt (Boston: Shambala, 1979), p. 1.

[10] Cf., e.g., Jacques Derrida, "Speech and Phenomena," *Speech and Phenomena and Other Essays on Husserl's Theory of Signs,* trans. David B. Allison (Evanston: Northwestern University Press, 1973), esp. Chap. 6 (pp. 70-83).

[11] Derrida, *Positions,* trans. Alan Bass (Chicago: University of Chicago Press, 1981), p. 20.

[12] Loc. cit.

[13] Anthony Burgess, "Is Translation Possible?" *Translation* 12 (Spring 1984), pp. 3-7.

only an imperfect instrument for communicating experience, the reason for Burgess' chagrin is clear. One cannot translate a world-view that has not been entirely comprehended within the native language of those possessing that world-view! Each language is developed among its speakers as a particular formulation of a particular world-view. As Jerome said – in defense of idiomatic translation – "Every word has its own meaning."[14] Every language has been developed to express a somewhat different, perhaps even grossly different, way of seeing and thinking. To translate sufficiently well, one would not only need to enter the world of the speakers of the source language; one would have to share language with others who spoke that language and possessed the world-view to which that language gives expression. One would have to translate, that is, for those who have no need of translation.

We can get beyond this paradox by conceding that even under the very best of circumstances translation does not convey everything that the source can mean. Translation is always selective. Even the most spirited advocates of translation acknowledge that in traducing from language to language one must leave something behind. Jerome, who in general promoted the style of translation that renders sense for sense rather than word for word, wrote of the "omissions, additions, and alterations" that a translator must make in "substituting the idioms of his own for those of another tongue."[15] The great Russian writer and translator Kornei Chukovsky praised the art of translation perhaps beyond anyone else. Yet, he was fully aware of its constraints. Not only did he recognize that "not even the semantics of words in Russian and other languages coincide," he discussed the "impossibility of conveying the musical form of poetry from one language to another."[16]

Nida and Taber must also concede that translation encounters limitations. When they say, "Anything than can be said in one language can be said in another," they add: "unless the form is an essential element of the meaning."[17] How essential style is to the meaning of discourse can be debated in every case. But their "unless"-clause indicates what is a perpetual latent obstruction in transferring sense from language to language. Where form or style affects meaning in a crucial way, translation must reach an impasse. For those, like the many artists and poets who regard form as an ineluctable part of their expression, all translation of literature must fail. Unless, that is, one is willing to accept translation as at best an approximation – or, in Derrida's term, a transformation – of sense rather than a reproduction of it.

---

[14]Jerome, "Preface to the Chronicle of Eusebius," in Jean Steinman, *St. Jerome and His Times,* trans. Ronald Matthews (Notre Dame: Fides, 1959), p. 95.

[15]Jerome, "Letter LVII," *The Principal Works of St. Jerome,* ed. W. H. Freemantle (1892), p. 114a.

[16]Kornei Chukovsky, *The Art of Translation [A High Art],* trans. and ed. Lauren G. Leighton (Knoxville: University of Tennessee Press, 1984), pp. 55, 150.

[17]See above, n. 2.

In fact, virtually all sophisticated translators have since ancient times distinguished between what of the source they seek to traduce and what they are resigned to dismiss. Each translation sets goals. These goals are in turn determined by the function(s) that the translation is meant to serve. In assessing the degree of a translation's success, one ought, it follows, to measure the translation's achievement against its avowed goals and functions.[18] One may dissent from the goals of a certain translation style or a particular translation effort; one may oppose a translation's function. But that is a political decision that is very different from evaluating the translation in its own terms.

In Chapter Five, I described the various types of Bible translation with respect both to their goals and functions, as well as their philosophical foundations. A shifting set of distinctions was drawn between the idiomatic and the literal, the philological and the literary, the evangelical and the source-oriented, the audience-oriented and the author-oriented. The different translation modes seek to accomplish different goals. In doing so they target for themselves different aspects of the source to reproduce in translation. An idiomatic translator attempts to bring the world reflected in the source text to the intended audience in its own idiom. There are a number of reasons for adopting this approach. One is that an unidiomatic rendering may lack the precision in conveying information that a translator wishes to achieve.

Let us take, for example, the Hebrew idiom כעת חיה in Gen. 18:10 and elsewhere. The literal sense is something like "at the time living," but the comparable expression in Gen. 17:21 and the Akkadian idioms *ana/adi/ina balāṭ* suggest the meaning "this time next year." The more literalist King James Version renders, "I will certainly return unto thee according to the time of life." In a similar vein, Fox offers: "I will return, yes, return to you when time revives."[19] Without the textual commentary Fox provides, a reader would have no idea of the precise intention of the Hebrew.[20] The New American Bible and the New International Version give an accurate English equivalent: "I will surely return to you about this time next year." The gist comes across clearly.[21] As a source of Jerome's had said, "A literal translation from one language into another

---

[18]Cf., e.g., Keith R. Crim, Review of the NJV's *The Prophets-Nevi'im, JBL* 99 (1980), p. 605. Crim, however, makes clear that he approves the NJV because it "abandon[s] misleading literalism for the appropriate English expression" (p. 606).

[19]Fox, *In the Beginning* (Chapter Five, n. 127), p. 66 with comment on p. 67.

[20]This is in keeping with the later formulation of Nida's approach in de Waard and Nida, *From One Language to Another*, pp. 154-58, in which literal translation of figurative expressions may be supplemented with marginal notes to facilitate transcultural intelligibility.

[21]Other recent translations, such as the Revised Standard Version, the New Jewish Version, and Today's English Version offer clear, but in my view incorrect, renderings, assuming that the phrase refers to a nine-month period of pregnancy.

obscures the sense."[22] An idiomatic rendering has the advantage of intelligibility.

Before proceeding to some of the other reasons behind idiomatic translation, let us take stock of what has been lost in choosing the idiomatic style here. A Hebrew idiom has been rendered by a prosaic phrase in English. Moreover, Gen. 17:21 employs the Hebrew expression למועד הזה בשנה אחרת. The New International Version translates, "by this time next year," nearly the same words it used to render the radically different idiom in Gen. 18:10. Fox, on the other hand, far more accurately reproduces the difference in style when he renders: "at this set-time, another year hence." The different translation modes each convey some aspect of the source while at the same time losing some other quality.

Idiomatic translation – or, more specifically, translating an idiom of one language by a native idiom in another language – tends to dull the actual meaning of the original by relating to only one of its usages and accommodating it to an imprecise gloss in the language of translation. Let us consider the following example of de Waard and Nida's.[23] They try to justify replacing the Biblical expression "to harden the heart" by a different, "dynamically equivalent" locution in an African language:

> In the Fulani language of Africa the biblical idiom "hardening the heart" can only be understood correctly when translated as "hardening the head." A literal translation of the Hebrew expression also makes sense, but it is the wrong sense, for in Fulani "to harden the heart" means "to be courageous"....

One cannot but sympathize with de Waard and Nida's concern that a literal rendering would obstruct comprehension. However, by seeking out a "dynamic equivalent" they fail to probe the full and precise meaning of Hebrew חזק לב. In certain contexts, the best known of which is the story of the pharaoh in Exodus, "to be hard of heart" does mean something like "to be obstinate." But, in fact, "to be hard of heart" can in other contexts mean exactly what de Waard and Nida say it means in Fulani: "to be courageous." Compare, for example, Ps. 27:14: חזק ויאמץ לבך, "Be strong and may your heart be firm," i.e., "be courageous" (cf. also Ps. 31:25). In light of the full expression חזק לב, "to strengthen the heart," i.e., "to give courage" in Josh. 11:20 and the numerous conjunctions of חזק and אמץ in such passages as Deut. 31:6, 7, 23; Josh. 1:6, 7, 9, 18; 10:25; etc., the usage of חזק to indicate courage is in all likelihood an ellipsis of חזק לב.[24] Hebrew "to be hard of heart," then means neither precisely "to be obstinate" nor

---

[22]Jerome, "Letter LVII," p. 114b.

[23]De Waard and Nida, *From One Language to Another*, p. 34.

[24]Some instances of חזק in the sense of "courageous" may result from an ellipsis of חזק יד, "to be strong of hand"; cf., e.g., Judg. 7:11; 9:24; 2 Sam. 2:7; Jer. 23:14; Ezek. 22:14; Zech. 8:9, 13. For analysis of ellipsis of body idioms in Semitic, cf. my "Trans-Semitic Idiomatic Equivalency and the Derivation of Hebrew *ml'kh*," *UF* 11 (1979), pp. 329-36.

"to be courageous," but rather something more general like "to be single-minded" or "resolute" toward one end or another. Only context governs its interpretation.

A second rationale for translating idiomatically is that the language of the traduction would then be as smooth and pure as the language of the source. Literal rendering must occasionally, if not frequently, warp the language of the translation. As Jerome wrote, quoting from another tract: "If I render word for word, the result will sound uncouth."[25] There is more than the translator's ego at stake here. For the idiomatic Bible translator, if the source makes sense, so should the translation. Chukovsky stresses a further dimension: art must be transmitted, even in another language, as art.[26] A poem in Hebrew should appear as a poem in the translation. This principle has explicitly guided the idiomatic Bible translators of the New Jewish Version, the American Bible Society, and such individuals as Marcia Falk, who rendered the Song of Songs into American poetry.[27] Yet, in heeding Jerome's caution one should not fail to take note of the other side: "a proper translation has always had to do some violence either to [the translation language], or to the language translated."[28]

Adherents of the idiomatic approach all too often denigrate the literal mode as though it were wrong-headed and mindlessly mechanical. If the translation sounds awkward, difficult, or obscure – because it follows the word order of the source and attempts to reproduce its idioms – many would condemn it. Chukovsky said that such a literalist rendering is "based on a fallacious theory."[29] One cannot help feeling that the critical move of deploring literal styles of translation as falsely conceived fails to distinguish between the goals of translation and the procedures of executing a translation. It is unproductive to criticize a method of translation for failing to attain goals that it does not espouse.

Literal modes of translation, as far as I can tell, have nearly always set different objectives from those of the idiomatic school. Ancient literalistic traducers sought to render each and every term of the source because they believed that the text's meaning inhered not only in the general sense and rhetorical impact of the language but in the atomic components, as it were, of the source text. Classical midrash drew significance out of configurations of words and letters, so that the translator would feel obliged to transfer the very shape of the language and not only its predigested message.[30] The King James translators in

---

[25]Jerome, "Letter LVII," p. 114b.
[26]Chukovsky, *A High Art*, p. 18 and passim.
[27]See above, Chapter Five.
[28]Paul Feyerabend, *Against Method* (London: Verso, 1978), p. 273, n. 130.
[29]Chukovsky, *A High Art*, p. 50.
[30]This iconic view of the scriptural text derives from the belief that even the wording originates in God. It is not, as Wendland asserts, "an attitude of idolatry" in which the text becomes an "object of worship"! Since Wendland adds that in

many ways admired the style of the Hebrew source and its classic rendering in Latin and in part modelled their own language after that of the Bible. Buber and Rosenzweig, in their literalistic "Germanization" of the Hebrew Bible,[31] wished to accomplish a variety of goals. Here, I shall dwell on only two of them.

One is literary. It is abundantly clear from the essays of Rosenzweig and especially Buber that they intended to convey in German literary features of the Hebrew source that they regarded as significant for interpreting the Biblical text. In recurring words and phrases they found literary allusions and connections, leading to interpretations made on the basis of narrative analogy. In repeating words they found the suggestion of key ideas and themes. For the interpreter who, with Buber and Rosenzweig, considers such literary properties crucial to a text's meaning, only a more literalistic rendering provides the data that are requisite for proper analysis. Even more: an idiomatic translation tends to suppress such data and in so doing may in fact convey meaning that is seriously at odds with the meaning that a more literal rendering might communicate.

In order to illustrate and substantiate my claims I shall contrast two modern translations of the Creation story in Gen. 1:1-2:4a into English, translations representing the two poles of highly idiomatic and fairly literal renderings. These are Today's English Version (TEV), produced by the American Bible Society in 1976 for non-native speakers of English, and the first version of Everett Fox's translation, published in 1972.[32] I use the earlier Fox version because it hews more closely to the (revised) Buber-Rosenzweig German translation (of 1930).

One of the most striking features of the TEV, and one in which it follows the 1926 translation by James Moffatt, is that it renders Hebrew שמים וארץ not as "heaven and earth" but as "the universe."[33] Their choice of terms is informed by their expectation that an English audience will respond to the word "universe" the way ancient Israelites would respond to the phrase "heaven and earth." In this example we may observe the contrast between the idiomatic and more literal approaches in focus. The idiomatic traducer calculates that what the ancients referred to by the dyad "heaven and earth" is expressed for today's English-speaking audience as "the universe."[34] This would be correct were the ancients referring to something that we identify by the term "universe" – a representation of a system of that which exists in which the elements of matter, energy, space,

---

Judaism's alleged literalization of the divine "Word" "its meaning was lost in the process" – citing Matthew 15:6-9 – this is nothing but an ignorant put-down of Judaism, scandalous only because it is published by the United Bible Societies and prefaced by Eugene Nida. See Ernst R. Wendland, *The Cultural Factor in Bible Translation* (London: United Bible Societies, 1987), p. 12.

[31]See Chapter Five.

[32]Fox, *In the Beginning* = *Response* 14 (Summer 1972).

[33]Cf., e.g., de Waard and Nida, *From One Language to Another*, p. 128.

[34]Cf. Harry M. Orlinsky, "The Plain Meaning of Genesis 1:1-3," *BA* 46/4 (December 1983), p. 208b.

and time are interactive and interdependent. But from an anthropological perspective, one could contend that the ancients had no such idea. They were not at all referring to what we mean by "universe." The modern's error results from an onomasiological approach to the problem, i.e., by asking "How did they say 'universe'?" rather than by asking "What does שמים וארץ mean?"

The ancients saw their world as two large geographical spaces above which and under which was water and within which species of vegetable and animal life lived. English seems not to have a common term for this conception of the world – not even the word "world." The translation "heaven and earth" represents the world as the ancients saw it more accurately than the term "universe." What led the idiomatic TEV translators to employ the modern word, however, appears to be more than the search for a modern equivalent.

The underlying assumption seems to have been that both Genesis and the translation of it are looking at more or less the same objective world. But if one understands that texts construct the world as those who speak the text's language imagine the world to be, then the Bible and the modern translation in fact present different conceptions. To transform the phrase "heaven and earth" to "universe" is not, then, simply to provide a contemporary equivalent; it is to supplant one world-view with a very different one. The superidiomatic TEV translation is not merely speaking today's English. It is teaching today's physics. The preface to the TEV denies this is its goal; it says rather: "Faithfulness in translation also includes a faithful representation of the cultural and historical features of the original, without any attempt to modernize."[35] In this instance, and, we shall see, in others, too, it would appear to be at odds with its goal.[36]

From a literary perspective the introduction of the dyad "heaven and earth" establishes two distinct areas to be created. The narrative devotes separate events on separate days to their creation. To collapse this distinction at the outset by converting "heaven and earth" into "universe" does more than remove a stylistic touch. It disturbs the literary order of the narrative, which duplicates in form, as

---

[35]*Good News Bible,* "Preface" (no pagination).

[36]De Waard and Nida, *From One Language to Another,* show a sophisticated concern for the complex process of finding functional equivalents for Biblical ideas and imagery in the culture for which the translation is made; Wendland, *The Cultural Factor,* is almost entirely devoted to this problem. De Waard and Nida would seem to violate their own principles when it comes to images that are conventional in the church. They write, for example: "Expressions such as 'Lamb of God', 'cross', and 'sacrifice' need to be preserved, but often with explanatory marginal notes. Readers may not be acquainted with execution by crucifixion, but this would not justify substituting 'lynching' or 'beheading', nor can one justify the use of 'little pig of God' rather than 'Lamb of God' merely because in the case of some peoples of Melanesia, pigs are highly praised and sheep are either unknown or despised" (*From One Language to Another,* p. 38). In this instance, the evangelical Christian interests of the American Bible Society supersede their arguments for "dynamic equivalent" translation.

it were, the orderliness of the described creation.[37] On the second day of creation, the narrative has God say, in Fox's words:

> Be there a vault in the midst of the waters,
> and be there division between waters and waters!

The repetition of the word "water" (מים), marking out water above from water below, shows what it tells – there is "water" here and there is "water" there. Although there does not seem to be anything unidiomatic about repeating the word "water," the TEV follows the lead of Moffatt in eliminating the repetition. It renders:

> Let there be a dome to divide the water and to keep it in two separate places.

By translating this way the TEV does not convey the fact that God has not yet created the idea of *place*. It is the act of dividing water from water that establishes the notion of space and place. Just as there was no time prior to God's division of the darkness by periods of light, there was no place until God separated water from water. To say that the dome will "divide the water and...keep it in two separate places" assumes a concept that has not yet been introduced. It is only on the third day that God had the water below the dome "blocked-up" – to use Fox's gloss – "in one place." The internal logic of the creation of order in Gen. 1:1-2:4a can be read in the very wording of the text. From a literary point of view, the TEV translation neglects the sequential construction of the created order and reads retrospectively by presupposing at the beginning what was first presented later.[38] The literary interpreter as well as the anthropologist might well argue that the idiomatic rendering of the TEV by belittling style fails to make sufficient sense of the passage.

On the fourth day of creation God commands that there be, in Fox's translation, "luminaries in the vault of the heavens." God makes two luminaries –

> the greater luminary for rule of the day and the smaller luminary for
>   rule of the night,
> and the stars.

The TEV seeks to render the references to the two luminaries in language that its audience would use. Accordingly, it translates "the greater luminary" by the term "the sun" and "the smaller luminary" by the term "the moon." One wonders whether the TEV translators asked themselves whether the text means something

---

[37]Cf., e.g., Michael Fishbane, *Text and Texture* (New York: Schocken, 1979), pp. 3-16.

[38]On the fallacy of retrospective reading, see now Mieke Bal, *Lethal Love: Feminist Literary Readings of Biblical Love Stories* (Bloomington: Indiana University Press, 1987), p. 108 and passim.

very different by saying "sun" and "moon" rather than "greater" and "smaller luminary." As I read it, it does.

For one thing, the narrative pattern of dividing water from water and continuing to render the two now-separate bodies of water as "water" and nothing more specific is reproduced in the creation of luminaries. The two most distinct luminaries are distinguished in this narrative by their size alone. The two luminaries are set off from the collectivity of "stars". God did not distinguish water from water by the assignation of names. (In v. 10 God names the water that was pulled back from the land "seas" [ימים].) Nor did God, in the Hebrew source, name the two distinctive luminaries other than to place one over day-time and the other over night-time. The significance of these luminaries is not in those things for which we typically appreciate the sun and moon. We enjoy the heat of the sun and the light of both the sun and moon. Genesis 1 stresses a different function: to indicate periods of time, including the specific occasions – מועדים – which the TEV elaborately but correctly glosses as "religious festivals." The observance of sacred time is an evident concern of this narrative, which caps off creation with God's blessing and hallowing of the Sabbath. By naming the sun and moon, the TEV elicits in its audience the various associations that "sun" and "moon" connote. By avoiding these names for the luminaries the Hebrew source suppresses such associations.

We may understand the suppression of the names "sun" and "moon" in the text to serve another function, too. The ancient Semitic terms for "sun" and "moon" denominated not only the luminaries but also certain powers within or behind the luminaries – gods; for example, Ugaritic Shapshu (the sun-goddess) and Yarihu (the moon-god), which are cognate with Hebrew שמש and ירח, "sun" and "moon," respectively. In Genesis 1's patently monotheistic account of creation, the invocation of other gods, even indirectly, by explicit reference to "sun" and "moon," is avoided by the Hebrew's circumlocutions.[39] This interpretation, as the nineteenth century Italian Jewish commentator S. D. Luzzatto pointed out,[40] dovetails with the fact that light was created prior to the luminaries. Its meaning, Luzzatto suggests, is that light derives directly from God and not from the luminaries. People should, therefore, not attribute power to the luminaries themselves and worship them on that account. Whether or not one is convinced by this interpretation, it should be apparent that different translation styles, by selecting different aspects of the text to translate, construct different meanings. In this instance the TEV has transmitted the (so to speak)

---

[39]Cf., e.g., John Skinner, *Genesis,* 2nd ed. (Edinburgh: T. & T. Clark, 1930), pp. 24-26; Gerhard von Rad, *Genesis,* trans. John Marks (Philadelphia: Westminster Press, 1961), p. 53. For an argument against the thesis that תהום in Gen. 1:2 alludes to the Babylonian sea-goddess Ti'amat, see Chapter Four, Part Four. See, too, e.g., von Rad, *Genesis,* pp. 47-48.

[40]*S. D. Luzzatto's Commentary on the Pentateuch,* ed. P. Schlesinger (Tel Aviv: Dvir, 1965; first published: Padua, 1871), ad Gen. 1:3 (p. 6) [in Hebrew].

"objective" reference of the source, while Fox has reflected the source's own conception or formulation of creation.

Let us consider one further illustration, which I adduce to argue that even subtler alterations of the source's locutions may affect the overall meaning of the text. The Genesis 1 account repeatedly describes God's creation as a series of singular and deliberate acts. By dividing the text into verse-like lines – Buber's "breathing units" – Fox positions God's actions at the beginning of each successive unit of discourse: "God said.../ God saw.../ God divided.../ God called...," and so on. God is the initiator and subject of the action. When various objects of creation are mentioned, especially toward the beginning of the account, they are spoken of in the passive voice, or, at the least, in a nondescript manner. Thus, for example, "God said: Be there light! There was light." – Fox's rendering. Already in the first century the Roman writer, said to be Longinus, interpreted the precise repetition of the command "Be there light!" in the command's fulfillment, "There was light," as a bold manifestation of God's power.[41] In the spirit of this style, Longinus went so far as to embellish Genesis with yet another command-fulfillment formula: "Let there be earth', and there was earth."

The TEV eliminates what it seems to perceive as an alien, oriental repetition and renders: "'Let there be light' – and light appeared." It adds color to the nondescript Hebrew. Not only do the American Bible Society translators blunt the force of the command's complete and immediate realization; they ascribe a modest activity to the light itself – "it appeared." Attributing such activity to subjects other than God detracts from the narrator's depiction of God in the grand role of creator. In a similar fashion, when the Hebrew uses its most nondescript verb, "to be" (היה), elsewhere in the story, the TEV rushes in with more explicit language. God intends the luminaries to "be signs" of the days and seasons; but the TEV has the luminaries "show the time when days, years, and religious festivals begin." Fox translates the formula that delineates the end of each day as "Evening was and morning was." The source employs the same verb, ויהי – "it was" – twice. The TEV reads: "Evening passed and morning came." It makes the evening and morning sound more interesting but has the effect of diminishing the austerity of God's creation.

On the third day, God orders the water to consolidate into one place so that the dry land could emerge. Emphasizing God's commanding role and the water's subordination, the Hebrew expresses the transformation of water and land in the passive voice. The passive conjugation of the Hebrew verbs is reflected in Fox's translation:

> Let the waters under the heavens be blocked-up to one place,
> and let the dry-land be seen.

---

[41] *"Longinus" on Sublimity*, trans. D. A. Russel (Oxford: Clarendon Press, 1965), pp. 11-12.

Consistent with its embellishment of the verb "to be" in this passage, the TEV lends the water and land greater independence of action by rendering the verbs in the active voice[42]:

> Let the water below the sky come together in one place, so that the land will appear.

Going even further toward ascribing power to creatures, the TEV also turns nouns into verbs. Where Fox translates "Let us make man in our image after our likeness!" the TEV makes the creature the subject of verbs:

> And now we will make human beings; they will be like us and resemble us.

My point is simply that the creation story accentuates God's activity not only semantically but through is use of verbs, too. A literal translation may by choosing to reproduce Hebraic verbal usage reinforce the semantic component with the stylistic one. This particular idiomatic version may convey some of the semantic sense more expressly than a literal version would. But at the same time, by neglecting the style of the original, a highly idiomatic rendering such as the TEV employs language that reduces the text's potential significance.

The literary goal, as I said, was one of Buber and Rosenzweig's purposes in adopting a fairly literal mode of translation. A second motive derived from their belief that each language expresses things that are unique to it and that every translation constitutes a text different from the source. Buber and, in this case especially, Rosenzweig sought to produce a translation that would sound like a translation. In an essay "On Translating Homer," Matthew Arnold explained the rationale behind such a move:

> On one side it is said that the translation ought to be such "that the reader should, if possible, forget that it is a translation at all, and be lulled into the illusion that he is reading an original work, – something original"...One the other hand [another] declares that he "aims at precisely the opposite: to retain every peculiarity of the original, so far as he is able, *with the greater care the more foreign it may happen to*

---

[42]This maneuver is in keeping with the TEV's policy of simplifying the language. In generative transformational grammar, passive sentences are analyzed as transformations of simple active sentences, "kernels." "What makes, *Today's English Version*...so popular and so helpful to translators," write Nida and Taber, "is that it is frequently restructured in the direction of kernel expressions, and is thus more readily understandable and provides a useful basis for transfer to other languages"; *Theory and Practice*, p. 47. Although I grant the syntactic analysis, I maintain that the "restructuring" alters the sense. Consider, for example, that the topic of transformationally related active and passive sentences differs, as in *Joe hits the ball* versus *The ball was hit by Joe*. These sentences, as I understand them, do not have the same meaning.

be"; so that it may "never be forgotten that he is imitating, and imitating in a different material."[43]

Rosenzweig inclined toward the latter position: no translation can serve in lieu of the source. The goal of translation is to share enough of the source with the reader that the reader will want to find the original.

For Buber and Rosenzweig their translation functioned to share the Biblical source with a Jewish audience that was unfamiliar with it, or unfamiliar with it except in Christian translations. The terminology used to render the Bible in German, like most English terminology,[44] carries specifically Christian associations. Buber and Rosenzweig wanted a different terminology, one that was molded according to the Hebrew. An offering to God was, therefore, a "bringing nigh," a קרבן – not a "sacrifice." The unnaturalness of the translation language that Buber and Rosenzweig developed was partly intended to mystify the Hebrew, to carry on the tradition that the Bible means something to Jews in its very Hebraic formulation. The Jew must hear the Bible in Hebrew, and if not Hebrew, then a German, or English, that is bent into a Hebraic shape. This is admittedly a Jewish function; but a translator plans the goals of a translation to further an envisaged function.

In Chapter Five I quoted Schleiermacher's classification of two translation types – the one that brings the source to the audience and the one that leads the audience to the source. A bridge extends in two directions. What I called there a "Jewish" translation maintains the mystique of the source text. The great Judaic scholar of a century ago, Solomon Schechter, explains the nature of this Jewish concern:

> Translation – it has been said – are the structures with which a kind of Providence has overbridged the deeps of human thought caused by the division of tongues at the Tower of Babel. The remark is as humble in spirit as it is prudent in practice. It is certainly safer to walk over the bridge than to swim the flood. But in this case we must be satisfied not to express opinions about the nature of the river, its various currents, and undercurrents, its depths and shallows, and the original formation of its bed. To form a judgment on these points, one must learn to swim and dive, nay, one must immerse himself in the very element against whose touch the bridge was meant to protect him.[45]

---

[43]Matthew Arnold, "On Translating Homer," quoted in Chukovsky, *A High Art*, p. 155; cf. the discussion above in Chapter Five.

[44]Cf., e.g., Cynthia Ozick, "Prayer Leader," *Prooftexts* 3 (1983), pp. 1-8; Barry W. Holtz, "Introduction," *Back to the Sources: Reading the Classic Jewish Texts*, ed. idem (New York: Summit Books, 1984), p. 20.

[45]Solomon Schechter, from his inaugural lecture as Goldsmith Professor of Hebrew at London University, quoted in Norman Bentwich, *Solomon Schechter* (London: George Allen & Unwin, 1931), pp. 29-30.

Idiomatic translations serve what I there called "evangelical" interests, a concern that is explicit in the work of the American Bible Society.

One should not overlook, however, that not only theological or philosophical interests motivate translators. One may have more specifically pragmatic goals in translating. Jacob Neusner, for example, has contrasted two approaches to rendering classical Jewish ("rabbinic") texts.[46] The one seeks to capture the rhetorical form of a work, the other the substance of the discourse. Neusner has himself applied the former approach to the Mishna, judging its orderly rhetorical patterning to reflect the essence of the Mishna's meaning. He has applied the latter, more idiomatic approach to the Talmuds, feeling that the rhetoric of the source is a sort of shorthand or code, intelligible only by means of elaboration. In a sense, Neusner allows that Talmudic discourse is formulated such that a literal version of the original would share the same difficulties that the original poses.

Because translators produce texts with different goals, expecting their work to perform different functions, there will always be different types of "translation." If partisans of one style or another would acknowledge translation's multiple functions, they would then evaluate translations on the basis of their projected aims, and not some absolute principle or "truth" about language (or God).

---

[46]E.g., Jacob Neusner, "Translating the Palestinian Talmud into English....," *Hebrew Studies* 23 (1982), pp. 85-98; "Translating Bavli: A Fresh Approach," *Major Trends in Formative Judaism, Second Series: Texts, Contents, and Contexts* (Chico, CA: Scholars Press, 1984), pp. 99-121; "Preface," *The Mishnah: A New Translation* (New Haven: Yale University Press, 1988), p. x. Neusner explains his preference for more literal renderings in "Translation and Paraphrase: The Differences and Why They Matter," *Hebrew Studies* 27 (1986), pp. 26-37.

Index

CPSIA information can be obtained
at www.ICGtesting.com
Printed in the USA
BVHW080127140620
581354BV00003B/125